Synthesis Lectures on Data Management

Series Editor

H. V. Jagadish, University of Michigan, Ann Arbor, USA

This series publishes lectures on data management. Topics include query languages, database system architectures, transaction management, data warehousing, XML and databases, data stream systems, wide scale data distribution, multimedia data management, data mining, and related subjects.

Mohammad Javad Amiri · Divyakant Agrawal · Amr El Abbadi

Blockchain-Enabled Large-Scale Transaction Management

Springer

Mohammad Javad Amiri
Department of Computer Science
Stony Brook University
Stony Brook, NY, USA

Divyakant Agrawal
Department of Computer Science
University of California, Santa Barbara
Santa Barbara, CA, USA

Amr El Abbadi
Department of Computer Science
University of California, Santa Barbara
Santa Barbara, CA, USA

ISSN 2153-5418 ISSN 2153-5426 (electronic)
Synthesis Lectures on Data Management
ISBN 978-3-031-91057-9 ISBN 978-3-031-91058-6 (eBook)
https://doi.org/10.1007/978-3-031-91058-6

This Springer imprint is published by the registered company Springer Nature Switzerland AG
The registered company address is: Gewerbestrasse 11, 6330 Cham, Switzerland

Contents

1 Introduction

Networked applications, the web, and diverse applications on mobile platforms have attracted hundreds of millions of end-users [1, 2] who interact and transact with services dispersed across the internet. Users use these services without being concerned about where the data and computation providing such services are located. Furthermore, the scale and reliability of such computational and data infrastructures have become limitless since users from across the world expect instantaneous responses to their requests twenty-four-seven. During the past two decades, unprecedented advances have facilitated the development of highly scalable and reliable infrastructures to host networked applications. In particular, large-scale data centers hosting tens to hundreds of thousands of computers with petabytes to exabytes of storage have become modern instruments of choice for deploying such services. This paradigm is referred to as *cloud computing* [3]. Internet companies have popularized this paradigm by providing simple, user-friendly services, e.g., Amazon Web Services (AWS) [4], Google Cloud [5], Microsoft Azure [6], etc. The cloud computing paradigm offers unlimited infrastructure-as-a-service with a pay-as-you-go billing model. Cloud computing is powered by geographically distributed core data centers and edge data centers that offer elastic compute, memory, storage, and network services for managing data and computation for Internet applications.

Although cloud computing and data centers have transformed the application infrastructure landscape over the past two decades, the unfortunate consequence of this technology has been that the over eight billion inhabitants of the planet today are at the mercy of (perhaps) a handful of dominant technology companies in the world. Ironically, the underlying technology deployed within a data center is itself highly distributed and parallelized; still, the networked deployment of services and applications in the cloud is highly centralized. For example, an outage of a data center can jeopardize the availability of all the applications and services on that data center. Cloud computing providers mitigate such risks by encouraging

M. J. Amiri et al., *Blockchain-Enabled Large-Scale Transaction Management*,
Synthesis Lectures on Data Management,
https://doi.org/10.1007/978-3-031-91058-6_1

their clients (service providers) to deploy their services redundantly on multiple data centers for increased fault tolerance. Even with such redundancy, there is an *implicit* trust assumption between the cloud computing clients and the cloud computing providers. In particular, cloud computing clients must entrust the cloud with their respective data. The problem with this trust model is that even if the cloud provider can be trusted and is honest, they are still vulnerable to malicious attacks from various types of actors in the network. Over the past decade, the issue of malicious attacks and failures has become of significant concern in the context of Internet applications.

Before the advent of cloud computing, in the early era of the Web and the Internet, another computational and storage paradigm successfully deployed global-scale networked services on the Internet. This paradigm was referred to as *peer-to-peer computing* (P2P). Unlike the cloud computing model that requires the availability of large-scale data centers, P2P computing is highly decentralized and distributed and only relies on the availability of individual machines. The P2P computing paradigm emerged in the context of network file-sharing applications. For example, it became highly popular among users to share media files (e.g., audio and video data). Unfortunately, media-sharing applications deployed on the P2P computing model got mired in copyright issues resulting in the eventual demise of these applications. Furthermore, with the demise of file-sharing applications, the P2P computing paradigm also went sideways and was quickly replaced by the cloud computing paradigm on top of large-scale data centers by powerful internet players. Although the mainstream application developers abandoned the P2P paradigm, it remained of interest to developers [7] who envisioned a notion of a currency independent of any central bank authority. The idea is that no single entity (e.g., a powerful Central Bank) can manipulate the world's economy by developing such an infrastructure. The key challenge to realizing this idealized notion is *where and how to maintain the state of this currency* since no single machine or even a group of machines can be entrusted with complete responsibility.

In 2008, the *mysterious Nakamoto* presented a novel decentralized peer-to-peer computation model that enabled Bitcoin [7], the first successful global scale peer-to-peer cash system or cryptocurrency. The original Bitcoin protocol allows financial transactions to be transacted among participants without the need for a trusted third party, e.g., banks, credit card companies, or PayPal. Bitcoin eliminates the need for such a trusted third party by replacing it with a distributed ledger that is fully replicated among a decentralized open network of computing nodes in the cryptocurrency system [8, 9]. This distributed data structure for recording transactions, which is maintained by several nodes without a central authority, is referred to *blockchain* [10, 11].

In a blockchain system, nodes agree on their shared states across a large network of possibly *untrusted* participants. While blockchain was originally devised for Bitcoin cryptocurrency [7], large-scale data management systems have recently focused on specific features of blockchains, such as transparency, provenance, and authenticity, to support a wide range of distributed applications. Bitcoin and most other cryptocurrencies are *permissionless* blockchains. In a permissionless blockchain, the network is public, and anyone can participate without a specific identity. Many other distributed applications, such as supply chain management and healthcare, are deployed on *permissioned* blockchain systems consisting of a set of known, identified, mutually distrustful entities. Such applications have different requirements that need to be supported by permissioned blockchain systems. In this monograph, we focus on four main requirements, *performance*, *scalability*, *confidentiality*, and *verifiability*, and show how permissioned blockchain systems address them.

Performance. Distributed applications, such as financial services, demand high performance in both throughput and latency. For instance, the Visa payment system can process over 10, 000 transactions per second. In contrast, typical blockchain-based services like Multichain [12] are limited to handling only a few hundred transactions per second.

Blockchain systems usually replicate a copy of the blockchain data on all nodes in the system. They use the State Machine Replication (SMR) approach [13] to ensure consistency among the data replicated on different nodes. SMR regulates the deterministic execution of client transactions on different nodes such that every non-faulty node executes every transaction in the same order. This is typically achieved using a consensus protocol. Permissioned blockchain systems process transactions using either an optimistic or pessimistic approach. These approaches offer trade-offs in performance depending on the degree and frequency of contention and conflict among transactions. In the optimistic approach, nodes execute transactions without a priori running a consensus protocol to definitively establish an ordering but run the consensus protocol later to ensure a consistent order. In the pessimistic approach, transactions are first ordered using a consensus protocol and then executed. Ordering and execution are the two main stages of any transaction processing system. From an architectural point of view, three main paradigms have been proposed for transaction processing systems and in particular, permissioned blockchain systems. The order-execute (OX) and the order-parallel execute (OXII) paradigms follow the pessimistic approach, while the execute-order-validate (XOV) paradigm follows the optimistic approach.

The order-execute paradigm is widely used in different permissioned blockchains such as Tendermint [14], Quorum [15], and Multichain [12]. In order-execute permissioned blockchains, a set of nodes (might be all of them) agrees on a total order for the transactions using Byzantine, e.g., PBFT [16], crash, e.g., Paxos [17], or hybrid, e.g., SeeMoRe [18], fault-tolerant protocols, generates blocks and multicasts them to all the nodes. Each node then executes the transactions sequentially in the specified order and updates its own copy of the ledger. The order-execute paradigm, however, suffers from performance limitations because of the *sequential execution* of transactions on all nodes.

Hyperledger Fabric [19], presents the XOV paradigm by switching the order of the execution and ordering phases. In Hyperledger Fabric, transactions of different enterprises are first executed in parallel and then ordered using a pluggable consensus protocol. Hyperledger Fabric improves performance by executing transactions in parallel and is able to detect the non-deterministic execution of transactions. However, in the presence of any contention (i.e., conflicting transactions) in the workload, which is common in most distributed applications, Fabric has to disregard the effects of conflicting transactions which negatively impacts the performance of the blockchain. To address this issue, different variants of Hyperledger Fabric, e.g., Fabric++ [20], FabricSharp [21], and XOX Fabric [22], employs different techniques such as (a) early aborting transactions, (b) reordering transactions after the order phase to reconcile the potential conflicts, (c) early filtering out transactions that can never be reordered, and (d) re-execution transactions that are invalidated due to read-write conflicts. In this monograph, we discuss these alternative paradigms and present a more efficient approach to deal with contentious workloads using the OXII paradigm, introduced by ParBlockchain [23]. In ParBlockchain, a *dependency graph* is generated for a block's transactions in the ordering stage. The dependency graph gives a partial order based on the conflicts between transactions and enables the parallel execution of non-conflicting transactions in the execution stage.

Scalability. Scalability is one of the main obstacles to the business adoption of blockchain systems. To support a large-scale data management system, a blockchain system should be able to scale efficiently by adding more resources to the system. The scalability of blockchain systems has been addressed in several studies using different on-chain, e.g., increasing the block size, and off-chain, e.g., Lightning Networks [24], techniques.

Permissioned blockchain systems mainly use *clustering* to improve scalability. In clustering approaches, e.g., Blockplane [25], nodes are partitioned into fault-tolerant clusters where each cluster processes (or at least orders) a disjoint set of transactions. Permissioned blockchain systems use *single-ledger* or *sharded-ledger* techniques to enhance scalability. In the single-ledger technique, e.g., ResilientDB [26], the entire ledger is replicated on all clusters and all nodes execute every transaction. In the sharded-ledger technique, e.g., AHL [27], SharPer [28], and Saguaro [29], on the other hand, the ledger is partitioned into multiple shards that are maintained by different clusters. Partitioning the data into multiple shards that are maintained by different subsets of nodes is a proven approach to enhance the scalability of databases [30]. Sharded-ledger permissioned blockchain systems process two types of *intra-shard* and *cross-shard* transactions. Cross-shard transactions can be processed either in a centralized manner using the coordinator-based approach or in a decentralized manner using the flattened approach.

In this monograph, we present SharPer [28, 31], a permissioned blockchain system that improves scalability by clustering (partitioning) the nodes and assigning different data shards to different clusters where each data shard is replicated on the nodes of a cluster. SharPer supports both intra-shard and cross-shard transactions and processes intra-shard transactions of different clusters as well as cross-shard transactions with non-overlapping clusters simultaneously. SharPer also incorporates a *flattened* protocol to establish consensus among clusters on the order of cross-shard transactions.

Confidentiality. Confidentiality of data is required in many collaborative distributed applications, e.g., supply chain management, where multiple enterprises collaborate with each other following Service Level Agreements (SLAs) to provide different services. To deploy distributed applications across different collaborating enterprises, a blockchain system needs to support the internal transactions of each enterprise as well as cross-enterprise transactions that represent the collaboration between enterprises. While the data accessed by cross-enterprise transactions should be *visible* to all enterprises, the internal data of each enterprise, which are accessed by internal transactions, might be *confidential*. In particular, in collaborative distributed applications where multiple enterprises work together, each enterprise can maintain its own independent and disjoint blockchains. They can utilize techniques such as atomic cross-chain transactions [32, 33] or the Interledger protocol [34] to facilitate cross-enterprise collaboration. However, these methods are often expensive, complex, and primarily designed for permissionless blockchains. Conversely, techniques that support collaborating applications on a single blockchain typically face challenges: they may not support internal transactions of individual enterprises (leading to data integration issues), suffer from confidentiality concerns since the entire ledger is accessible to all enterprises (e.g., single-channel Fabric [19]), or require a trusted channel among enterprises (e.g., multi-channel Fabric [35]).

While cryptographic techniques can be used to achieve confidentiality, the considerable overhead of such techniques makes them impractical [19]. Hyperledger Fabric [19] ensures the confidentiality of data using private data collections [36]. Private data collections manage confidential data that two or more enterprises on a single channel want to keep private from other enterprises on that channel. However, the blockchain ledger is still maintained by the nodes of every enterprise within a channel.

To address this problem, this monograph presents a permissioned blockchain system, Caper [37]. In Caper, transactions are either internal, which are maintained by a single enterprise, or cross-enterprise, which are maintained by all enterprises. Each enterprise also maintains two types of private and public data. Caper supports both internal and cross-enterprise transactions of collaborating distributed applications. In Caper, each enterprise orders and executes its internal transactions locally while cross-enterprise transactions are public and visible to every node. In addition, the blockchain ledger of Caper is a directed acyclic graph that includes the internal transactions of every enterprise and all cross-enterprise transactions. Nonetheless, for the sake of confidentiality, the blockchain ledger is not maintained by any node. In fact, each enterprise maintains its own *local view* of the ledger including its internal and all cross-enterprise transactions. Since ordering cross-enterprise transactions requires global agreement among all enterprises, Caper introduces different consensus protocols to globally order cross-enterprise transactions.

While Caper's solution is simple and suitable for collaboration workflows with internal and public transactions, Caper does not support confidential collaboration among subsets of enterprises (i.e., it only supports internal or public transactions) To support confidential collaboration (i.e., data sharing), in addition to public transactions among all enterprises and internal transactions within each enterprise, any subset of enterprises might process transactions *confidentially* from other enterprises.

To deal with this challenge, this monograph presents Qanaat [38], a more generalized confidentiality solution for scalable multi-enterprise applications. Qanaat presents *data col-*

lections that enable any subset of enterprises involved in a collaboration workflow to keep their collaboration private from other enterprises. Moreover, Qanaat utilizes the privacy firewall technique [39, 40] to prevent confidential data leakage despite the Byzantine failure of nodes.

Verifiability. In addition to confidentiality, many cross-enterprise systems require enterprises to verify transactions initiated by other parties to ensure compliance with global constraints while maintaining privacy. This situation often arises in environments like crowdworking, where multiple untrustworthy platforms must collaboratively enforce regulations such as limiting a worker to a maximum of 40 h per week. Thus, the system must support *verifiability* without compromising transaction confidentiality.

Verifiability is also crucial for cryptocurrencies that prioritize privacy, such as Zcash [41], where transaction details remain confidential yet need verification by nodes without revealing the sender, receiver, or transaction amount. Zero-knowledge proofs have been employed for this purpose in systems like ZebraLancer [42] (within the crowdsourcing context) and Quorum [15]. In cryptography, a zero-knowledge proof enables one party (the prover) to confirm to another party (the verifier) that they possess knowledge of a value x, without disclosing any information beyond their knowledge of x. Although zero-knowledge proofs effectively achieve verifiability in Quorum and ZebraLancer, they come with significant overhead costs [19]. Furthermore, replicating every transaction across all enterprises can be expensive due to the necessity for each transaction's verification.

Confidentiality techniques cannot support all the requirements of such systems, especially since internal transactions might need to be verified as well. For instance, crowdworking platforms need to be integrated within society and in particular to interface with legal and social institutions. Global regulations must be enforced, such as minimal and maximal work hours that participants can spend on crowdworking platforms. Crowdworking platforms are also naturally distributed and need to collaborate to process complex tasks, resulting in the rise of *multi-platform crowdworking systems*. Moreover, while collaborating to enforce global regulations requires the *transparent* sharing of information about the tasks, the system needs to preserve the *privacy (confidentiality)* of all participants. In this monograph, we present Separ [43], a blockchain-based *multi-platform* crowdworking system that enforces global *constraints* on distributed independent entities. In Separ, *Privacy* is ensured using *lightweight and anonymous tokens*, while *transparency* is achieved using a *permissioned blockchain* shared across multiple platforms.

Contributions. The primary contribution of this monograph is to illustrate how permissioned blockchains can effectively tackle the key challenges associated with processing transactions in large-scale data management systems. Our objective is to enhance understanding of the fundamental issues in transaction processing and to present techniques that facilitate the development of efficient systems. We showcase the practicality of these techniques through real-world applications and design various systems to implement them successfully.

Organization. The rest of the monograph is organized as follows. Chapter 2 introduces the preliminary concepts of data management and blockchains. Then, the monograph addresses the performance, scalability, and confidentiality challenges of large-scale data management systems in Chaps. 3–5. A generalized notion of confidentiality is presented in Chap. 6. Chapter 7 discusses the verifiability challenge using a multi-platform crowdworking application and finally, Chap. 8 summarizes the monograph and discusses future direction in large-scale data management and blockchains.

References

1. Facebook company info. http://newsroom.fb.com/company-info/ (2018)
2. Twitter: number of active users 2010–2018. https://www.statista.com/statistics/282087/number-of-monthly-active-twitter-users/ (2018)
3. Regalado, A.: Who coined 'cloud computing'? https://www.technologyreview.com/s/425970/who-coined-cloud-computing/ (2011)
4. Announcing amazon elastic compute cloud (amazon ec2)—beta. https://aws.amazon.com/about-aws/whats-new/2006/08/24/announcing-amazon-elastic-compute-cloud-amazon-ec2---beta/. 2006
5. Google cloud. https://cloud.google.com/
6. Microsoft azure. https://azure.microsoft.com/
7. Nakamoto, S.: Bitcoin: A peer-to-peer electronic cash system (2008)
8. Maiyya, S., Zakhary, V., Amiri, M.J., Agrawal, D., El Abbadi, A.: Database and distributed computing foundations of blockchains. In: SIGMOD International Conference on Management of Data, pp. 2036–2041. ACM (2019)
9. Amiri, M.J., Maiyya, S., Zakhary, V., Agrawal, D., El Abbadi, A.: Blockchain system foundations. In: The Brazilian Symposium on Databases (SBBD). SBC (2020)
10. Cachin, C., Vukolić, M.: Blockchain consensus protocols in the wild. In: International Symposium on Distributed Computing (DISC), pp. 1–16 (2017)
11. Agrawal, D., El Abbadi, A., Amiri, M.J., Maiyya, S., Zakhary, V.: Blockchains and databases: opportunities and challenges for the permissioned and the permissionless. In: European Conference on Advances in Databases and Information Systems, pp. 3–7. Springer (2020)
12. Greenspan, G.: Multichain private blockchain-white paper. http://www.multichain.com/download/MultiChain-White-Paper.pdf (2015)
13. Lamport, L.: Time, clocks, and the ordering of events in a distributed system. Commun. ACM **21**(7), 558–565 (1978)
14. Kwon, J.: Tendermint: consensus without mining (2014)
15. Chase, J.M.: Quorum White Paper (2016)
16. Castro, M., Liskov, B.: Practical byzantine fault tolerance. In: Symposium on Operating Systems Design and Implementation (OSDI), pp. 173–186. USENIX Association (1999)
17. Lamport, L.: Paxos made simple. ACM Sigact News **32**(4), 18–25 (2001)
18. Amiri, M.J., Maiyya, S., Agrawal, D., El Abbadi, A.: SeeMoRe: A fault-tolerant protocol for hybrid cloud environments. In: International Conference on Data Engineering (ICDE), pp. 1345–1356. IEEE (2020)
19. Androulaki, E., Barger, A., Bortnikov, V., Cachin, C., Christidis, K., De Caro, A., Enyeart, D., Ferris, C., Laventman, G., Manevich, Y.: Hyperledger fabric: a distributed operating system for permissioned blockchains. In: European Conference on Computer Systems (EuroSys), pp. 30:1–30:15. ACM (2018)

20. Sharma, A., Schuhknecht, F.M., Agrawal, D., Dittrich, J.: Blurring the lines between blockchains and database systems: the case of hyperledger fabric. In: SIGMOD International Conference on Management of Data, pp. 105–122. ACM (2019)
21. Ruan, P., Loghin, D., Ta, Q.T., Zhang, M., Chen, G., Ooi, B.C.: A transactional perspective on execute-order-validate blockchains. In: SIGMOD International Conference on Management of Data, pp. 543–557. ACM (2020)
22. Gorenflo, C., Golab, L., Keshav, S.: Xox fabric: A hybrid approach to transaction execution. In: International Conference on Blockchain and Cryptocurrency (ICBC), pp. 1–9. IEEE (2020)
23. Amiri, M.J., Agrawal, D., El Abbadi, A.: ParBlockchain: leveraging transaction parallelism in permissioned blockchain systems. In: International Conference on Distributed Computing Systems (ICDCS), pp. 1337–1347. IEEE (2019)
24. Poon, J., Dryja, T.: The bitcoin lightning network: Scalable off-chain instant payments. https://lightning.network/lightning-network-paper.pdf (2016)
25. Nawab, F., Sadoghi, M.: Blockplane: a global-scale Byzantizing middleware. In: International Conference on Data Engineering (ICDE), pp. 124–135. IEEE (2019)
26. Gupta, S., Rahnama, S., Hellings, J., Sadoghi, M.: Resilientdb: global scale resilient blockchain fabric. Proceed. VLDB Endowment **13**(6), 868–883 (2020)
27. Dang, H., Dinh, T.T.A., Loghin, D., Chang, E.C., Lin, Q., Ooi, B.C.: Towards scaling blockchain systems via sharding. In: SIGMOD International Conference on Management of Data, pp. 123–140. ACM (2019)
28. Amiri, M.J., Agrawal, D., El Abbadi, A.: SharPer: Sharding permissioned blockchains over network clusters. In: SIGMOD International Conference on Management of Data, pp. 76–88. ACM (2021)
29. Amiri, M.J., Lai, Z., Patel, L., Loo, B.T., Lo, E., Zhou, W.: Saguaro: An edge computing-enabled hierarchical permissioned blockchain. In: International Conference on Data Engineering (ICDE), pp. 259–272. IEEE (2023)
30. Corbett, J.C., Dean, J., Epstein, M., Fikes, A., Frost, C., Furman, J.J., Ghemawat, S., Gubarev, A., Heiser, C., Hochschild, P.: Spanner: Google's globally distributed database. Trans. Comput. Syst. (TOCS) **31**(3), 8 (2013)
31. Amiri, M.J., Agrawal, D., El Abbadi, A.: On sharding permissioned blockchains. In: International Conference on Blockchain, pp. 282–285. IEEE (2019)
32. Herlihy, M.: Atomic cross-chain swaps. In: Symposium on Principles of Distributed Computing (PODC), pp. 245–254. ACM (2018)
33. Zakhary, V., Agrawal, D., El Abbadi, A.: Atomic commitment across blockchains. Proc. of the VLDB Endowment **13**, 1319–1331 (2020)
34. Thomas, S., Schwartz, E.: A protocol for interledger payments. https://interledger.org/interledger.pdf (2015)
35. Androulaki, E., Cachin, C., De Caro, A., Kokoris-Kogias, E.: Channels: horizontal scaling and confidentiality on permissioned blockchains. In: European Symposium on Research in Computer Security (ESORICS), pp. 111–131. Springer (2018)
36. Hyperledger: Private data collections: a high-level overview. https://www.hyperledger.org/blog/2018/10/23/private-data-collections-a-high-level-overview
37. Amiri, M.J., Agrawal, D., El Abbadi, A.: CAPER: a cross-application permissioned blockchain. Proc. of the VLDB Endowment **12**(11), 1385–1398 (2019)
38. Amiri, M.J., Loo, B.T., Agrawal, D., El Abbadi, A.: Qanaat: a scalable multi-enterprise permissioned blockchain system with confidentiality guarantees. Proc. VLDB Endowment **15**(11), 2839–2852 (2022)
39. Yin, J., Martin, J.P., Venkataramani, A., Alvisi, L., Dahlin, M.: Separating agreement from execution for byzantine fault tolerant services. Oper. Syst. Rev. (OSR) **37**(5), 253–267 (2003)

40. Duan, S., Zhang, H.: Practical state machine replication with confidentiality. In: Symposium on Reliable Distributed Systems (SRDS), pp. 187–196. IEEE (2016)
41. Hopwood, D., Bowe, S., Hornby, T., Wilcox, N.: Zcash Protocol Specification. San Francisco, CA, USA, GitHub (2016)
42. Lu, Y., Tang, Q., Wang, G.: Zebralancer: Private and anonymous crowdsourcing system atop open blockchain. In: International Conference on Distributed Computing Systems (ICDCS), pp. 853–865. IEEE (2018)
43. Amiri, M.J., Duguépéroux, J., Allard, T., Agrawal, D., El Abbadi, A.: Separ: Towards regulating future of work multi-platform crowdworking environments with privacy guarantees. In: The Web Conf. (WWW), pp. 1891–1903 (2021)

2 Preliminaries

2.1 Blockchain-Enabled Decentralized Data Management

A blockchain system, e.g., bitcoin [1] and Ethereum [2], typically consists of a *storage* layer and an *application* layer [3], as illustrated in Fig. 2.1. The storage layer comprises a decentralized distributed ledger managed by a network of computing nodes. In a permissioned blockchain system, all computing nodes are known a priori, while in a permissionless blockchain system, computing nodes can join or leave the network at any moment without obtaining permission from a centralized authority. Each computing node, sometimes called a *miner* in permissionless blockchains, maintains a copy of the ledger, the main underlying data structure in blockchain systems. The blockchain ledger is an append-only fully replicated tamper-proof data structure that records transactions in the form of a hash chain. The blockchain ledger is shared among all participants and provides a consistent view of all user transactions by all participants in the system. Each block contains a set of valid transactions, e.g., asset transfer among end-users. The application layer comprises end-users who communicate with the storage layer via message passing through a client library. End-users have identities, defined by their public keys, and signatures, generated using their private keys. Digital signatures are the mechanism used by the end-users to generate transactions. End-users submit their transactions, e.g., transferring assets from one identity to another, to the storage layer through a client library. End-users multicast their transaction messages to computing nodes in the storage layer. In a permissionless blockchain, computing nodes, e.g., miners, validate the received transactions and add valid transactions to the current (but *pending* to be finalized) block. The block proposer, e.g., a computing node that successfully mines a transaction block in bitcoin, gets the right to add its *current but pending* block to the chain and multicasts it to other computing nodes. Computing nodes accept the valid block after verifying it and start working on the next block. On the other hand, in a permissioned blockchain, only a designated computing node, i.e., the leader, validates transactions, con-

M. J. Amiri et al., *Blockchain-Enabled Large-Scale Transaction Management*,
Synthesis Lectures on Data Management,
https://doi.org/10.1007/978-3-031-91058-6_2

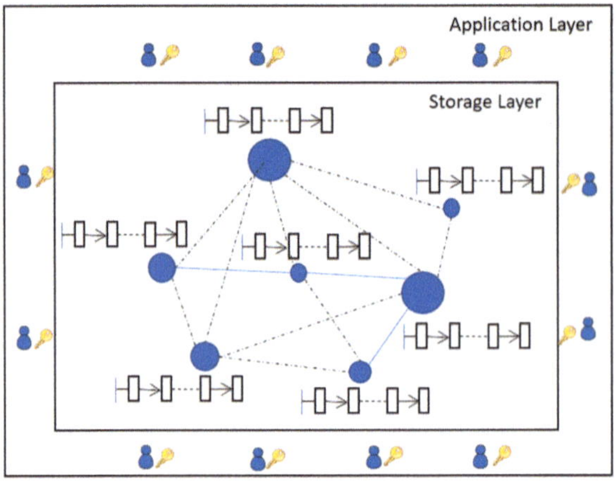

Fig. 2.1 Blockchain architecture overview

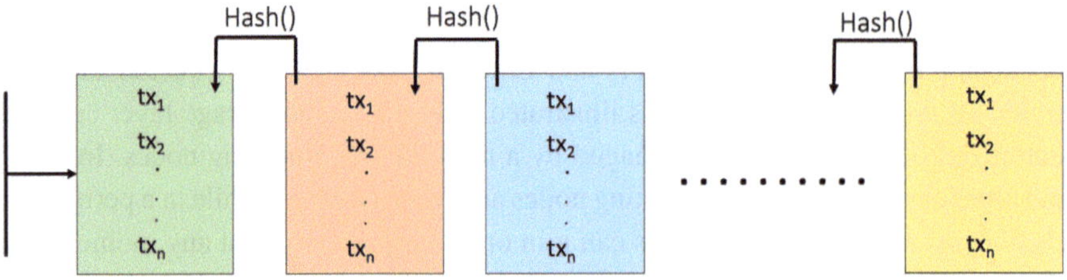

Fig. 2.2 Blockchain is a chain of blocks of transactions linked by hash pointers

structs a transaction block, and multicasts it to other computing nodes. A consensus protocol runs among computing nodes to establish agreement on the order of transaction blocks.

Blockchain ledger, as shown in Fig. 2.2, is a secure list of blocks linked by *hash pointers* each block containing a set of transactions. A blockchain system maintains a consistent view of this blockchain ledger in a secure and Byzantine fault-tolerant manner. Blockchain systems, and specifically bitcoin, build on foundations developed over the last few decades from diverse fields [4], but primarily from the fields of **cryptography** [5, 6], **distributed systems** [7–9], and **data management** [10–12].

2.2 Basic Cryptography Concepts

Cryptographic hash functions have been extensively used in different blockchain systems and, especially, in bitcoin. Secure Hash Algorithms, also known as SHA, are a family of cryptographic functions designed to keep data secure. It works by transforming the data using a hash function: an algorithm consisting of bitwise operations, modular additions, and compression functions. The family of SHA algorithms maps an input of any size to a fixed size output, hence the values in a large input domain can be *compacted* into a fixed size domain. In addition, they are *one-way* functions, i.e., they are practically infeasible to invert. A popular cryptographic hash function used extensively in blockchain is *SHA-256*, which takes an arbitrary string and outputs a 256-bit output. A cryptographic hash function H has several important characteristics that are important for both the correctness of blockchains and to ensure that the data structures are tamper-free [13]:

1. *Collision-free*: No two different values hash to the same output, i.e., for any two values x and y such that $x \neq y$ the probability that $H(x) = H(y)$ is extremely low.
2. *One-Way or Hiding*: Given the output of a hash function, it is very difficult to compute the input. That is, given $H(x)$ it is practically infeasible to compute x efficiently.
3. *Puzzle-Friendly*: A corollary of the *hiding* property is that given a random string k, and a target output pattern S, it is computationally expensive to find a string x, such that $H(k||x) \in S$.

Merkle trees extend the notion of cryptographic hashes from one element to a set of elements. A merkle hash tree (MHT) [14] is a (binary) tree where each leaf node is labeled with the cryptographic hash of a data item in the set, and each internal node is labeled with the cryptographic hash of the concatenated labels of its child nodes. Merkle trees are often used for efficient and secure verification of the contents of large datasets as the label of the root reflects the content of all data items in the set.

A digital signature, similar to an actual signature, authenticates messages. A public-key signature [5] consists of a public key, pk, known to all participants, and a secret key, sk, known only to the message author. The author, A, signs message m using her secret key sk, while A's public key represents her identity. Digital signatures are unique to the specific document being signed. They are mathematically hard to forge, but are computationally easy to verify. Given the message m and the signature, any receiver can verify whether the author A sent the message m by decrypting the signature using A's public key. Public-key signature schemes are used to prevent forgery as it is computationally infeasible for author B to sign a message with author A's signature.

2.3 Data, Ledger, and Transactions

2.3.1 Banks and Transactions

To introduce and motivate blockchain systems in the context of cryptocurrencies, we start by using the more traditional analogy of real *fiat cash*. In the world of banks and finances, if Alice wants to transfer \$50 to Bob, one standard approach is for Alice to write a check to Bob. If Alice and Bob have different banks, the check requests Alice's Bank to withdraw \$50 from Alice's account; Alice's bank transfers $50 to Bob's account; and finally Bob's bank deposits $50 in Bob's account (ignoring all fees). We highlight several instructive aspects of this fairly traditional and standard transfer.

- **Identities and Signatures**: The check should contain the public identity of Bob so that the bank can identify which account to deposit the $50. Also, the check needs to include Alice's signature. This analog signature is typically uniquely identified with Alice, as this guarantees to the bank that Alice in fact does want to transfer the $50 of her account. The standard assumption is that nobody can *forge* Alice's signature. In the digital world, digital signatures replace analog signatures. Public signatures are used as identities, while private signatures are used to sign documents in a manner that cannot be forged by others.
- **Ledger**: Each bank typically maintains a ledger. Since banks are trusted, this ledger is considered to contain a true record of all transfer operations executed on all accounts in this bank.
- **Transactions**: All operations on bank accounts are executed as *transactions* [15]. Transactions have ACID properties, namely, atomicity, consistency, isolation, and durability. To ensure these properties, foundational protocols and data structures have been developed. Two important sets of protocols for the correct behavior of databases are *concurrency control* and *recovery* protocols. Concurrency control ensures that all transactions involving transfers among accounts are serializable. Serializability guarantees a total serial order on all transactions executed on a database. This is critical for the correct functioning of the banking system, e.g., only one transaction succeeds when multiple concurrent transactions are withdrawing $50 each from an account with only $50. Recovery protocols, on the other hand, ensure that even when failures occur, no information is lost, even if the failure occurs during the execution of a transaction. Recovery protocols traditionally use *logs* that are stored on persistent storage, e.g., disk. The standard assumption in banking systems is that the only type of failure that occurs is machine crashes, i.e., the bank is trusted and hence the design of the underlying database does not have to tolerate malicious failures or any tampering with the data. Once we move to the cryptocurrency world, this assumption might no longer hold. In the cryptocurrency world, all these properties need to be correctly and reliably supported.

2.3.2 Digital Cash and Its Basic Cryptocurrency Model

The original concepts of cryptocurrencies can be traced back to David Chaum's pioneering work on *digital cash* [16]. The basic concept is quite simple. If Alice owns digital cash, she can transfer its ownership to Bob as follows:

1. Alice appends Bob's public signature pk_{Bob} to the string associated with the digital cash to create a message m.
2. Alice signs the message m using Alice's private signature sk_{Alice}.

This creates a transaction that transfers the digital cash from Alice to Bob. Since both Alice and Bob's public signatures are public, anybody can decrypt this message and verify that Alice actually signed this message and Alice transferred the digital cash to Bob. Now that Bob owns the digital cash, he can also transfer ownership to Carol by appending her public key and signing it using his private key. Hence, in general, once digital cash is created, it can be transferred securely from one owner to another. Only the current owner can transfer it using their private key, but everybody can verify and validate the provenance of the current ownership of a unit of digital cash.

2.3.3 The Blockchain Ledger

The blockchain ledger is a linked list of blocks connected by pointers. Each block consists of a header in addition to its content, which is a set of transactions, as illustrated in Fig. 2.2. To ensure that the structure is tamper-free, instead of a simple pointer between blocks, pointers are replaced with *hash pointers*. A hash pointer is a pointer to the previous block and the hash of the previous block's header. In bitcoin, SHA-256 is used as the hash function. A block header includes the Merkle Tree root hash on the transactions in the block. Hence, any malicious manipulation of the contents of any of the transactions will require a new Merkle Tree root hash (otherwise, any validator can detect the inconsistency between the contents of the block and the Merkle Tree root hash stored in the header). In this manner, any change in the contents of a header will require a recalculation of the subsequent block's hash pointer, and so on. Such recalculations involve significant computational power, and hence will ensure that any tampering with the contents of a block will be very difficult and require significant computational power. To ensure persistence, the blockchain is replicated among all participants of the blockchain system.

2.3.4 Transaction Model

Two main transaction models are used in blockchain systems: UTXO (unspent transaction output) and account based. In the context of cryptocurrencies, transactions transfer the ownership of a cryptocurrency from one identity to another. End-users use their private keys [5] to digitally sign coins linked to their identity to transfer these coins to other identities, identified by their public keys. Using transactions, the provenance of a coin can be tracked from its registration in the blockchain, the first owner, to its latest owner in the blockchain.

In bitcoin and many other cryptocurrencies, new coins are generated and transferred in the blockchain through mining. In a traditional banking database, the balance of the account associated with a user is updated by each user's transaction to reflect their current balance. In bitcoin, on the other hand, each user owns a collection of coins. Coins can be split or merged using transactions. Each transaction takes one or more input coins owned by one user and outputs one or more coins where each output coin is owned by one user. Indeed, a transaction references previous transaction outputs as new transaction inputs and dedicates all input coin values to new outputs. The summation of a transaction's input assets matches the summation of its output assets assuming that no transaction fees are imposed. This transactional model is the *Unspent Transaction Output (UTXO)* model. The naming refers to the fact that if Alice wants to transfer x coins to Bob, she issues a transaction with input as the number of coins she owns, whose sum, s, is greater than x. The output of the transaction typically consists of two outputs: x coins to Bob and the *unspent* amount, $s - x$, back to Alice.

In traditional databases, end-user transactions execute arbitrary updates as long as the semantic and access control rights of a transaction are validated by a correct concurrency control protocol. On the other hand, in permissionless blockchain systems, this validation is explicitly enforced in the miners and hence end-users are allowed to transact only on the assets they own. This is in contrast to the database systems model where individual transactions in isolation and in the absence of concurrency are assumed to be *correct*. Indeed, the database concurrency control component provides the guarantee that the interleaved execution of multiple transactions will be equivalent to some serial execution.

In the blockchain context, the correctness of individual user transactions cannot be assumed due to the absence of a trust model and hence the miners need to check the validity of the user transactions, i.e., they need to validate that end-users can transact only on their own assets. If an end-user digitally signs an asset that is not owned by this end-user, the resulting transaction is invalid and will be rejected by the miners. In addition, miners validate that an asset cannot be spent twice and hence prevent double spending of assets. Hence, creating a new block requires the miner to (1) validate that all the transactions in the block do not conflict with each other, i.e., no two transactions in the block consume the same cryptocurrency owned by a user and (2) validate that all the transactions in the new block are consistent with cryptocurrencies owned by any user desiring to transfer some of its ownership to another user.

Note that this is only feasible due to the restrictive semantics of the currency-based asset model. More complex applications on permissionless blockchain also need to deal with the lack of assumption of the *correct transaction model* that is made in traditional database systems.

2.3.5 Smart Contract

The blockchain model is similar to an object-oriented programming language (OOPL). Similar to the primitive data types, user-defined functions, and classes in an OOPL, each blockchain also has primitive data types (e.g., an asset, asset ownership, etc.) and primitive functions operating on these primitive data types (e.g., transactions that move currency units from one user identity to another). Classes and complex functionalities are implemented in the blockchain using smart contracts. A *smart contract*, as exemplified by Ethereum [2], is a computer program that self-executes once established and deployed. Smart contracts have been used in a wide range of blockchain-enabled distributed applications to manage digital assets, including auctions [17], financial contracts [18], elections [19], trading platforms [20], and permission management [21]. A smart contract can be seen as a class in an object-oriented programming language where assets are the objects of that class and transactions update the state (ownership) of the objects. The state transformation of a smart contract is made persistent in the blockchain by ensuring that every state change appears as a record in the blockchain. Smart contracts have the advantages of supporting real-time updates, accurate execution, and little human intervention. Smart contracts can be written in different languages such as Solidity and Vyper. A smart contract can also handle automatic conditional payments from escrow. When a payment function is triggered, the smart contract automatically checks the defined conditions and transfers the money according to the defined rules [22].

While permissionless blockchains mostly support cryptocurrency assets, smart contracts are more generic and can support any type of asset. Indeed, a smart contract, like a class in object-oriented programming, could potentially have different attributes and functions. Once a smart contract is written, it can be deployed on a blockchain and different transactions can call the functions of the smart contract to change its attributes or even destroy the contract (using a destructor function), making it void [23]. It should be noted that smart contracts are error-prone, and this has led to significant financial losses resulting from attacks such as Dice2win [24], King of Ether [25], Parity Multisig Bug [26], Accidental [27], and DAO [28]. Over the past few years, different analysis and verification techniques have been proposed to address vulnerabilities of smart contracts [29–34].

2.4 Reaching Agreement Through Mining

In bitcoin, once the transactions in the block are validated, the miner creates a block and tries to add the block to the head of the blockchain. In general, there can be multiple miners in the system, each competing to add a block (with similar or different content, depending on the transactions that reached that miner) to the head of the blockchain. To ensure consistency, there needs to be "agreement" among all miners on *the new block*. This problem has been studied extensively in the distributed system's literature known as *consensus* or *Byzantine Agreement*.

Byzantine agreement protocols are typically defined for a given set of processes n to tolerate at most an *a priori* known number of failures f. The goal of the protocol is for the n processes to agree on a given value (in our case, the block to be added to the head of the blockchain), irrespective of the failures that occur during the execution of the protocol. In a cryptocurrency setting, typically the number of miners is not known and can dynamically change at any moment. Hence, traditional Byzantine agreement protocols are not useful in this context. For applications where the number of participants is known, as in supply chain applications, Byzantine Agreement protocols can be used, and the resulting system is often referred to as *Permissioned Blockchain*. When the number of participants is unknown, the system is called *permissionless blockchain*. Bitcoin and most cryptocurrencies are *permissionless* blockchain systems.

Traditional Byzantine Agreement protocols use communication to achieve consensus. This is typically achieved by communicating with a *quorum* of sites (usually two-thirds of the processes in the system in the case of malicious failures and a majority of the processes in the case of crash or fail-stop failures). Since the number of participating miners is not known, *permissionless blockchain* systems replace communication with *computation*. We focus here on the *proof-of-work (PoW)* approach used by bitcoin.

Whenever a user wants to perform a transfer transaction, they issue the transaction and broadcast it in the peer-to-peer network to as many miners as possible. A miner collects such transactions and immediately creates a block with its corresponding header. The miner has a copy of the current blockchain and, hence, can construct the hash pointer to the current head of the blockchain using its header information. Based on the current transactions in the candidate block, the miner also constructs a Merkle Tree and calculates the corresponding Merkle Tree root hash. Finally, it tries to find the *nonce*, which will qualify it to add that block to the head of the blockchain. A nonce is a string of bits that when concatenated to the current header information, and hashed (using SHA-256) will result in a string with D leading *zero bits*. Given that the cryptographic hash function is a one-way function, it is impossible to efficiently construct an inverse function, hence, the miner keeps trying different values until a qualifying *nonce* is found.

Proof-of-Work (PoW) mining has several advantages. Paramount among these is that any participant in the system can easily verify it. Given a block in the blockchain, a verifier just hashes, using SHA-256 the header content, including the nonce. The outcome should have the specified number, D, of leading zeros. SHA-256 is an easily computed function, and hence verification is straightforward and not costly (unlike the mining process, which takes 10 min on average). Furthermore, a miner cannot cheat the system by *pre-computing* the nonce, as the nonce depends critically on the actual content of the block. More specifically, the nonce is a function of the current header contents, which includes the Merkle Tree root hash. The Merkle Tree root hash is a function of the transfer transactions in the blocks, which are dynamically added to the systems when users issue transfer transactions. SHA-256 is a cryptographic one-way function where no two output values depend on the input in any way. Hence, any pre-computation does not help find a nonce more efficiently.

As an incentive for a miner to create a new block, a miner is awarded a *reward* if successful. This is instantiated as a *reward transaction* which creates the reward amount and awards it to the miner. The reward transaction is issued and signed to the public key of the miner and is added to the block content. This is the primary way in which new bitcoins are created. In bitcoin, the initial reward amount in 2009 was 50 bitcoins. Every 210,000 blocks or approximately every 4 years, this reward amount is halved. Since 2009, the reward has been halved 4 times, from 50 to 25 to 12.5 to 6.25, and the latest on April 19, 2024, the reward value became 3.125 bitcoins. This halving will continue until 2040, when no more reward transactions will be executed and hence no new bitcoins will be created. At this point, there will be 21,000,000 bitcoins in existence. As an incentive for miners to continue mining, a miner also charges a processing fee per transaction.

In bitcoin, the difficulty bits, D, are adapted dynamically to ensure that the average mining time is 10 min. This recalculation is performed after every 2016 blocks. Hence, if each block takes about 10 min to mine, the difficulty is changed approximately every 20160 min, i.e., every 2 weeks. This recalculation, as with most decisions in bitcoin, is completely decentralized. Each miner calculates the actual time it took to produce 2016 blocks based on its own local clock, i.e., *actual time* = time to produce 2016th block—time when *first* block was produced. The miner then calculates the new difficulty number of bits as the old difficulty number of bits * (20160/*actual time*. Hence, if the difficulty increases if 20160 is greater than the actual time, and vice versa, the difficulty decreases if the actual time is greater than 20160. This dynamic adaptation adjusts the mining time to changes in the number of miners, hardware, the underlying infrastructure, and, in general, the bitcoin network computing power. The number of difficulty bits, D, is recorded in the header, and hence provides a disincentive for malicious behavior.

2.5 Permissionless Blockchain System's Limitations

Bitcoin [1] is considered the first successful global-scale peer-to-peer cryptocurrency. Bitcoin and other permissionless blockchain systems eliminate the need for a trusted third party by replacing it with a distributed ledger that is fully replicated among all participants in the cryptocurrency system. This section briefly discusses some of the limitations of permissionless blockchains, especially bitcoin.

2.5.1 Low Performance and Scalability

Despite their current success, permissionless blockchain systems mostly suffer from scalability and performance limitations represented by the number of transactions executed per second, especially when compared with commercially successful online transaction processing (OLTP) financial systems, such as credit card companies. While the Visa payment service is able to handle on average 2000 transactions per second, Bitcoin and Ethereum 1.0 can handle at most 7 and 15 transactions per second, respectively.

In bitcoin, miners need to perform a computationally challenging proof-of-work (PoW) puzzle before they can add (i.e., finalize) any block of transactions to the replicated blockchain. Since the PoW puzzle is computationally hard, very few miners can successfully solve the puzzle, and hence a successful miner can add a block to the blockchain and be guaranteed, with very high probability, to be unique. Many concerns have been raised about the wasted massive energy requirements to mine one transaction block [35]. In addition, the difficulty of bitcoin's Proof of Work (PoW) discourages miners from mining independently and pushes them to form powerful mining farms. Concentrating most of the mining power in a few hands, or pools, risks derailing the whole idea of decentralization.

This mining approach to determine the node eligible to add a new block to the blockchain is in contrast to the distributed system's approach, which has been promoting the use of Byzantine Agreements or consensus, which is efficient and more egalitarian. In fact, consensus protocols such as Paxos [7] have been quite successful in recent years in laying the foundations of global large-scale data management systems. However, Paxos requires a permissioned setting and is only able to tolerate crash failures. An alternative to Paxos that tolerates malicious failures is Practical Byzantine Fault Tolerance (PBFT) [9]. Although it tolerates malicious failures, PBFT still requires a permissioned setting where the number of participants is known. PBFT also requires a large number of message exchanges and hence does not scale to the large number of participants expected in modern-day permissionless environments. Recently, the security and distributed systems communities have been aggressively exploring alternative scalable solutions to resolve the bitcoin protocol shortcomings, e.g., BitcoinNG [36], Byzcoin [37], Elastico [38], and Algorand [39], using efficient and practical off-chain (layer two) and on-chain (layer one) solutions that integrate cryptographic and consensus mechanisms.

Off-chain solutions, which are built on top of the main chain, do not increase the throughput of the protocol, rather move a portion of the transactions off the chain. For example, in Lightning Networks [40, 41], assets are transferred between two different clients via a network of micro-payment channels instead of the main blockchain. While off-chain solutions increase the throughput of the system, they suffer from security issues, e.g., denial-of-service attacks.

In general, security, decentralization, and performance are known as the *scalability trilemma* in blockchain systems [42]. Security requires resistance to threats such as the denial-of-service attacks, 51% attack, or Sybil attacks; decentralization means no single entity can hijack the chain, censor it, or introduce changes in governance; and performance is the ability to handle thousands of transactions per second.

On-chain (layer one) solutions, on the other hand, increase the throughput of the main chain. Layer one solutions are categorized into vertical and horizontal techniques. In vertical scalability, more power is added to each node to perform more tasks. One trivial solution is to increase the block size which results in processing more transactions at once, thus enhancing performance. Increasing the block size, however, increases both the propagation time and the verification time of the block which makes operating full nodes more expensive, which, in turn, could cause less decentralization in the network.

Horizontal techniques, on the other hand, increase the number of nodes in the network to process more transactions. However, most blockchain systems require every transaction to be processed by every single node in the network. As a result, increasing the number of nodes does not necessarily enhance the performance of the system. Another horizontal solution to enhance the scalability of blockchain systems is sharding. Partitioning the data into multiple shards maintained by different subsets of nodes is a proven approach to enhance the scalability of databases [43]. Data sharding techniques are commonly used in globally distributed databases such as H-store [44], Calvin [45], Spanner [43], Scatter [46], Google's Megastore [47], Amazon's Dynamo [48], Facebook's Tao [49], and E-store [50]. However, in such systems, servers (nodes) are assumed to be known and crash-only and a coordinator node is used to process crash-shard transactions. Sharding techniques have also been used in permissionless blockchains, e.g., Elastico [38], OmniLedger [51], and Rapidchain [52].

2.5.2 Probabilistic Finality

Given that there is no specific bound on the time taken to generate a new block, any given node in the system must accept the first valid block it receives as the next head of the blockchain. Since various miners may be competing to generate the next header block, multiple miners may succeed in generating nonces for the new block simultaneously, or at least in close enough times. In this case, a node might receive multiple competing next header blocks, resulting in a *fork*. Forks are a major challenge in a blockchain, which, by definition, is a linear totally ordered linked list. Forks are also problematic since each fork branch is verified *independently* by a different miner. Hence, it is possible that a user Bob may issue conflicting transfer transactions that consume all of Bob's resources. Assume Bob has x bitcoins. If the two concurrent blocks collectively include transfer transactions that consume more than x bitcoins, the blockchain becomes inconsistent. This problem is referred to as *double spending* and needs to be avoided. Not that in the real world with fiat currencies, double spending is not possible. In cash transactions, the physical banknote cannot be replicated (this is guaranteed using watermarks and other forgery hampering physical techniques). In electronic bank transactions, concurrency control protocols ensure that conflicting transactions are not executed concurrently, and when a transaction is executed, the system invariants are checked and validated.

Forks in the Blockchain need to be eliminated. Bitcoin uses a heuristic approach by requiring miners to join the longest chain fork. Initially, when a fork occurs the miner picks either branch at random, however, eventually, one branch will be longer than the other. All honest miners follow the *longest branch* and, eventually, the other branch is abandoned. Note that all transactions in the blocks of the abandoned branch are discarded. This longest branch approach ensures that the blockchain is consistent and is a totally ordered linked list. However, it raises an important question: when is a transfer considered *committed*? In traditional databases, a transaction is committed once all its sub-components have been executed and all the new data is updated on disk. In bitcoin, the heuristic used is to wait till the transfer transaction is stored in a block that is d blocks deep from the current head of the blockchain. In general, bitcoin uses depth 6 to ascertain that a transaction is committed, i.e., the probability of having two concurrent blocks with depth 6 is negligible (0.01% even if an attacker amass more than 10% of the network computing power).

In summary, a transaction in bitcoin becomes increasingly secure and considered "final" over time as more blocks are added to the blockchain, but there is still a very small theoretical chance that it could be reversed. This is called *probabilistic finality*. The likelihood of a transaction being irreversible grows with each new block added, making it practically impossible to change with enough confirmations, but not absolutely guaranteed.

2.5.3 51% and Selfish Mining Attack

Bitcoin is susceptible to an attack by malicious colluding miners if they can gather a majority of the computing resources in the network. A malicious cohort of miners with a majority of the computing power in the network could add a block to the head of the blockchain that includes a transfer transaction for x bitcoins. They wait till that block is d deep, and thus are able to cash the x bitcoins. However, concurrently, and using their majority computing power, they violate the longest chain rule and create a fork just before the block with the x bitcoin transfer. Given that they have more resources, they can now force a longer branch, which contains another transaction that transfers x bitcoins. Since they have a majority of the resources, eventually, the original branch will be discarded, but the malicious miners will have been able to double-spend the x bitcoins. Bitcoin assumes that it is unlikely that 51% of the computing power will be concentrated in the hands of a malicious subset, and hence the 51% attack will not take place.

Another type of attack is *selfish mining* where a single or group of miners exploits Blockchain to gain an unfair advantage over other miners [53]. In selfish mining, selfish miners withhold mined blocks (i.e., creating a private branch) and release them only after honest miners have wasted resources mining alternative blocks. It has been shown that by leveraging a selfish mining attack, a mining pool can attack Bitcoin with even one-third computation power (i.e., less than 51%).

2.6 Reaching Agreement Through Consensus Protocols

In April 1980, Pease, Shostak, and Lamport addressed the problem of consensus in the presence of faults for the first time in the domain of distributed systems [54]. In this fundamental problem, a set of known distributed nodes needs to reach agreement on a single value [55]. Modern large-scale distributed systems such as cloud and blockchain rely on consensus protocols to provide robustness and performance. In cloud data management systems, such as Google's Spanner [43], Amazon's Dynamo [48], and Facebook's Tao [49], consensus protocols are extensively used to enhance fault tolerance. Similarly, permissioned blockchain systems [56–75] use consensus protocols to establish agreement on the order of transaction blocks among a set of known, identified nodes that might not fully trust each other. In the last four decades, numerous consensus protocols have been designed to satisfy the two main requirements of distributed systems, robustness, and performance, using State Machine Replication (SMR) [76] techniques. SMR regulates the deterministic execution of client requests on multiple copies of a server, called replicas, such that every non-faulty replica must execute every request in the same order [76, 77]. The SMR algorithm has to satisfy four main properties [78]: (1) *Agreement*: Every correct node must agree on the same value. (2) *Validity (integrity)*: If a correct node commits a value, then the value must have been proposed by some correct node. (3) *Consistency (total order)*: All correct nodes commit the same value in the same order. (4) *Termination*: Eventually every node commits some value. The first three properties are known as *safety* and the termination property is known as *liveness*.

Synchronous distributed systems assume known bounds on message delays and process speeds [79]. In synchronous systems, all communication proceeds in rounds. In one round, a process may send all the messages it requires, while receiving all messages from other processes. In this manner, no message from one round may influence any messages sent within the same round. On the other hand, in *asynchronous* distributed systems, there are no bounds on the amount of time a node might take to complete its work and then respond with a message [79]. In such systems, there is no global clock nor consistent clock rate, each node processes independently of others, and coordination is achieved via events such as message arrival [80]. As shown by Fischer et al. [81], in an asynchronous system, where nodes can fail, consensus has no solution that is both safe and live. As a result, asynchronous consensus protocols rely on techniques such as randomization [82–85], failure detectors [86, 87], hybridization/wormholes [88, 89], and partial synchrony [90, 91] to circumvent the FLP impossibility.

Each node in a distributed system follows either the crash or Byzantine failure model. In the crash failure model, nodes operate at arbitrary speed, may fail by stopping, and may restart; however, they may not collude, lie, or otherwise attempt to subvert the protocol. Whereas, in the Byzantine failure model, faulty nodes may exhibit arbitrary, potentially malicious, behavior. Crash fault-tolerant protocols, e.g., Paxos [7], guarantee safety in an asynchronous network using $2f+1$ nodes to overcome the simultaneous crash failure of any

f nodes while in Byzantine fault-tolerant protocols, e.g., PBFT [9], $3f+1$ nodes are needed to provide the safety property in the presence of f malicious nodes [92]. In a Byzantine failure model, it is usually assumed that a strong adversary can coordinate malicious nodes and delay communication to compromise the replicated service. However, the adversary cannot subvert standard cryptographic assumptions about collision-resistant hashes, encryption, and signatures. A hybrid failure model admits both crash and malicious failures. Indeed, in a hybrid network, some nodes might crash whereas some others behave maliciously. Hybrid fault-tolerant protocols, e.g., UpRight [93] and SeeMoRe [94], assume a known bound on the maximum number of crash and malicious failures.

We now briefly introduce Paxos [7] and PBFT [9, 95] as well-known crash and Byzantine fault-tolerant protocols.

In Paxos [7], which guarantees safety in an asynchronous network using $2f+1$ nodes, upon receiving a request from a client, the primary (assuming it is already elected) initiates a consensus protocol among the agents of the enterprises by multicasting an accept message including the transaction. Once an agent receives an accept message, it sends an accepted message to the primary. The primary waits for f accepted messages from different agents (plus itself becomes $f + 1$) multicast a commit message to all the agents and send a reply to the client. Upon receiving a commit message from the primary, each agent executes the transaction. Figure 2.3a shows the normal case operation of the Paxos protocol.

In the presence of malicious nodes, PBFT [9, 95] can be used. In PBFT, which guarantees safety in an asynchronous network using $3f+1$ nodes, during a normal case execution, a client sends a request to a (primary) replica. The primary assigns a sequence number to the request to determine the execution order of the request and multicasts a pre-prepare message to all other replicas (*backups*). Upon receiving a valid pre-prepare message from the primary, each backup replica multicasts a prepare message to all replicas and waits for prepare messages from $2f$ different replicas (including the replica itself) that match the pre-prepare message. The goal of the prepare phase is to guarantee safety within the view, i.e., $2f$ replicas received matching pre-prepare messages from the primary replica and agree with the order of the request.

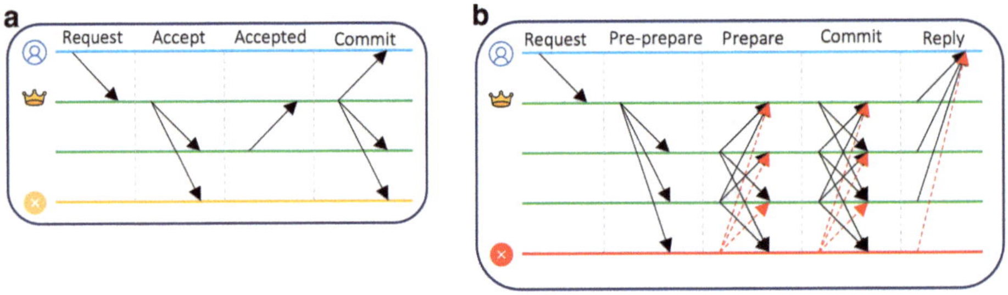

Fig. 2.3 Normal case operation in **a** Paxos [7] and **b** PBFT [9]

Each replica then multicasts a commit message to all replicas. Once a replica receives $2f + 1$ valid commit messages from different replicas, including itself, that match the pre-prepare message, it commits the request. The goal of the commit phase is to ensure safety across views, i.e., the request has been replicated on a majority of non-faulty replicas and can be recovered after (leader) failures. The second and third phases of PBFT have $O(n^2)$ message complexity. If the replica has executed all requests with lower sequence numbers, it executes the request and sends a reply to the client. Finally, the client waits for $f + 1$ valid matching responses from different replicas to make sure at least one correct replica executed its request. PBFT also has a view-change routine that provides liveness by allowing the system to make progress when the primary fails. Figure 2.3(b) shows the normal case operation of PBFT protocol.

References

1. Nakamoto, S.: Bitcoin: A peer-to-peer electronic cash system (2008)
2. Wood, G.: Ethereum: a secure decentralised generalised transaction ledger. Ethereum Project Yellow Paper **151**, 1–32 (2014)
3. Maiyya, S., Zakhary, V., Amiri, M.J., Agrawal, D., El Abbadi, A.: Database and distributed computing foundations of blockchains. In: SIGMOD International Conference on Management of Data, pp. 2036–2041. ACM (2019)
4. Narayanan, A., Clark, J.: Bitcoin's academic pedigree. Commun. ACM **60**(12), 36–45 (2017)
5. Rivest, R.L., Shamir, A., Adleman, L.: A method for obtaining digital signatures and public-key cryptosystems. Commun. ACM **21**(2), 120–126 (1978)
6. Back, A., et al.: Hashcash-a denial of service counter-measure (2002)
7. Lamport, L.: Paxos made simple. ACM Sigact News **32**(4), 18–25 (2001)
8. Lamport, L., Shostak, R., Pease, M.: The byzantine generals problem. Trans. Program. Lang. Syst. (TOPLAS) **4**(3), 382–401 (1982)
9. Castro, M., Liskov, B.: Practical byzantine fault tolerance. In: Symposium on Operating Systems Design and Implementation (OSDI), pp. 173–186. USENIX Association (1999)
10. Bernstein, P.A., Hadzilacos, V., Goodman, N.: Concurrency Control and Recovery in Database Systems (1987)
11. Weikum, G., Vossen, G.: Transactional Information Systems: Theory, Algorithms, and the Practice of Concurrency Control and Recovery. Morgan Kaufmann (2002)
12. Mohan, C., Haderle, D., Lindsay, B., Pirahesh, H., Schwarz, P.: Aries: a transaction recovery method supporting fine-granularity locking and partial rollbacks using write-ahead logging. ACM Trans. Database Syst. (TODS) **17**(1), 94–162 (1992)
13. Narayanan, A., Bonneau, J., Felten, E., Miller, A., Goldfeder, S.: Bitcoin and Cryptocurrency Technologies: A Comprehensive Introduction. Princeton University Press (2016)
14. Merkle, R.C.: A certified digital signature. In: Conference on the Theory and Application of Cryptology, pp. 218–238. Springer (1989)
15. Gray, J., et al.: The transaction concept: Virtues and limitations. In: VLDB, vol. 81, pp. 144–154. Citeseer (1981)
16. Chaum, D.: Blind signatures for untraceable payments. In: Advances in Cryptology: Proceedings of Crypto, vol. 82, pp. 199–203. Springer (1983)

17. Hahn, A., Singh, R., Liu, C.C., Chen, S.: Smart contract-based campus demonstration of decentralized transactive energy auctions. In: Power & Energy Society Innovative Smart Grid Technologies Conference (ISGT), pp. 1–5. IEEE (2017)
18. Biryukov, A., Khovratovich, D., Tikhomirov, S.: Findel: Secure derivative contracts for Ethereum. In: International Conference on Financial Cryptography and Data Security (FC), pp. 453–467. Springer (2017)
19. McCorry, P., Shahandashti, S.F., Hao, F.: A smart contract for boardroom voting with maximum voter privacy. In: International Conference on Financial Cryptography and Data Security (FC), pp. 357–375. Springer (2017)
20. Notheisen, B., Gödde, M., Weinhardt, C.: Trading stocks on blocks-engineering decentralized markets. In: International Conference on Design Science Research in Information System and Technology, pp. 474–478. Springer (2017)
21. Azaria, A., Ekblaw, A., Vieira, T., Lippman, A.: Medrec: Using blockchain for medical data access and permission management. In: International Conference on Open and Big Data (OBD), pp. 25–30. IEEE (2016)
22. Weber, I., Xu, X., Riveret, R., Governatori, G., Ponomarev, A., Mendling, J.: Untrusted business process monitoring and execution using blockchain. In: International Conference on Business Process Management (BPM), pp. 329–347. Springer (2016)
23. Zakhary, V., Amiri, M.J., Maiyya, S., Agrawal, D., El Abbadi, A.: Towards global asset management in blockchain systems. arXiv preprint arXiv:1905.09359 (2019)
24. Peng, Z.: Not a fair game—fairness analysis of dice2win. https://blogs.360.net/post/Fairness_Analysis_of_Dice2win_EN.html (2018)
25. King of the ether throne—post-mortem investigation. https://www.kingoftheether.com/postmortem.html (2016)
26. Technologies, P.: Parity security alert (2017)
27. Browne, R.: 'accidental' bug may have frozen $ 280 million worth of digital coin ether in a cryptocurrency wallet. https://www.cnbc.com/2017/11/08/accidental-bug-may-have-frozen-280-worth-of-ether-on-parity-wallet.html (2017)
28. Siegel, D.: Understanding the DAO attack (2016)
29. Grishchenko, I., Maffei, M., Schneidewind, C.: Foundations and tools for the static analysis of Ethereum smart contracts. In: International Conference on Computer Aided Verification (CAV), pp. 51–78. Springer (2018)
30. Permenev, A., Dimitrov, D., Tsankov, P., Drachsler-Cohen, D., Vechev, M.: Verx: Safety verification of smart contracts. In: symposium on Security and Privacy (S&P), pp. 1661–1677. IEEE (2020)
31. Albert, E., Gordillo, P., Livshits, B., Rubio, A., Sergey, I.: Ethir: A framework for high-level analysis of ethereum bytecode. In: International symposium on automated technology for verification and analysis (ATVA), pp. 513–520. Springer (2018)
32. Tsankov, P., Dan, A., Drachsler-Cohen, D., Gervais, A., Buenzli, F., Vechev, M.: Securify: Practical security analysis of smart contracts. In: Conference on Computer and Communications Security (CCS), pp. 67–82. ACM SIGSAC (2018)
33. Schneidewind, C., Grishchenko, I., Scherer, M., Maffei, M.: ethor: Practical and provably sound static analysis of Ethereum smart contracts. In: Conference on Computer and Communications Security (CCS), pp. 621–640. ACM (2020)
34. Chen, H., Whitters, G., Amiri, M.J., Wang, Y., Loo, B.T.: Declarative smart contracts. In: Joint Meeting on European Software Engineering Conference and Symposium on the Foundations of Software Engineering (ESEC/FSE), pp. 281–293. ACM (2022)
35. Li, J., Li, N., Peng, J., Cui, H., Wu, Z.: Energy consumption of cryptocurrency mining: a study of electricity consumption in mining cryptocurrencies. Energy **168**, 160–168 (2019)

36. Eyal, I., Gencer, A.E., Sirer, E.G., Van Renesse, R.: Bitcoin-ng: A scalable blockchain protocol. In: NSDI, pp. 45–59 (2016)
37. Kogias, E.K., Jovanovic, P., Gailly, N., Khoffi, I., Gasser, L., Ford, B.: Enhancing bitcoin security and performance with strong consistency via collective signing. In: Security Symposium, pp. 279–296. USENIX Association (2016)
38. Luu, L., Narayanan, V., Zheng, C., Baweja, K., Gilbert, S., Saxena, P.: A secure sharding protocol for open blockchains. In: SIGSAC Conference on Computer and Communications Security (CCS), pp. 17–30. ACM (2016)
39. Gilad, Y., Hemo, R., Micali, S., Vlachos, G., Zeldovich, N.: Algorand: Scaling byzantine agreements for cryptocurrencies. In: Symposium on Operating Systems Principles (SOSP), pp. 51–68. ACM (2017)
40. Miller, A., Bentov, I., Bakshi, S., Kumaresan, R., McCorry, P.: Sprites and state channels: payment networks that go faster than lightning. In: International Conference on Financial Cryptography and Data Security (FC), pp. 508–526. Springer (2019)
41. Poon, J., Dryja, T.: The Bitcoin Lightning Network: Scalable Off-chain Instant Payments. https://lightning.network/lightning-network-paper.pdf (2016)
42. Wiki Project, E.: Ethereum wiki project on Sharding blockchains. https://github.com/ethereum/wiki/wiki/Sharding-FAQ (2018)
43. Corbett, J.C., Dean, J., Epstein, M., Fikes, A., Frost, C., Furman, J.J., Ghemawat, S., Gubarev, A., Heiser, C., Hochschild, P.: Spanner: Google's globally distributed database. Trans. Comput. Syst. (TOCS) **31**(3), 8 (2013)
44. Kallman, R., Kimura, H., Natkins, J., Pavlo, A., Rasin, A., Zdonik, S., Jones, E.P., Madden, S., Stonebraker, M., Zhang, Y.: H-store: a high-performance, distributed main memory transaction processing system. Proc. VLDB Endowment **1**(2), 1496–1499 (2008)
45. Thomson, A., Diamond, T., Weng, S.C., Ren, K., Shao, P., Abadi, D.J.: Calvin: fast distributed transactions for partitioned database systems. In: SIGMOD International Conference on Management of Data, pp. 1–12. ACM (2012)
46. Glendenning, L., Beschastnikh, I., Krishnamurthy, A., Anderson, T.: Scalable consistency in scatter. In: Symposium on Operating Systems Principles (SOSP), pp. 15–28. ACM (2011)
47. Baker, J., Bond, C., Corbett, J.C., Furman, J., Khorlin, A., Larson, J., Leon, J.M., Li, Y., Lloyd, A., Yushprakh, V.: Megastore: Providing scalable, highly available storage for interactive services. In: Conference on Innovative Data Systems Research (CIDR) (2011)
48. DeCandia, G., Hastorun, D., Jampani, M., Kakulapati, G., Lakshman, A., Pilchin, A., Sivasubramanian, S., Vosshall, P., Vogels, W.: Dynamo: Amazon's highly available key-value store. Oper. Syst. Rev. (OSR) **41**(6), 205–220 (2007)
49. Bronson, N., Amsden, Z., Cabrera, G., Chakka, P., Dimov, P., Ding, H., Ferris, J., Giardullo, A., Kulkarni, S., Li, H.: Tao: Facebook's distributed data store for the social graph. In: Annual Technical Conference (ATC), pp. 49–60. USENIX Association (2013)
50. Taft, R., Mansour, E., Serafini, M., Duggan, J., Elmore, A.J., Aboulnaga, A., Pavlo, A., Stonebraker, M.: E-store: Fine-grained elastic partitioning for distributed transaction processing systems. Proc. VLDB Endowment **8**(3), 245–256 (2014)
51. Kokoris-Kogias, E., Jovanovic, P., Gasser, L., Gailly, N., Syta, E., Ford, B.: Omniledger: A secure, scale-out, decentralized ledger via sharding. In: Symposium on Security and Privacy (SP), pp. 583–598. IEEE (2018)
52. Zamani, M., Movahedi, M., Raykova, M.: Rapidchain: Scaling blockchain via full sharding. In: SIGSAC Conference on Computer and Communications Security, pp. 931–948. ACM (2018)
53. Eyal, I., Sirer, E.G.: Majority is not enough: bitcoin mining is vulnerable. Commun. ACM **61**(7), 95–102 (2018)
54. Pease, M., Shostak, R., Lamport, L.: Reaching agreement in the presence of faults. J. ACM (JACM) **27**(2), 228–234 (1980)

55. Lamport, L.: The part-time parliament. Trans. Comput. Syst. (TOCS) **16**(2), 133–169 (1998)
56. Baudet, M., Ching, A., Chursin, A., Danezis, G., Garillot, F., Li, Z., Malkhi, D., Naor, O., Perelman, D., Sonnino, A.: State machine replication in the libra blockchain. The Libra Association, Technical Report (2019)
57. Amiri, M.J., Agrawal, D., El Abbadi, A.: CAPER: a cross-application permissioned blockchain. Proc. VLDB Endowment **12**(11), 1385–1398 (2019)
58. Chase, J.M.: Quorum White Paper (2016)
59. Amiri, M.J., Agrawal, D., El Abbadi, A.: SharPer: Sharding permissioned blockchains over network clusters. In: SIGMOD International Conference on Management of Data, pp. 76–88. ACM (2021)
60. Gupta, S., Rahnama, S., Hellings, J., Sadoghi, M.: Resilientdb: Global scale resilient blockchain fabric. Proceed. VLDB Endowment **13**(6), 868–883 (2020)
61. Kwon, J.: Tendermint: consensus without mining (2014)
62. Androulaki, E., Barger, A., Bortnikov, V., Cachin, C., Christidis, K., De Caro, A., Enyeart, D., Ferris, C., Laventman, G., Manevich, Y.: Hyperledger fabric: a distributed operating system for permissioned blockchains. In: European Conference on Computer Systems (EuroSys), pp. 30:1–30:15. ACM (2018)
63. Gorenflo, C., Lee, S., Golab, L., Keshav, S.: Fastfabric: Scaling hyperledger fabric to 20,000 transactions per second. In: International Conference on Blockchain and Cryptocurrency (ICBC), pp. 455–463. IEEE (2019)
64. Gorenflo, C., Golab, L., Keshav, S.: Xox fabric: a hybrid approach to transaction execution. In: International Conference on Blockchain and Cryptocurrency (ICBC), pp. 1–9. IEEE (2020)
65. Sharma, A., Schuhknecht, F.M., Agrawal, D., Dittrich, J.: Blurring the lines between blockchains and database systems: the case of hyperledger fabric. In: SIGMOD International Conference on Management of Data, pp. 105–122. ACM (2019)
66. Ruan, P., Loghin, D., Ta, Q.T., Zhang, M., Chen, G., Ooi, B.C.: A transactional perspective on execute-order-validate blockchains. In: SIGMOD International Conference on Management of Data, pp. 543–557. ACM (2020)
67. Hyperledger iroha. https://github.com/hyperledger/iroha
68. Corda. https://github.com/corda/corda
69. Greenspan, G.: Multichain private blockchain-white paper. http://www.multichain.com/download/MultiChain-White-Paper.pdf (2015)
70. Amiri, M.J., Loo, B.T., Agrawal, D., El Abbadi, A.: Qanaat: a scalable multi-enterprise permissioned blockchain system with confidentiality guarantees. Proc. VLDB Endowment **15**(11), 2839–2852 (2022)
71. Chain. http://chain.com
72. Qi, J., Chen, X., Jiang, Y., Jiang, J., Shen, T., Zhao, S., Wang, S., Zhang, G., Chen, L., Au, M.H., et al.: Bidl: a high-throughput, low-latency permissioned blockchain framework for datacenter networks. In: Symposium on Operating Systems Principles (SOSP), pp. 18–34. ACM (2021)
73. Buchnik, Y., Friedman, R.: Fireledger: a high throughput blockchain consensus protocol. Proceed. VLDB Endowment **13**(9), 1525–1539 (2020)
74. Amiri, M.J., Lai, Z., Patel, L., Loo, B.T., Lo, E., Zhou, W.: Saguaro: An edge computing-enabled hierarchical permissioned blockchain. In: International Conference on Data Engineering (ICDE), pp. 259–272. IEEE (2023)
75. Amiri, M.J., Maiyya, S., Shu, D., Agrawal, D., El Abbadi, A.: Ziziphus: Scalable data management across byzantine edge servers. In: International Conference on Data Engineering (ICDE), pp. 490–502. IEEE (2023)
76. Lamport, L.: Time, clocks, and the ordering of events in a distributed system. Commun. ACM **21**(7), 558–565 (1978)

77. Schneider, F.B.: Implementing fault-tolerant services using the state machine approach: a tutorial. Comput. Surv. (CSUR) **22**(4), 299–319 (1990)
78. Cachin, C., Guerraoui, R., Rodrigues, L.: Introduction to Reliable and Secure Distributed Programming. Springer Science & Business Media (2011)
79. Lynch, N.A.: Distributed Algorithms. Elsevier (1996)
80. Amiri, M.J., Agrawal, D., El Abbadi, A.: Modern large-scale data management systems after 40 years of consensus. In: International Conference on Data Engineering (ICDE), pp. 1794–1797. IEEE (2020)
81. Fischer, M.J., Lynch, N.A., Paterson, M.S.: Impossibility of distributed consensus with one faulty process. J. ACM (JACM) **32**(2), 374–382 (1985)
82. Cachin, C., Kursawe, K., Shoup, V.: Random oracles in Constantinople: practical asynchronous byzantine agreement using cryptography. J. Cryptol. **18**(3), 219–246 (2005)
83. Ben-Or, M.: Another advantage of free choice: Completely asynchronous agreement protocols (extended abstract). In: Symposium on Principles of Distributed Computing (PODC), pp. 27–30. ACM (1983)
84. Rabin, M.O.: Randomized byzantine generals. In: Symposium on Foundations of Computer Science (SFCS), pp. 403–409. IEEE (1983)
85. Gao, Y., Lu, Y., Lu, Z., Tang, Q., Xu, J., Zhang, Z.: Efficient asynchronous byzantine agreement without private setups. In: International Conference on Distributed Computing Systems (ICDCS), pp. 246–257. IEEE (2022)
86. Chandra, T.D., Toueg, S.: Unreliable failure detectors for reliable distributed systems. J. ACM (JACM) **43**(2), 225–267 (1996)
87. Malkhi, D., Reiter, M.: Unreliable intrusion detection in distributed computations. In: Computer Security Foundations Workshop, pp. 116–124. IEEE (1997)
88. Correia, M., Neves, N.F., Lung, L.C., Veríssimo, P.: Low complexity byzantine-resilient consensus. Distrib. Comput. **17**(3), 237–249 (2005)
89. Neves, N.F., Correia, M., Verissimo, P.: Solving vector consensus with a wormhole. IEEE Trans. Parallel Distrib. Syst. **16**(12), 1120–1131 (2005)
90. Dwork, C., Lynch, N., Stockmeyer, L.: Consensus in the presence of partial synchrony. J. ACM (JACM) **35**(2), 288–323 (1988)
91. Dolev, D., Dwork, C., Stockmeyer, L.: On the minimal synchronism needed for distributed consensus. J. ACM (JACM) **34**(1), 77–97 (1987)
92. Bracha, G., Toueg, S.: Asynchronous consensus and broadcast protocols. J. ACM (JACM) **32**(4), 824–840 (1985)
93. Clement, A., Kapritsos, M., Lee, S., Wang, Y., Alvisi, L., Dahlin, M., Riche, T.: Upright cluster services. In: Symposium on Operating Systems Principles (SOSP), pp. 277–290. ACM (2009)
94. Amiri, M.J., Maiyya, S., Agrawal, D., El Abbadi, A.: SeeMoRe: a fault-tolerant protocol for hybrid cloud environments. In: International Conference on Data Engineering (ICDE), pp. 1345–1356. IEEE (2020)
95. Castro, M., Liskov, B.: Practical byzantine fault tolerance and proactive recovery. Trans. Comput. Syst. (TOCS) **20**(4), 398–461 (2002)

3 Performance

3.1 Introduction

Large-scale data management systems require high performance in terms of throughput and latency. Permissioned blockchain systems process transactions using either an optimistic or pessimistic approach. These approaches offer trade-offs in performance depending on the degree and frequency of contention and conflict among transactions. In the optimistic approach, nodes speculatively execute transactions without running a consensus protocol to definitively establish an order, whereas, in the pessimistic approach, transactions are first ordered and then executed.

Most early permissioned blockchains, e.g., Tendermint [1] and Multichain [2], employ the traditional *order-execute (OX)* paradigm where nodes agree on the total order of the transaction blocks using a consensus protocol and then the transactions are sequentially executed on all nodes in the same order. The OX paradigm suffers from performance degradation due to the sequential execution of transactions on all nodes. Hyperledger Fabric [3], on the other hand, presents a new paradigm for permissioned blockchains by switching the order of the execution and order phases. In Hyperledger Fabric, the order-execute-validate (XOV) paradigm has been used where transactions of different applications are first executed in parallel and then an ordering service consisting of a set of nodes uses a consensus protocol to establish agreement on the total order of all transactions. Fabric improves performance by executing transactions in parallel. However, the workloads of distributed applications might be contentious, i.e., include a high percentage of conflicting transactions. Under these workloads, several transactions simultaneously perform conflicting operations on a few popular records. As a result, in the presence of any contention in the workload, the validation phase of Fabric has to disregard the effects of conflicting transactions, which negatively impacts the system's performance.

M. J. Amiri et al., *Blockchain-Enabled Large-Scale Transaction Management*,
Synthesis Lectures on Data Management,
https://doi.org/10.1007/978-3-031-91058-6_3

This chapter discusses the OX and XOV paradigms and then presents OXII: an order-parallel execute paradigm for permissioned blockchains. OXII targets distributed applications processing workloads with *some degree of contention*. In the OXII paradigm, ordered nodes generate a dependency graph for the transactions within a block after the order phase. The dependency graph enables higher concurrency by allowing the parallel execution of non-conflicting transactions.

We then present ParBlockchain [4], a permissioned blockchain system designed specifically in the OXII paradigm. ParBlockchain processes transactions in the order and execution phases. In the order phase, transactions are ordered in a dependency graph and put in blocks. In the execution phase, the executors of each application execute the transactions of the corresponding application following the dependency graph. As long as the partial order of transactions in the dependency graph is preserved, the transactions of different applications can be executed in parallel.

A key contribution of this chapter is to show how workloads with conflicting transactions can be handled efficiently by a blockchain system without rolling back (aborting) the processed transactions or executing all transactions sequentially.

The rest of this chapter is organized as follows. Sections 3.2 and 3.3 briefly describe OX and XOV paradigms and their limitations. The OXII paradigm is introduced in Sect. 3.4. Section 3.5 presents ParBlockchain, a permissioned blockchain system designed specifically in the OXII paradigm. Section 3.6 discusses the performance of different paradigms under different workloads, and Sect. 3.7 concludes the chapter.

3.2 Order-Execute (OX) Paradigm

The two main stages of transaction processing are "Order" and "execution". Most permissioned blockchain systems follow the *order-execute* paradigm where the system first orders transactions and then executes them in the same order on all replicas sequentially. Since a permissioned blockchain system consists of known and identified nodes, traditional consensus protocols can be used to establish consensus on the order of requests [5].

In order-execute permissioned blockchains, a set of nodes (i.e., orderers) establishes agreement on a unique order of the incoming transactions using consensus protocols. Depending on the failure model of nodes, a Byzantine fault-tolerant protocol, e.g., PBFT [6], Hotstuff [7], a crash fault-tolerant protocol, e.g., Paxos [8], Raft [9], or even a hybrid, e.g., SeeMoRe [10], UpRight [11], fault-tolerant protocol can be used. Orderer nodes then generate and multicast blocks to other nodes (i.e., executors). Executor nodes (could be the same as ordered nodes) execute the transactions of a block sequentially in the same order, append transactions to the blockchain ledger, and update the blockchain state (i.e., datastore).

The order-execute paradigm is widely used in different permissioned blockchain systems, such as Tendermint [1], Quorum [12], Multichain [2], Chain Core [13], Hyperledger Iroha

[14], ResilientDB [15], and Corda [16]. Existing permissioned blockchains that employ the order-execute paradigm differ mainly in their ordering routines. For example, Tendermint [1] uses a PBFT-based consensus protocol which differs from the original PBFT in several ways. First, only a subset of nodes, called validators, participates in the consensus protocol where to become a validator, nodes need to lock their coins. Second, Tendermint uses the leader rotation technique and switches the leader after each round (i.e., each attempt to construct a block) in a round-robin manner. Third, Tendermint implements a proof-of-stake consensus mechanism where validators do not have the same "weight" in the consensus protocol, and the voting power of a validator corresponds to the number of its bounded coins. As a result, one-third or two-thirds of the validators are defined based on the proportions of the total voting power not the number of validators. Quorum [12] as an Ethereum-based [17] permissioned blockchain introduces a consensus protocol based on Raft [9]: a well-known crash fault-tolerant protocol. Quorum supports public and private transactions and uses the zero-knowledge proof technique to ensure the confidentiality of private transactions.

In order-execute permissioned blockchain systems, every transaction is executed on every node. The sequential execution of transactions on every node, however, reduces the blockchain performance in terms of throughput and latency.

3.3 Execute-Order-Validate (XOV) Paradigm

In contrast to the order-execute paradigm, Hyperledger Fabric [3] presents a new paradigm for permissioned blockchains by switching the order of execution and order stages. The execute-order paradigm was first presented in Eve [18] in the context of Byzantine fault-tolerant SMR. In Eve peers execute transactions concurrently, achieve consensus on the order of transactions, and then verify that they all reach the same output state. Eve uses an Optimistic Concurrency Control (OCC) [19] by assuming low data contention where conflicts are rare.

Hyperledger Fabric uses a similar strategy; a client sends a request to a subset of peers, called endorsers (the nodes that run smart contracts). Each endorser executes the request and sends the result back to the client. When the client receives a sufficient number of endorsements (specified by an endorsement policy), it assembles a transaction including all the endorsements and sends it to the ordering peers to establish a *total order* on transactions. This set of nodes establishes consensus on the order of transactions, creates blocks, and broadcasts them to every node. Finally, each peer validates a transaction within a received block by checking the endorsement policy and read-write conflicts and then updates the ledger. Since a validation phase occurs at the end, the paradigm is called *execute-order-validate*. Note that in Fabric the consensus protocol is pluggable and the system can use a crash fault-tolerant protocol, e.g., Paxos [8] or Raft [9], or a Byzantine fault-tolerant protocol, e.g., PBFT [20].

While Fabric improves performance by executing transactions in parallel (instead of sequentially as the order-execute paradigm does), in the presence of any contention, i.e., conflicting transactions, in the workload (which is common in distributed applications), it has to disregard the effects of conflicting transactions which negatively impacts the performance of the system. Two transactions *conflict* if they access the same record and one of them makes a write operation on the record. In such a situation, the order of executing the transactions is important, indeed, the later transaction in a block has to wait for the earlier transaction to be executed first. As a result, if two conflicting transactions execute in parallel, the result is invalid. Although Fabric guarantees correctness by checking the conflicts in the validation phase (the last phase) and disregarding the effects of invalid transactions, such conflicts significantly reduce the performance of the system. Different techniques have been proposed to improve the performance of Fabric while still following its XOV paradigm [21–29].

FastFabric [22] uses different data structures and caching techniques, and parallelizes the transaction validation pipeline to increase Fabric's throughput for conflict-free transaction workloads. Fabric++ [25] employs concurrency control techniques from databases to early abort transactions or reorder them after the order phase to reconcile the potential conflicts. FabricSharp [24] goes one step further and presents an algorithm to early filter out transactions that can never be reordered and also proposes a reordering technique that eliminates unnecessary aborts (resulting from strong serializability guarantees of Fabric++ while Fabric requires serializability guarantees). Finally, XOX Fabric [21] model consists of a pre-order and a post-order execution step where the post-order execution is added after the validation step to re-execute transactions that are invalidated due to read-write conflicts.

3.4 Order-Parallel-Execute Paradigm (OXII)

This section discusses OXII, an order-execute paradigm for permissioned blockchain systems. OXII is mainly designed to support applications with contentious workloads. In OXII, each node has one of the following roles:

- *Clients* that send operations to be executed by the system.
- *Orderers* that agree on a total order of all transactions.
- *Executors* that validate and execute transactions.

The set of nodes in OXII is denoted by $N = O \cup X$ where O is the set of orderers and X is the set of executors. OXII supports distributed applications running concurrently on the blockchain. For each application, a program code including the logic of that application (*smart contract*) is installed on a (non-empty) subset of executor peers called the *agents* of the application. We use $\mathcal{A} = \{A_1, ..., A_n\}$ to denote the set of applications (ids) and $\Sigma(A_i)$ to specify the non-empty set of agents of each application A_i where $\Sigma : \mathcal{A} \mapsto 2^X - \emptyset$. Every peer in the system is aware of the agents of each application and the set of orderers.

Each pair of peers is connected with point-to-point bi-directional communication channels. Network links are pairwise authenticated, which guarantees that a Byzantine node cannot forge a message from a correct node, i.e., if node i receives a message m in the incoming link from node j, then node j must have sent message m to i beforehand.

3.4.1 Orderers

Orderers use an asynchronous fault-tolerant protocol to establish consensus. OXII, similar to Fabric [3], uses a pluggable consensus protocol for ordering. Depending on the characteristics of the network and peers, OXII might employ a Byzantine, a crash, or a hybrid fault-tolerant protocol. The number of orderers is also determined by the utilized protocol and the maximum number of simultaneous failures in the network. Furthermore, orderers do not have access to any smart contract or the application state, nor do they participate in the execution of transactions. This makes orderers independent of other peers and adaptable to a changing environment.

Orderers batch multiple transactions into blocks to improve the system's performance by making data transfers more efficient, especially in a geo-distributed setting. It also amortizes the cost of cryptography.

In the OXII paradigm, as shown in Fig. 3.1, clients send requests (transactions) to be executed. Here, transactions t_1 and t_3 are for application A_1 and t_2, t_4, and t_5 are for another application A_2. The ordered nodes (o_1, o_2, o_3, and o_4) order transactions using a consensus protocol, e.g., PBFT protocol [20] in this example, and put them into a block. The resulting block contains five transactions ordered as $[t_1, t_5, t_4, t_3, t_2]$.

Next, orderers generate a "dependency graph" for the transactions within a block. In order to generate dependency graphs a priori knowledge of transactions' read-set and write-

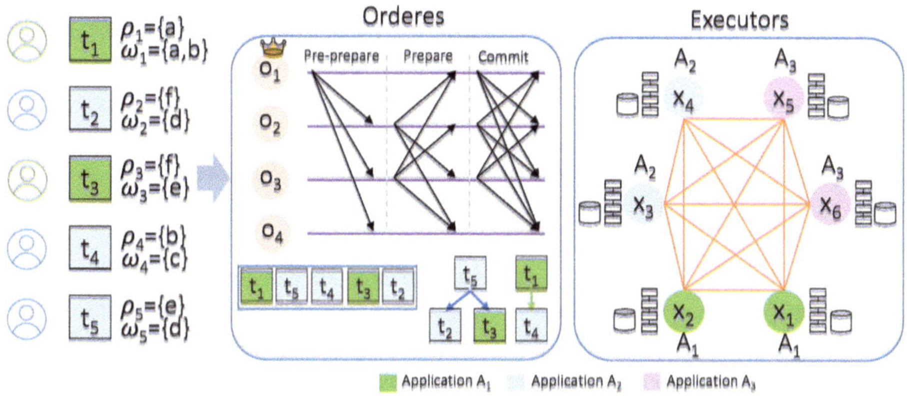

Fig. 3.1 Components of the OXII paradigm

set is needed. Each transaction consists of a sequence of read and write operations, each accessing a single record. Here we assume that the read-set and write-set are pre-declared or can be obtained from the transactions via a static analysis, e.g., all records involved in a transaction are accessed by their primary keys. Note that even if that assumption does not hold, the system can use techniques like speculative execution [30] to obtain the read-set and write-set of each transaction.

Given a transaction t, we use $\omega(t)$ and $\rho(t)$ to represent the write-set and read-set of the transaction, respectively. Each transaction t is also associated with a timestamp $ts(t)$ where for each two transactions t_i and t_j within a block such that t_i appears before t_j, $ts(t_i) < ts(t_j)$.

We define "ordering dependencies" to show possible conflicts between two transactions of the same or different applications. Two transactions are conflicting transactions if they both access some data object o and (at least) one of the transactions performs a write operation on data object o.

Definition 3.1 Given two transactions t_i and t_j. An *ordering dependency* $t_i \succ t_j$ exists if and only if $ts(t_j) > ts(t_i)$ and one of the following holds:

- $\rho(t_i) \cap \omega(t_j) \neq \varnothing$,
- $\omega(t_i) \cap \rho(t_j) \neq \varnothing$,
- $\omega(t_i) \cap \omega(t_j) \neq \varnothing$.

Definition 3.2 Given a block of transactions, the *dependency graph* of the block is a directed graph $G = (T, E)$ where T is the set of transactions within the block and $E = \{(t_i, t_j) \mid t_i \succ t_j\}$ represents the set of edges (i.e., ordering dependencies).

We use the example in Fig. 3.1 to illustrate the dependency graph construction process. As can be seen, the block consists of five transactions which are ordered as $[t_1, t_5, t_4, t_3, t_2]$, i.e., $ts(t_1) < ts(t_5) < ts(t_4) < ts(t_3) < ts(t_2)$. Since t_4 reads data object b which is written by an earlier transaction t_1 there is an ordering dependency $t_1 \succ t_4$, thus (t_1, t_4) is an edge of the dependency graph. Similarly, t_2 writes data object d which is also written by t_5 ($t_5 \succ t_2$) and t_3 writes data object e which is read by t_5 ($t_5 \succ t_3$). As a result, edges (t_5, t_2) and (t_5, t_3) are also added to the graph. The executors then use the constructed graph to execute independent transactions, e.g., t_1 and t_2, in parallel.

The dependency graph generator is an independent module in the OXII paradigm. Therefore, it can also be adapted to a multi-version database system [31] where each write operation creates a new version of a data object, and reads are directed to the correct version based on the position of the corresponding transaction in the block (log). Since writes do not overwrite each other, the system has more flexibility to manage the order of reads and writes. As a result, for any two transactions t_i and t_j within a block where t_i appears before t_j, t_i and

t_j can concurrently write the same data item or t_i reads and t_j writes the same data item. However, if t_i includes a write and t_j includes a read operation to the same data object, they cannot be executed in parallel.

A dependency graph exposes conflicts between transactions to give a partial order of transactions. Hence, as long as the order of transaction execution is consistent with the dependency graph, the execution results are valid. Using dependency graphs leads to higher concurrency by enabling the parallel execution of non-conflicting transactions within a block. Such parallelism highly improves the performance of the OXII paradigm compared to the traditional order-execute paradigm where transactions are executed sequentially.

When the dependency graph is generated, orderers multicast a message including the block and its dependency graph to all executors. Depending on the employed consensus protocol, either the leader (in case of crash fault-tolerant protocols) or all the orderers (in case of Byzantine fault-tolerant protocols) multicast the message.

3.4.2 Executors

Executing and validating transactions, updating the ledger and the application state, and multicasting the application state after executing transactions are the main services of executor peers. Executors in OXII correspond to the endorsers in Hyperledger [3]. Each executor peer maintains (a) the blockchain ledger, (b) the application state (database), and (c) the application logic (smart contracts).

When a block of transactions is executed and validated, each executor peer appends the block to its copy of the blockchain ledger. Each executor node is an agent for one or more applications and maintains the corresponding smart contracts. Upon receiving a transaction block from the orderers, an executor executes its related transactions (transactions where the executor is an agent for the corresponding applications) following the dependency graph and multicasts the execution results to all other peers.

For each transaction within a block where the executor is not an agent of the transaction's application, the executor waits for a specified number of matching updates from different executors, who are the agents of the transaction, before committing the update. This is needed to prevent a malicious executor from committing an invalid result. It also tolerates the non-deterministic execution of transactions. The required number of matching results from executors is decided by the system and known to all executors (similar to endorsement policies in Fabric). We use $\tau(A)$ to denote the required number of matching updates for the transactions of application A.

In Fig. 3.1, executor nodes x_1 and x_2 are the agents of application A_1 (with transactions t_1 and t_3) and executor nodes x_3 and x_4 are the agents of application A_2 (with transactions t_2, t_4, and t_5).

3.5 ParBlockchain

In this section, we present ParBlockchain [4], a permissioned blockchain system designed specifically in the OXII paradigm. We first give a summary of ParBlockchain and then explain its order and execution phases in detail.

3.5.1 ParBlockchain Overview

The normal case operation for ParBlockchain to execute transactions proceeds as follows. Clients send requests to the orderers and the orderers run a consensus protocol to reach agreement on the order of transactions. Orderers then construct a block of transactions and generate a dependency graph for the transactions within the block.

Once the dependency graph is generated, the block along with its dependency graph is multicast to all the executor nodes. The executors which are the agents of the applications of transactions within the block execute the corresponding transactions and multicast the results, i.e., updated records in the datastore, to every executor node. Each executor node in the network waits for the required number of matching results from the executors before updating the ledger and application state (database). Multiple matching results are needed to deal with malicious executors and the non-deterministic execution of transactions. The required number of matching results for each application is determined by the system and might be different for different applications.

The flow of transactions in ParBlockchain can be seen in Fig. 3.2 where p_3, p_4, and p_5 are the orderer nodes, and p_1, p_2, and p_6 are the executor nodes from which p_1 and p_2 are the agents for the received request. Upon receiving requests from clients, orderers order the requests, put them into a block, generate the dependency graph for the block, and multicast the block along with the graph to all the executor nodes. The agents of the corresponding application (e.g., p_1 and p_2) execute the transactions and multicast the updated state of the application data to the other executor nodes. Upon receiving the required number of matching messages for each transaction (e.g., two in this example), each executor commits (or aborts) the transaction by updating the state. The block is also appended to the ledger.

3.5.2 Order Phase

The goal of the order phase is to establish a total order on client requests. A client c requests an operation op for some application A by sending a message $\langle \text{REQUEST}, op, A, ts_c, c\rangle_{\sigma_c}$ to the orderer o it believes to be the *primary* (an orderer node that initiates the consensus protocol). Here, ts_c is the client's timestamp and the entire message is signed with the client signature σ_c. We use timestamps of clients to totally order the requests of each client and to ensure exactly once semantics for the execution of client requests.

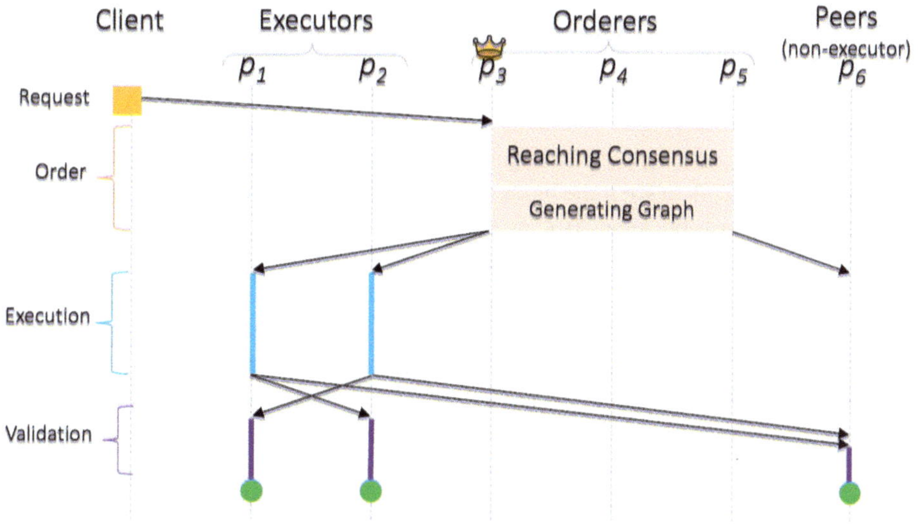

Fig. 3.2 Processing transactions in ParBlockchain

Upon receiving a client request, the primary orderer o checks the signature to ensure it is valid, makes sure the client is allowed to send requests for application A (by checking access control policies), and then initiates a consensus protocol by multicasting the request to all other ordered nodes. Depending on the utilized consensus protocol, several rounds of communication between orderers are needed to achieve consensus on the order of each transaction.

Once the orderers agree on the order of a transaction, they put the transaction in a block. Batching multiple transactions into blocks improves the throughput of the broadcast protocol. Blocks have a pre-defined maximal size, maximal number of transactions, and maximal time the block production takes since the first transaction of a new block was received. When any of these three conditions is met, a block is full. Since transactions are received in order, the first two conditions are deterministic. In the third case, to ensure that the produced blocks by all orderers are the same, the primary sends a cut-block message in the consensus step of the last request.

When a block is completed, each ordered node independently generates a dependency graph for the block, as explained in Sect. 3.4.1. Generating dependency graphs requires a priori knowledge of transactions' read- and write-set. Here, we assume that the requests include the read-set and write-set.

When the graph is constructed, each orderer node o multicasts a message $\langle \text{NEWBLOCK}, n, B, G(B), \mathbf{A}, o, h \rangle_{\sigma_o}$ to all executor nodes where n is the sequence number of the block, B is the actual block with all the request messages, $G(B)$ is the dependency graph of B, $\mathbf{A}$ is the set of applications that have transactions in block B, and $h = H(B')$ where $H(.)$ denotes the cryptographic hash function and B' is the block with sequence number $n-1$.

3.5.3 Execution Phase

Each application request is executed on the specified set of executors, i.e., agents of that application. Upon receiving a newBlock message $\langle \text{NEWBLOCK}, n, B, G(B), \mathbf{A}, o, h \rangle_{\sigma_o}$ from some orderer o, executor x checks the signature and the hash to be valid and logs the message. It also checks the set $\mathbf{A}$ to see if the block contains any transaction that needs to be executed by the node, i.e., an application $A_i \in \mathbf{A}$ such that $x \in \Sigma(A_i)$.

When an executor node receives a sufficient number of matching newBlock messages, e.g., $f + 1$ messages if the consensus protocol is PBFT, it marks block B as a valid block and enters the execution phase. The execution phase consists of two main procedures that are run concurrently: (1) executing transactions following the dependency graph and multicasting commit messages including the execution results to other executor nodes and (2) updating the application state upon receiving commit messages from a sufficient number of executor nodes.

If an executor node is not an agent of any transaction within the block, the node becomes a *passive* node and only the third procedure is run to update the state. However, if a node is an agent for some transaction's application in the block, it runs all three procedures, executes the corresponding transactions following the dependency graph, multicasts the results, and also updates the state.

A transaction can be executed only if all of its "predecessors" in the dependency graph have been executed. We define functions $Pre()$ and $Suc()$ to present the set of predecessors and successors of a node in a dependency graph, respectively. More formally, given a dependency graph $G = (T, E)$, and a node (transaction) t in $\mathcal{T}$, $Pre(t) = \{t' \mid (t', t) \in E\}$ and $Suc(t) = \{t' \mid (t, t') \in E\}$.

The execution procedure on an executor node x is shown in Algorithm 1. An empty set T_x is initiated to keep the transactions that will be executed by executor x, i.e., x is an agent for the application of those transactions. Set X stores the executed transactions. Such transactions are (1) executed by x or (2) executed by some other agents and x has received their execution results. Set R_x maintains the execution results that will be shared with other executor nodes. First, we add all transactions of the dependency graph with no incoming edges to set T_x. A transition t in T_x is executed if all its predecessors are executed.

To multicast the execution results, depending on the transactions' applications, three different situations could happen. If all the transactions within a block belong to the same application, an agent x executes all of the transactions following the dependency graph and multicast a commit message $\langle \text{COMMIT}, S, x \rangle_{\sigma_x}$ to all other executor nodes. Here, S presents the state of the blockchain and consists of a set of pairs (t, r) where t is a transaction (id) and r is the set of updated records resulting from the execution of t on the datastore. Note that if a transaction t is invalid, the executor puts $(t, \texttt{"abort"})$ in S.

If the transactions within a block are for different applications but the transactions of each application access a disjoint set of records, the agents still can execute the corresponding transactions independently and multicast a single commit message with all the results to

Algorithm 1 Execution of Transactions on an executor x

Input: A transaction block B and its dependency graph $G(B) = (T, E)$

```
Initiate Set Tx = ∅                                  ▷ transactions to be executed by x
Initiate Set X = ∅                                   ▷ executed transactions
Initiate Set Rx = ∅                                  ▷ execution results to be shared
Cut = False           ▷ Cut is used to determine when the results should be multicast
for every transaction t in T where Pre(t) = ∅ do     ▷ transactions with no incoming edges
    Tx.add(t)
end for
while Tx in not empty do
    choose a transaction t ∈ Tx
    if Pre(t) ⊆ X then
        r ← Execute(t)                               ▷ r is the result of executing transaction t
        Tx.remove(t)
        X.add(t)
        Rx.add(t, r)
        for every ts ∈ Suc(t) do
            if x is an agent of ts's application then
                Tx.add(ts)
            end if
            if ts's application is different from t's application then
                Cut = True
            end if
        end for
        if Cut = True then
            Multicast ⟨COMMIT, Rx, x⟩σx to all executors
            Rx.empty()
            Cut = False
        end if
    end if
end while
if Rx ≠ ∅ then
    Multicast ⟨COMMIT, Rx, x⟩σx to all executors
end if
```

other executor nodes. In this case, the dependency graph is disconnected and can be decomposed into different components where the transactions of each component are for the same application and no edge connects any two components.

However, if there are some dependencies between the transactions of two applications, the agents of those two applications cannot execute the transactions independently. In fact, the agents of one application have to wait for the agents of other applications to execute all their transactions and send the commit message which might result in a deadlock situation.

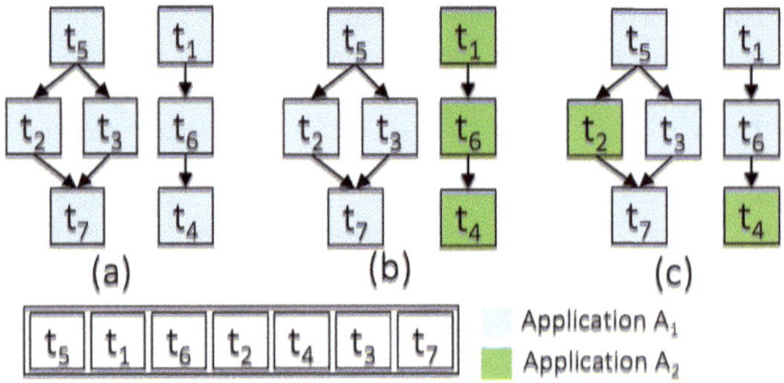

Fig. 3.3 Three dependency graphs

Figure 3.3 shows three dependency graphs for a block of seven transactions t_1–t_7. In Fig. 3.3a, all the seven transactions belong to the same application, A_1. Therefore, the agents of application A_1 can execute the transactions following the dependency graph and multicast the results of all transactions together when they are all executed. In Fig. 3.3b although the transactions belong to different applications (t_2, t_3, t_5, and t_7 are for application A_1 and t_1, t_4, and t_6 are for application A_2), there is no dependency between the transactions of application A_1 and the transactions of application A_2. As a result, the agents can still execute independently and multicast the results once the execution of their transactions is completed. However, in Fig. 3.3c, since there are some dependencies between the transactions of the two applications, the agents cannot execute their transactions independently. For example, to execute transaction t_2, the agents of application A_2 need the execution results of transaction t_5 from the agents of A_1. Similarly, transaction t_4 cannot be executed before committing the execution results of transaction t_6.

To prevent a deadlock situation, one possibility is that agents send commit messages as soon as the execution of each transaction is completed. While this approach solves the blocking problem, the number of exchanged commit messages will be large. Indeed, if a block includes n transactions and each application has (on average) m agents, there will be $n * m$ exchanged commit messages for the block.

A more efficient way is to send commit messages when the execution results are needed by some other agents. Basically, an agent keeps executing the transactions and collecting the results until the results of an executed transaction are needed by some other transactions that belong to other applications. At that time, the agent generates a commit message including the results of all the executed transactions (that have not been shared) and multicasts it to all executor nodes. Upon receiving a commit message from an executor, the node validates the signature and logs the message. Once the node receives a sufficient number of matching results for a transaction, the results are reflected in the datastore and the transaction is marked as committed.

Algorithm 2 Updating the Blockchain State

Input: Transaction block B along its dependency graph $G(B) = (T, E)$

for every transaction t in B **do**
    Initialize set $log_x(t)$ to be empty
end for
Upon Receiving a valid $\langle \text{COMMIT}, S, n \rangle_{\sigma_n}$ message from node n
for every record $(t, r) \in S$ **do**
    Add (r, n) to $log_x(t)$
    if Matching records in $log_x(t)$ is equal to the predefined threshold **then**
        Update the blockchain state
        Add t to X
    end if
end for

As shown in Algorithm 1, when the execution of a transaction t is completed, the node checks all the successor nodes of t in the dependency graph. If any of the successor nodes of t belongs to an application different from the application of t, the execution result of transaction t might be needed by other agents. Hence, node x multicasts the results of executed transactions, R_x, to all other executors.

For example, in Fig. 3.3c, upon executing the transaction t_5, since t_5 has a successor node t_2 that belongs to another application, the executor node multicasts a commit message including the execution results of t_5 to all other executor nodes. Note that if t_1 is already executed, the executor node puts the execution results of t_1 in the commit message as well. Similarly, when the execution of t_6 is completed, the executor node multicasts a commit message including the execution results of t_6 and any other executed but not yet multicast transactions.

When an executor receives commit messages from other executor nodes, it updates its copy of the blockchain state. The updating procedure on a node x is presented in Algorithm 2. The procedure first initializes an empty set $log_x(t)$ to collect execution results for every transaction t. When node x receives a valid commit message $\langle \text{COMMIT}, S, n \rangle_{\sigma_n}$ from some executor n, node x checks set S, which includes pairs of transactions and their execution results. For each pair (t, r) in set S of a commit message received from node n, if n is an agent for the application of transaction t (i.e., the result is valid), a pair of (r, n) (execution result and the executor) is added to set $log_x(t)$. If the number of the matching tuples in $log_x(t)$ reaches the predefined threshold for transaction t's application, τ, the execution results are valid. As a result, the procedure updates the blockchain state (datastore) and adds the transaction t to the set of executed transactions X (which then be used by Algorithm 1 to traverse the graph).

3.6 Discussion

To conclude this section, we first examine, both intuitively and experimentally, why different blockchain paradigms perform differently across different workloads. In this chapter, we highlighted a number of blockchain paradigms and illustrated their advantages and disadvantages. The point here is not that some blockchain paradigms are always "better" or "worse" than others, but rather that each blockchain paradigm performs well under some conditions and poorly under others. We argue that a blockchain that can adaptively switch between multiple paradigms is able to achieve "best of all worlds" performance [32].

Table 3.1 lists representative blockchain systems and their paradigms, where the design space consists of six performance dimensions (block size, early execution capability, dependency graph construction, early abort capability, cross-block conflict detection, parallel execution capability) and two correctness dimensions (multi-version concurrency control and isolation level). Figure 3.4 shows their performance under four different workloads. Here, we use *effective* throughput as the performance metric, i.e., the number of successfully committed transactions per second.

The workloads `A` to `D` are characterized in Table 3.2. Blockchain workloads embody a large extent of variations. For instance, different transactions might invoke different percentages of write operations to the underlying key-value store, as represented by the *write ratio*. These transactions might also contend to access or update the same set of popular keys (or hot keys), as indicated by the *contention level*. In addition, the runtime *load* on a blockchain can be determined by the frequency of issued transactions by each client and the number of active clients varying with time. Last, *compute intensity* is an important characterization of blockchain workloads, as pointed out by [24, 34, 35]. This is because permissioned blockchains support a wide range of applications, some of which are compute intensive (e.g., those that provide security and correctness guarantees for machine learning applications).

Below, we briefly describe the design principles of each paradigm and explain the intuition behind why the performance of each paradigm can vary under different workloads.

Order-Execute (OX). In the order-execute paradigm, transactions are totally ordered and batched into blocks and then transactions of a block are executed sequentially. As a result, the OX paradigm does not require a Multi-version Concurrency Control (MVCC) validation phase, which is used to resolve conflicts between transactions, and hence no transactions will be aborted due to conflicts. As shown in Fig. 3.4, this design principle makes OX outstanding at workload `D`, where transactions are write-heavy and contentious, i.e., transactions update a small set of hot keys. On the other hand, OX performs comparatively poorly on workloads `A` and `C`, which are compute intensive. Due to the lack of parallel execution mechanisms, OX cannot take advantage of modern servers' multi-core processing power.

Order-Parallel Execute (OXII). In the OXII paradigm, used by ParBlockchain [4], as discussed earlier, transactions are first totally ordered and batched into blocks. OXII then constructs a dependency graph for transactions within a block based on their positions, which is then used to execute transactions in parallel, i.e., a transaction can be executed once all

Table 3.1 Comparing design principles of existing permissioned blockchain paradigms. Here, X stands for execution, O stands for order, and V stands for validation

Paradigm	System	B. Size	Early X.	Dep. Graph	Early Abort	C-B Conf.	Par. X.	MVCC	Isolation
OX	Tendermint [1]	Tunable	✗	✗	✗	–	✗	✗	Strong serializable
OXII	ParBlockchain [4]	Tunable	✗	✓	✗	–	Partial	✗	Strong serializable
XOV	Fabric [3]	Tunable	✓	✗	✗	V	Fully	✓	Strong serializable
XOV++	Fabric++ [25]	Tunable	✓	✓	X, O	V	Fully	✓	Strong serializable
XOV#	Fabric# [24]	Tunable	✓	✓	O	O	Fully	✗	Serializable
XOV	StreamChain [33]	1	✓	✗	✗	V	Fully	✓	Strong serializable

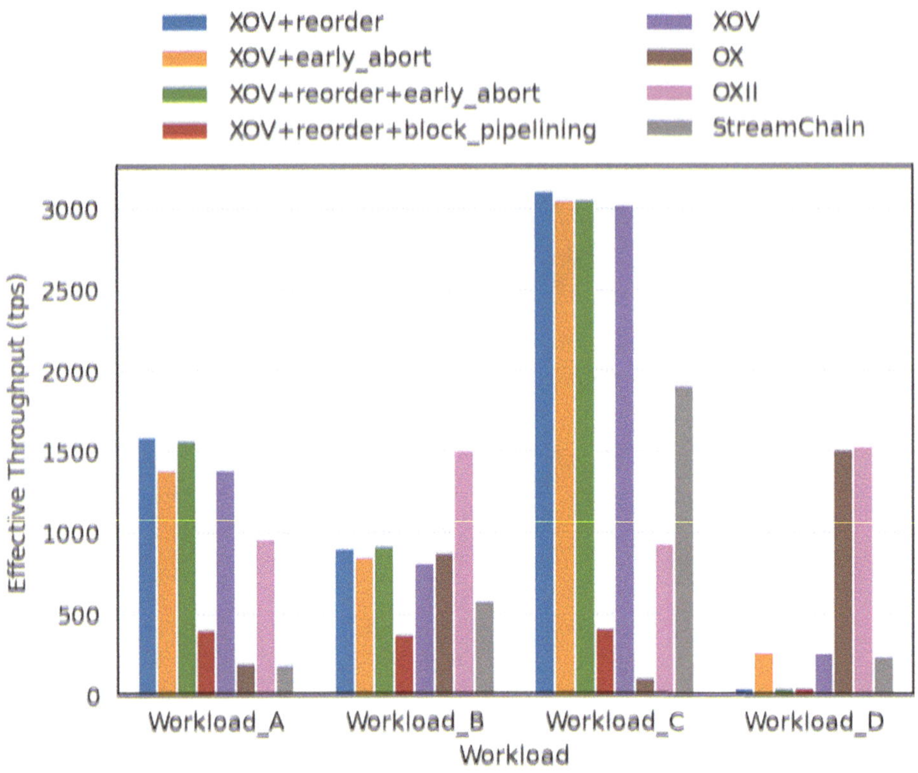

Fig. 3.4 Performance of different blockchain paradigms under various workloads. The performance of different paradigms can vary significantly between workloads. Workloads and paradigms are described in Tables 3.1 and 3.2

Table 3.2 Characterizing workloads A, B, C, and D. Specific workload parameters are presented in Table 3.3

Workload	Write ratio	Contention level	Load	Compute intensity
A	Low	High	High	High
B	Moderate	High	Moderate	Low
C	Moderate	Low	High	Very high
D	High	Very high	Moderate	Very low

its predecessors have finished execution. Given a higher level of execution parallelism than OX, OXII performs better than OX under computation-heavy workloads such as A and C. However, when the workload is contention-free, e.g., C, OXII performs worse than the XOV paradigm and its variants due to the overhead of dependency graph construction. Note that even for a given workload, OXII requires careful tuning of block size; a large block

Table 3.3 Specific workload parameters

Workload	P_w	P_{hot}	N_{hot}	N_{trans}	T_{fire} (ms)	$T_{compute}$ (ms)
A	0.2	0.95	5	300	50	5
B	0.5	0.99	10	100	50	1
C	0.5	0.1	10	300	50	10
D	0.9	0.95	1	100	50	0
E	0.5	0.99	10	100	50	5

results in high overhead in dependency graph construction, while a small block results in less parallelism and higher communication overhead.

Execute-Order-Validate (XOV). Hyperledger Fabric [3] presents the XOV paradigm by switching the order of the order and execution phases such that transactions are simulated fully in parallel before being ordered in the order phase. Since it utilizes early execution, XOV requires an MVCC validation phase to invalidate all transactions that are simulated on stale data, and commits only the validated transactions to the world-state and the blockchain ledger. This early execution enables XOV to perform well on contention-free workloads such as `C`. On the other hand, XOV demonstrates poor performance under contentious and write-heavy workloads, such as `B` and `D`, due to the high percentage of invalidated transactions. Interestingly, while fully parallel execution results in poor performance of XOV under workload `B`, OXII outperforms all other paradigms by finding the proper level of parallelism using a dependency graph. Similarly, as network delay increases, XOV suffers from inconsistent world states among peers as well as stale reads, and thus significantly degraded performance [36].

XOV with early abort and reordering (XOV++). The XOV++ paradigm, as introduced in Fabric++ [25], follows the XOV paradigm but with some modifications. First, a dependency graph is constructed in the order phase to capture RW conflicts between each pair of transactions within the same block. When the graph is constructed, all elementary cycles in the graph are aborted greedily. Unlike OXII, which utilizes the graph for concurrency control, XOV++ uses the graph for transaction reordering; when there is a RW conflict between t_i and t_j, it (re)orders t_i before t_j in the block. Second, it adopts early abort techniques in both the simulation and order phases. Whenever XOV++ detects that a transaction operates on stale data, XOV++ immediately aborts that transaction without waiting for the final MVCC validation. As an effect of transaction reordering, XOV++ has outstanding performance on workload `A`, where the conflicts are reconcilable given a low write ratio. On the other hand, XOV++ performs poorly on workload `D` with a near-zero effective throughput. This is because, under a contentious and update-heavy workload, very few conflicts can be reconciled through reordering. Moreover, reordering becomes more expensive when there are a large number of cycles in the dependency graph, resulting in more pending blocks and, thus, more transactions that simulate on stale data. Interestingly, the early abort technique itself is ineffective in all workloads A–D.

XOV with serializable isolation (XOV#). The XOV# paradigm, presented in Fabric# [24], is mainly different from XOV and XOV++ in that XOV# is serializable, while XOV and XOV++ are strongly serializable. To achieve this isolation level, XOV# incrementally constructs a dependency graph that keeps track of all dependencies, including those that span across blocks in the order phase. Once a transaction is ordered, XOV# immediately drops this transaction if there is a dependency cycle involved. The resulting acyclic schedule is guaranteed to be serializable, thus, no extra MVCC validation is needed in XOV#. To ensure a fair comparison with other paradigms, we run XOV# under the strong serializability isolation level while keeping the remaining design dimensions the same as the original XOV# (the XOV+reorder+block_pipelining bar). XOV# performs worse than vanilla XOV in all workloads A to D due to the overhead of maintaining a large dependency graph and detecting cycles. This suggests that the performance improvement reported in Fabric# is mainly due to a more relaxed isolation level.

Stream XOV. StreamChain [33] switches from block processing to stream transaction processing. Specifically, StreamChain follows the XOV paradigm while fixing the block size to 1. The motivation behind stream processing is simple: while the original, permissionless blockchains were forced to use proof-of-work (PoW) consensus techniques to maintain fault tolerance, a permissioned blockchain environment allows more efficient consensus protocols to be used. Thus, stream processing can reduce transaction latency. In terms of effective throughput, StreamChain has relatively good performance when the workload is lightweight or not contentious, such as in workloads B and C. Otherwise, the high block construction overhead in terms of cryptographic operations and excessive disk I/Os leads to a large number of pending blocks in StreamChain, making incoming transactions simulate on stale data. As expected, StreamChain is more sensitive to the type of storage hardware used than OX: the system has poor performance without RAM disk [36]. StreamChain also highlights that the *parameters* of a given paradigm can impact performance. A large block size leads to higher block formation overhead and latency, while a small block size results in higher communication and disk overhead.

3.7 Summary

In this chapter, we discussed different paradigms for processing transactions in permissioned blockchain systems. We specifically focus on the OXII paradigm that is able to handle the workload with conflicting transactions without rolling back the processed transactions or executing transactions sequentially. We also presented ParBlockchain, a high-performance permissioned blockchain system designed specifically in the OXII paradigm. We concluded with a discussion of some experimental results that contrast the different paradigms and highlight the workloads where each performs better or worse.

References

1. Kwon, J.: Tendermint: Consensus Without Mining (2014)
2. Greenspan, G.: Multichain Private Blockchain-White Paper (2015). http://www.multichain.com/download/MultiChain-White-Paper.pdf
3. Androulaki, E., Barger, A., Bortnikov, V., Cachin, C., Christidis, K., De Caro, A., Enyeart, D., Ferris, C., Laventman, G., Manevich, Y.: Hyperledger fabric: a distributed operating system for permissioned blockchains. In: European Conference on Computer Systems (EuroSys), pp. 30:1–30:15. ACM (2018)
4. Amiri, M.J., Agrawal, D., El Abbadi, A.: ParBlockchain: Leveraging transaction parallelism in permissioned blockchain systems. In: International Conference on Distributed Computing Systems (ICDCS), pp. 1337–1347. IEEE (2019)
5. Cachin, C.: Architecture of the hyperledger blockchain fabric. In: Workshop on Distributed Cryptocurrencies and Consensus Ledgers, vol. 310 (2016)
6. Castro, M., Liskov, B.: Practical byzantine fault tolerance. In: Symposium on Operating Systems Design and Implementation (OSDI), pp. 173–186. USENIX Association (1999)
7. Yin, M., Malkhi, D., Reiter, M.K., Gueta, G.G., Abraham, I.: Hotstuff: BFT consensus with linearity and responsiveness. In: Symposium on Principles of Distributed Computing (PODC), pp. 347–356. ACM (2019)
8. Lamport, L.: Paxos made simple. ACM Sigact News **32**(4), 18–25 (2001)
9. Ongaro, D., Ousterhout, J.K.: In search of an understandable consensus algorithm. In: Annual Technical Conference (ATC), pp. 305–319. USENIX Association (2014)
10. Amiri, M.J., Maiyya, S., Agrawal, D., El Abbadi, A.: SeeMoRe: a fault-tolerant protocol for hybrid cloud environments. In: International Conference on Data Engineering (ICDE), pp. 1345–1356. IEEE (2020)
11. Clement, A., Kapritsos, M., Lee, S., Wang, Y., Alvisi, L., Dahlin, M., Riche, T.: Upright cluster services. In: Symposium on Operating Systems Principles (SOSP), pp. 277–290. ACM (2009)
12. Chase, J.M.: Quorum White Paper (2016)
13. Chain. http://chain.com
14. Hyperledger iroha. https://github.com/hyperledger/iroha
15. Gupta, S., Rahnama, S., Hellings, J., Sadoghi, M.: Resilientdb: global scale resilient blockchain fabric. Proceed VLDB Endowment **13**(6), 868–883 (2020)
16. Corda. https://github.com/corda/corda
17. Ethereum blockchain app platform (2017). https://www.ethereum.org
18. Kapritsos, M., Wang, Y., Quema, V., Clement, A., Alvisi, L., Dahlin, M., et al.: All about eve: Execute-verify replication for multi-core servers. In: Symposium on Operating Systems Design and Implementation (OSDI), vol. 12, pp. 237–250. USENIX Association (2012)
19. Kung, H.T., Robinson, J.T.: On optimistic methods for concurrency control. Trans. Database Syst. (TODS) **6**(2), 213–226 (1981)
20. Castro, M., Liskov, B.: Practical byzantine fault tolerance and proactive recovery. Trans. Comput. Syst. (TOCS) **20**(4), 398–461 (2002)
21. Gorenflo, C., Golab, L., Keshav, S.: Xox fabric: a hybrid approach to transaction execution. In: International Conference on Blockchain and Cryptocurrency (ICBC), pp. 1–9. IEEE (2020)
22. Gorenflo, C., Lee, S., Golab, L., Keshav, S.: Fastfabric: Scaling hyperledger fabric to 20,000 transactions per second. In: International Conference on Blockchain and Cryptocurrency (ICBC), pp. 455–463. IEEE (2019)
23. Raman, R.K., Vaculin, R., Hind, M., Remy, S.L., Pissadaki, E.K., Bore, N.K., Daneshvar, R., Srivastava, B., Varshney, K.R.: Trusted multi-party computation and verifiable simulations: a scalable blockchain approach (2018). arXiv preprint arXiv:1809.08438

24. Ruan, P., Loghin, D., Ta, Q.T., Zhang, M., Chen, G., Ooi, B.C.: A transactional perspective on execute-order-validate blockchains. In: SIGMOD International Conference on Management of Data, pp. 543–557. ACM (2020)
25. Sharma, A., Schuhknecht, F.M., Agrawal, D., Dittrich, J.: Blurring the lines between blockchains and database systems: the case of hyperledger fabric. In: SIGMOD International Conference on Management of Data, pp. 105–122. ACM (2019)
26. Sousa, J., Bessani, A., Vukolic, M.: A byzantine fault-tolerant ordering service for the hyperledger fabric blockchain platform. In: International Conference on Dependable Systems and Networks (DSN), pp. 51–58. IEEE (2018)
27. Thakkar, P., Nathan, S.: Scaling hyperledger fabric using pipelined execution and sparse peers (2020). arXiv preprint arXiv:2003.05113
28. Thakkar, P., Nathan, S., Vishwanathan, B.: Performance benchmarking and optimizing hyperledger fabric blockchain platform (2018). arXiv preprint arXiv:1805.11390
29. Xu, L., Chen, W., Li, Z., Xu, J., Liu, A., Zhao, L.: Locking mechanism for concurrency conflicts on hyperledger fabric. In: International Conference on Web Information Systems Engineering, pp. 32–47. Springer (2020)
30. Faleiro, J.M., Abadi, D.J., Hellerstein, J.M.: High performance transactions via early write visibility. Proc. VLDB Endowment **10**(5), 613–624 (2017)
31. Bernstein, P.A., Goodman, N.: Multiversion concurrency control-theory and algorithms. Trans. Database Syst. (TODS) **8**(4), 465–483 (1983)
32. Wu, C., Mehta, B., Amiri, M.J., Marcus, R., Loo, B.T.: AdaChain: a learned adaptive blockchain. Proc. VLDB Endowment **16**(8), 2033–2046 (2023)
33. István, Z., Sorniotti, A., Vukolić, M.: Streamchain: Do blockchains need blocks? In: Workshop on Scalable and Resilient Infrastructures for Distributed Ledgers (SERIAL), pp. 1–6. ACM (2018)
34. Wu, C., Amiri, M.J., Asch, J., Nagda, H., Zhang, Q., Loo, B.T.: FlexChain: an elastic disaggregated blockchain. Proc. VLDB Endowment **16**(01), 23–36 (2022)
35. Gramoli, V., Guerraoui, R., Lebedev, A., Natoli, C., Voron, G.: Diablo: a benchmark suite for blockchains. In: European Conference on Computer Systems (EuroSys). ACM (2023)
36. Chacko, J.A., Mayer, R., Jacobsen, H.A.: Why do my blockchain transactions fail? a study of hyperledger fabric. In: SIGMOD International Conference on Management of Data, pp. 221–234. ACM (2021)

Scalability

4

4.1 Introduction

Scalability is the ability of a blockchain system to process an increasing number of transactions by adding resources to the system. The scalability of blockchain systems has been addressed in several studies using different on-chain, e.g., increasing the block size, and off-chain, e.g., lightning networks [1, 2], techniques. Increasing the block size, however, increases both the propagation time and the verification time of the block which makes operating full nodes more expensive, and this in turn could cause less decentralization in the network [3]. Off-chain solutions also suffer from security issues [4], especially denial-of-service attacks.[1]

Partitioning the data into multiple shards that are maintained by different subsets of trustworthy nodes is a proven approach to improve the scalability of distributed databases [5]. In such an approach, the performance of the database scales near-linearly with the number of nodes. Recently, sharding has been utilized in the presence of Byzantine nodes in both permissionless and permissioned blockchain systems. Sharded permissionless blockchains, e.g., Elastico [6], OmniLedger [7], and Rapidchain [8], ensure *probabilistic* correctness by randomly assigning nodes to *committees* (partitions) resulting in a uniform distribution of faulty nodes in committees. OmniLedger and Rapidchain also support cross-shard transactions using BFT consensus protocols.

Sharding techniques have been adopted by various permissioned blockchain systems, such as Fabric [9], Cosmos [10], RSCoin [11], and AHL [12]. In Fabric, channels are utilized to partition blockchain data. Each channel represents a segmented state of the overall system, managed independently by a logically distinct set of nodes while remaining aware of the larger system it is part of [13]. This approach allows Fabric to efficiently handle intra-

[1] https://www.trustnodes.com/2018/03/21/lightning-network-ddos-sends-20-nodes.

M. J. Amiri et al., *Blockchain-Enabled Large-Scale Transaction Management*,
Synthesis Lectures on Data Management,
https://doi.org/10.1007/978-3-031-91058-6_4

shard transactions. However, executing cross-shard transactions requires either a trusted channel among participants or an atomic commit protocol [13]. Cosmos [10] introduces inter-blockchain communication (IBC) for initiating operations across different blockchains. For chains interacting via IBC to function effectively, they must be aware of each other's state, necessitating the establishment of bi-directional trusted channels between them. In AHL [12], Dang et al. leverage trusted hardware to reduce the number of nodes required in each cluster. They randomly assign nodes to clusters and ensure safety with high probability when each cluster contains at least 80 nodes—significantly fewer than the approximately 600 needed in OmniLedger. However, implementing Byzantine fault-tolerant protocols among 80 nodes still leads to considerable latency. Moreover, in AHL, achieving consensus on the ordering of cross-shard transactions not only necessitates an additional cluster of nodes known as a *reference committee*, but also results in numerous phases of intra- and cross-cluster communication. Furthermore, since all cross-shard transactions are processed by a single reference committee, AHL cannot execute independent cross-shard transactions in parallel.

In general, large-scale sharded systems, such as Spanner [5], typically partition data into shards and replicate each shard on the nodes of a *pre-determined fault-tolerant* cluster, e.g., based on physical constraints such as a data center with a majority of non-faulty nodes, to guarantee *deterministic* safety. Maintaining data on pre-determined fault-tolerant clusters for the purpose of scalability has also been studied in permissioned blockchains ResilientDB [14] and Blockplane [15]. However, most sharded blockchain systems, e.g., Elastico, OmniLedger, and AHL, operate on a flat homogeneous network of peers and hence *configure* fault-tolerant units by randomly assigning nodes to clusters and provide a *probabilistic* safety guarantee. To guarantee safety with a high probability, such systems need to uniformly distribute faulty nodes across all clusters, resulting in large-size clusters, e.g., ~600 nodes in OmniLedger.

In this chapter, we present a permissioned blockchain system called *SharPer* [16, 17], designed to enhance scalability. SharPer, similar to large-scale sharded systems, assumes pre-determined fault-tolerant clusters and is able to provide deterministic safety guarantees with clusters each consisting of either $2f + 1$ crash-only nodes or $3f + 1$ Byzantine nodes. This architecture is particularly effective in networks with a high proportion of non-faulty nodes. Data shards are assigned to these clusters, with each cluster processing transactions that pertain to its designated shard. For transactions that interact with only a single shard—referred to as *intra-shard transactions*—the respective cluster can order and execute the transaction locally. This independent handling allows intra-shard transactions from different clusters to be processed in parallel. In contrast, *cross-shard transactions* necessitate agreement among all involved clusters exclusively. However, if two cross-shard transactions do not share any overlapping clusters, they can still be executed concurrently. Given that the ordering of various transactions may occur in parallel and that the system accommodates cross-shard interactions, SharPer represents its blockchain ledger as a *directed acyclic graph (DAG)* encompassing both intra- and cross-shard transactions. To optimize performance, it's important to note that no single node maintains the entire blockchain ledger; instead, each cluster's node preserves only their own view of the ledger including their intra-shard transactions along with the cross-shard ones they participate in. The primary contribution of this chapter is demonstrating how a permissioned blockchain system can facilitate concurrent transaction processing through node clustering and data sharding.

The remainder of this chapter is structured as follows: Sect. 4.2 presents the system model; Sects. 4.3 and 4.3.5 detail how consensus operates within SharPer; and, finally, Sect. 4.5 wraps up the discussion.

4.2 The SharPer Model

SharPer is a permissioned blockchain system designed specifically to achieve high scalability in networks with a very large percentage of non-faulty nodes. SharPer consists of a set of nodes in an asynchronous distributed system where nodes might be placed in data centers, public clouds, or local infrastructures. Nodes in SharPer either follow the crash or Byzantine failure model. SharPer organizes the nodes into clusters and assigns a data shard to each cluster. Each node, in addition to a data shard, maintains a view of the blockchain ledger. SharPer uses point-to-point bi-directional communication channels to connect nodes. Network channels are pairwise authenticated, which guarantees that a malicious node cannot forge a message from a correct node. Furthermore, messages might contain public-key signatures and message digests [18]. Similar to other systems and for signature verification, we assume that all nodes have access to the public keys of all other nodes. We assume that a strong adversary can coordinate malicious nodes and delay communication to compromise the replicated service. However, the adversary cannot subvert standard cryptographic assumptions. In this section, we show how clusters and shards are formed, and then introduce the blockchain ledger.

4.2.1 Cluster and Shard Formation

In existing sharded permissionless blockchain systems, such as OmniLedger [7], nodes are randomly assigned to clusters (or committees). To ensure that each cluster contains at most one-third faulty nodes with a high probability (approximately $1–2^{-20}$), these clusters must comprise hundreds of nodes. In AHL [12], safety is achieved with the same level of probability using only 80 nodes per cluster by leveraging trusted hardware. However, as previously mentioned, executing Byzantine fault-tolerant protocols among 80 nodes leads to significant latency issues. In contrast, SharPer utilizes predefined fault-tolerant clusters that are sufficiently large to tolerate f failures. Consequently, SharPer offers a *deterministic* safety guarantee rather than a probabilistic one. It's important to note that both the proba-

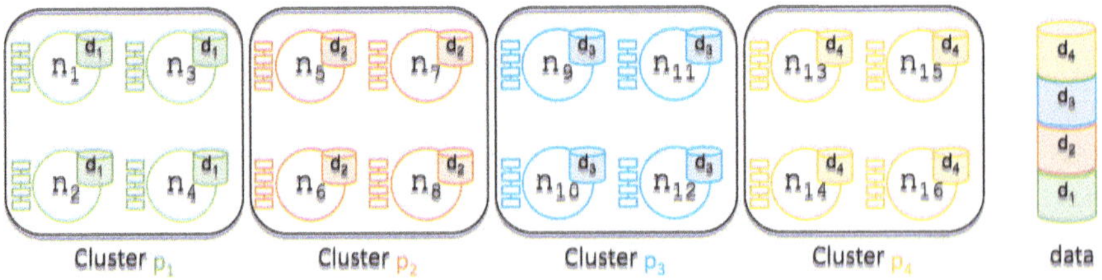

Fig. 4.1 The infrastructure of SharPer with 16 Byzantine nodes where $f = 1$

bilistic approach and the trusted hardware technique can also be integrated into SharPer for improved performance.

Within SharPer and in scenarios involving crash-only nodes, each cluster consists of $2f + 1$ nodes; for Byzantine failure models, each includes $3f + 1$ nodes. We denote the set of clusters as $P = \{p_1, p_2, ...\}$. When dealing with crash-only scenarios, the number of clusters $|P|$ equals $\frac{N}{2f+1}$ where N is the total number of nodes. Similarly, for Byzantine node configurations, it amounts to $|P| = \frac{N}{3f+1}$. Since there are $|P|$ clusters present in the system, data is partitioned into an equal number of shards, thus each cluster maintains its own unique shard replicated across its member nodes. The shards are labeled as $d_1, d_2, \ldots, d_{|P|}$, with each data shard d_i being replicated on all the nodes within cluster p_i.

Figure 4.1 depicts the architecture of SharPer within a blockchain system consisting of 16 nodes operating under a Byzantine failure model where $f = 1$. As illustrated, this configuration yields four clusters ($|P| = \frac{16}{4}$) consisting of four members each ($3f + 1$). Data is divided into four shards corresponding to these clusters; every shard d_i is replicated across all members in cluster p_i. Additionally within every individual cluster, not only do they maintain their data shard but also store their version of the blockchain ledger.

Effective sharding should be *workload-aware*, meaning it requires prior knowledge regarding both data structure and access patterns from various transactions. Workload-aware data sharding enhances the likelihood that records accessed by single transactions remain within a single shard [19]. Various strategies have been proposed to reduce transaction occurrences in sharded systems [20], and recent advancements employing machine learning techniques have aimed at further minimizing these distributed transactions [21]. Nonetheless, there will still be some transactions that span multiple shards. Therefore, SharPer supports two transaction types: *intra-shard* transactions which operate solely within one shard and *cross-shard* transactions which involve accessing records from different shards.

4.2.2 Blockchain Ledger

In SharPer, each data shard is replicated on all nodes of a cluster. As a result, to ensure data consistency, a total order among transactions (both intra- and cross-shard) that access

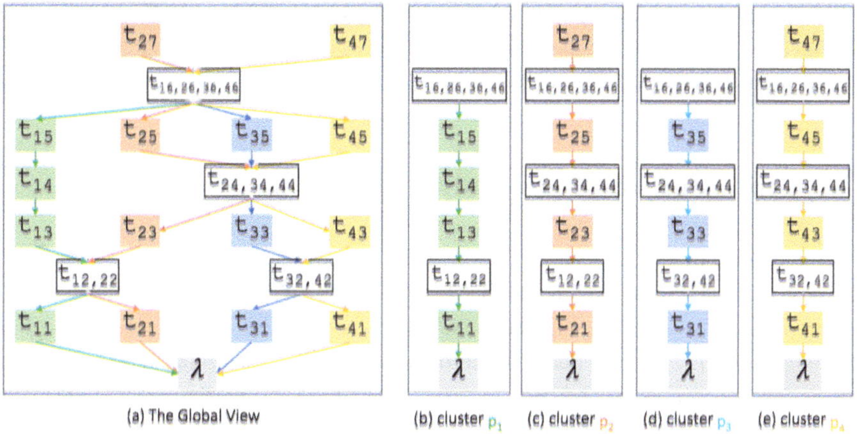

Fig. 4.2 **a** The global view of the blockchain ledger, **b–e** Different views of the blockchain maintained on clusters p_1–p_4

to the same data shard is needed. The total order of transactions in the blockchain ledger is captured by *chaining* transaction blocks (without loss of generality, we assume each block consists of a single transaction). To support both types of transactions, we generalize the notion of a blockchain ledger from a linear chain to a *directed acyclic graph (DAG)* where nodes of the graph are transactions and edges enforce the order of transactions. The ledger also includes a unique initialization block, λ, called the *genesis* block.

Figure 4.2a shows a sample blockchain ledger created in the SharPer model consisting of four clusters p_1, p_2, p_3, and p_4 (data shards d_1, d_2, d_3, and d_4). In this figure, λ is the genesis block of the blockchain. The model includes multiple intra- and cross-shard transactions. For example, t_{11}, t_{13}, t_{14}, and t_{15} are the intra-shard transactions of cluster p_1. Each cross-shard transaction is labeled with $t_{o_1,\ldots,o_k}$ where k is the number of involved clusters and o_i indicates the order of the transaction among the transactions of the ith involved cluster. This is needed to ensure that cross-shard transactions are ordered correctly with regard to the intra-cluster transactions of all involved clusters. For example, $t_{12,22}$ and $t_{16,26,36,46}$ are two cross-shard transactions where $t_{12,22}$ accesses data shards d_1 and d_2, whereas $t_{16,26,36,46}$ accesses all four data shards.

As can be seen, there is a total order among the transactions (both intra- and cross-shard) that access a data shard, e.g., t_{11}, $t_{12,22}$, t_{13}, t_{14}, t_{15}, and $t_{16,26,36,46}$ are chained together. In addition, intra-shard transactions of different clusters can be added to the blockchain ledger in parallel, e.g., t_{11}, t_{21}, t_{31}, and t_{41} can be processed by different clusters in parallel. Similarly, if two cross-shard transactions access disjoint subsets of shards, they can be added to the ledger in parallel as well, e.g., $t_{12,22}$ and $t_{32,42}$.

In SharPer, the entire blockchain ledger is *not maintained* by any cluster and each cluster maintains only its own *view* of the blockchain ledger including the transactions that access the data shard of the cluster. The blockchain ledger's global view is the union of all these physical views.

Figure 4.2b–e shows the views of the ledger for clusters p_1, p_2, p_3, and p_4 respectively.

4.3 Consensus with Crash-Only Nodes

In a permissioned blockchain system, nodes establish consensus on a unique order in which entries are appended to the blockchain ledger. To establish consensus, asynchronous fault-tolerant protocols have been used. Fault-tolerant protocols use the State Machine Replication (SMR) algorithm [22] where nodes agree on an ordering of incoming requests. The algorithm, as discussed in Sect. 2.6, has to satisfy four main properties: agreement, validity, consistency (total order), and termination [23]. Consistency is a trivial property in consensus protocols with a single ordering routine, however, since multiple clusters with different ordering routines are involved in SharPer, consistency between different instances of the consensus algorithm needs to be guaranteed. Due to the trust assumptions of blockchains, most existing blockchain systems employ Byzantine fault-tolerant protocols. Studying crash fault-tolerant protocols, however, is beneficial for two main reasons. First, it can be used in permissioned blockchain systems with more federated settings, e.g., Hyperledger Fabric [9] uses crash fault-tolerant protocol Raft [24]. Second, from a development point of view, it is pedagogically easier to introduce the complex concepts used in Byzantine consensus protocols. In this section, we first show how consensus is established in SharPer for intra-shard and cross-shard transactions in the presence of crash-only nodes. Then, the primary failure handling routine of SharPer is presented, and finally the correctness of SharPer is proven.

4.3.1 Intra-shard Consensus

Crash fault-tolerant protocols, e.g., Paxos [25], guarantee safety in an asynchronous network using $2f+1$ nodes to overcome the simultaneous crash failure of any f nodes. SharPer uses multi-Paxos, a variation of Paxos, where *the primary* (a pre-elected node that initiates consensus) is relatively stable, to establish consensus on the order of intra-shard transactions. The multi-Paxos protocol has been presented in Sect. 2.6. Here we briefly discuss how multi-Paxos has been integrated into SharPer. In SharPer, upon receiving a signed request (i.e., transaction) from a client, the primary assigns a sequence number to the request (to provide a total order among requests) and multicasts a propose message (called accept in Paxos) including the transaction to every node within the cluster. Instead of a sequence number, the primary can also include the cryptographic hash of the previous transaction block, $H(b)$, in the message where $H(.)$ denotes the hash function and b is the previous block that is ordered by the cluster. Using hashes instead of sequence numbers improves the overall security of the system. However, it prevents the primary node from initiating the next instance of consensus before the commitment of the previous instances (out-of-order processing). Upon receiving a valid propose message from the primary, each node sends an accept (i.e., accepted) message to the primary. The primary waits for f accept messages from different nodes (plus itself becomes $f + 1$), multicasts a *signed* commit message to every node within the cluster, appends the transaction block including the transaction and the signed commit message (as evidence of the transaction's validity) to the blockchain ledger, executes the transaction, updates the blockchain state (data shard), and sends a reply to the client. We assume that all transactions are executed deterministically in the system. Upon receiving a commit message from the primary, each node appends the transaction block (i.e., the transaction and the received commit message) to its blockchain ledger, executes the transaction, and updates the state. The client also waits for a valid reply from the primary to accept the result. Since commit messages include the digest (cryptographic hash) of the corresponding transactions, appending valid signed commit messages to the blockchain ledger in addition to the transactions provides the same level of *immutability* guarantee as including the cryptographic hash of the previous transaction in the transaction block, i.e., any attempt to alter the block data can easily be detected.

4.3.2 Cross-Shard Consensus

Cross-shard transactions access records from different data shards which are maintained by different clusters. To ensure data consistency, cross-shard transactions have to be appended to the blockchain ledgers of all involved clusters in the same order. As a result, consensus among all involved clusters on the order of cross-shard transactions is needed. In this section, we show how SharPer processes cross-shard transactions in a network consisting of crash-only nodes.

A client sends its request message to the (pre-elected) primary node of a cluster (i.e., one of the clusters that store data records accessed by the cross-shard transaction). Note that once a primary node of a cluster is elected, it initiates all intra-shard transactions of the cluster as well as cross-shard transactions that are sent to the cluster by clients. Upon receiving a valid request from a client, primary node π initiates the protocol among the involved clusters by multicasting a propose message including the transaction to *all* nodes of all involved clusters, i.e., all clusters that store data records accessed by the cross-shard transaction. Once a node receives a valid propose message, it assigns a sequence number to the transaction and sends an accept message to the primary. The primary waits for matching accept messages from $f + 1$ different nodes of *every* involved cluster to ensure that the majority of every cluster agrees with the order of the transaction (recall that each cluster includes $2f + 1$ nodes). The primary then multicasts a commit message to all nodes of every involved cluster, appends the transaction block to its ledger, executes the transaction, and sends a reply to the client. Upon receiving a commit message from the primary, each node also appends the transaction block to its ledger.

Algorithm 3 Cross-shard Consensus with Crash-Only Nodes

1: **init()**:
2: $r := node\_id$
3: $p_i :=$ the cluster that initiates the consensus instance
4: $\pi(p) :=$ the primary node of cluster p
5: $P :=$ set of all nodes in the involved clusters
6: **if** $r == \pi(p_i)$ and receiving valid request $m = \langle \text{REQUEST}, op, ts, c\rangle_{\sigma_c}$ **then**
7: multicast $\langle\langle \text{PROPOSE}, h_i, d\rangle, m\rangle$ to P
8: **end if**
9: **if** $r \in P$ and receiving valid $\langle \text{PROPOSE}, h_i, d\rangle, m\rangle$ and r is not waiting for commit message of request m' where m and m' intersect in some other cluster p_k **then**
10: assign sequence number h_j to m ▷ assuming r is a member of cluster p_j
11: send $\langle \text{ACCEPT}, h_i, h_j, d, r\rangle$ to primary node $\pi(p_i)$
12: **end if**
13: **if** $r == \pi(p_i)$ and receiving $f+1$ valid matching $\langle \text{ACCEPT}, h_i, h_j, d, r\rangle$ from every cluster p_j in P **then**
14: multicast $\langle \text{COMMIT}, h_i, h_j, ..., h_k, d\rangle_{\sigma_{\pi(p_i)}}$ to P
15: append the transaction and commit message to the ledger
16: **end if**
17: **if** $r \in P$ and receiving $\langle \text{COMMIT}, h_i, h_j, ..., h_k, d\rangle_{\sigma_{\pi(p_i)}}$ **then**
18: append the transaction and commit message to the ledger
19: **end if**

Algorithm 3 presents the normal case operation for SharPer to process a cross-shard transaction in the presence of crash-only nodes. Although not explicitly mentioned, every sent and received message is logged by nodes. As indicated in lines 1–5 of the algorithm, p_i is the cluster that initiates the transaction, $\pi(p_j)$ represents the primary node of cluster p_j, and P is the set of involved clusters in the transaction.

As shown in lines 6–8, upon receiving a valid signed cross-shard request $m = \langle \text{REQUEST}, op, ts, c\rangle_{\sigma_c}$ from an authorized client c (with timestamp ts used to ensure exactly once semantics for the execution of client requests) to execute operation op, the primary node $\pi(p_i)$ of the initiator cluster p_i assigns sequence number h_i to the request and multicasts a propose message $\langle \text{PROPOSE}, h_i, d, m\rangle$ to the nodes of every involved cluster where m is the client's request message and $d = D(m)$ is the digest of m. The sequence number h_i represents the correct order of the transaction block in the initiator cluster p_i. Since all nodes are crash-only, there is no need to sign messages.

Upon receiving a propose message, as indicated in lines 9–12, each node r of an involved cluster p_j validates the message and its sequence number. If node r is currently waiting for a commit message of some cross-shard request m' where the involved clusters of two requests m and m' intersect in some other cluster p_k, the node does not process the new request m before the earlier request m' gets committed. This ensures that requests are committed in the same order on different clusters. Otherwise, node r sends an accept message

$\langle$ACCEPT, $h_i, h_j, d, r\rangle$ to primary node $\pi(p_i)$ where h_j is the sequence number, assigned by r, that represents the correct order of request m in cluster p_j and d is the digest of m.

Once primary $\pi(p_i)$ receives valid matching accept messages from $f+1$ nodes of *every* involved cluster p_j with matching h_j and also h_i and d that match to the propose message sent by $\pi(p_i)$, as presented in lines 13–16, it collects all valid sequence numbers (e.g., $h_i, h_j, ..., h_k$) from the accept messages of all involved clusters (e.g., $p_i, p_j, ..., p_k$) and multicasts a commit message $\langle$COMMIT, $[h_i, h_j, ..., h_k], d\rangle_{\sigma_{\pi(p_i)}}$ to the nodes of all involved clusters. The order of sequence numbers h_i, h_j, ..., h_k in the message is an ascending order determined by their cluster IDs. The sequence number, indeed, consists of multiple sub-sequence numbers where each sub-sequence number presents the local order of the transaction in one of the involved clusters. The primary signs its commit message because it might be used later by nodes to prove the correctness of the transaction block.

Finally, as shown in lines 17–19, once a node of some cluster p_j receives a valid commit message from primary $\pi(p_i)$, the node considers the transaction as committed (even if the node has not sent an accept message for that request). If all transactions with lower sequence numbers than h_j have been committed, the node appends the transaction as well as the corresponding commit message to the ledger and executes it. This ensures that all replicas execute requests in the same order as required to provide the safety property.

Figure 4.3 shows the normal case operation for SharPer to execute two concurrent cross-shard transactions in the presence of crash-only nodes where the first transaction accesses clusters p_1 and p_2 and the second transaction accesses the other two clusters, p_3 and p_4. The network consists of four clusters and each cluster includes three nodes ($f = 1$).

4.3.3 Dealing with Conflicting Messages

In the presented consensus protocol and after multicasting a propose message, the primary might not receive a quorum of *matching* accept messages from $f+1$ nodes of every involved cluster after some predefined time τ_a because the primary nodes of different clusters might multicast their propose messages in parallel, hence, different nodes in an overlapping cluster might receive these *conflicting messages* in different orders and assign them inconsistent sequence numbers in their corresponding accept messages. A special case of conflicting messages is when there is more than one cluster in the intersection of conflicting propose messages, hence, to ensure consistency, as explained earlier, nodes of overlapping clusters do not send accept messages for later transactions before committing the earlier ones, thus, the system might face a *deadlock* situation. It is important to note that this issue primarily arises from our assumption that the read-set and write-set of transactions are not known in advance. If this information were available, locking mechanisms could potentially address the problem. We propose two techniques, the first for the general case of conflicting messages and the second to deal specifically with deadlocks.

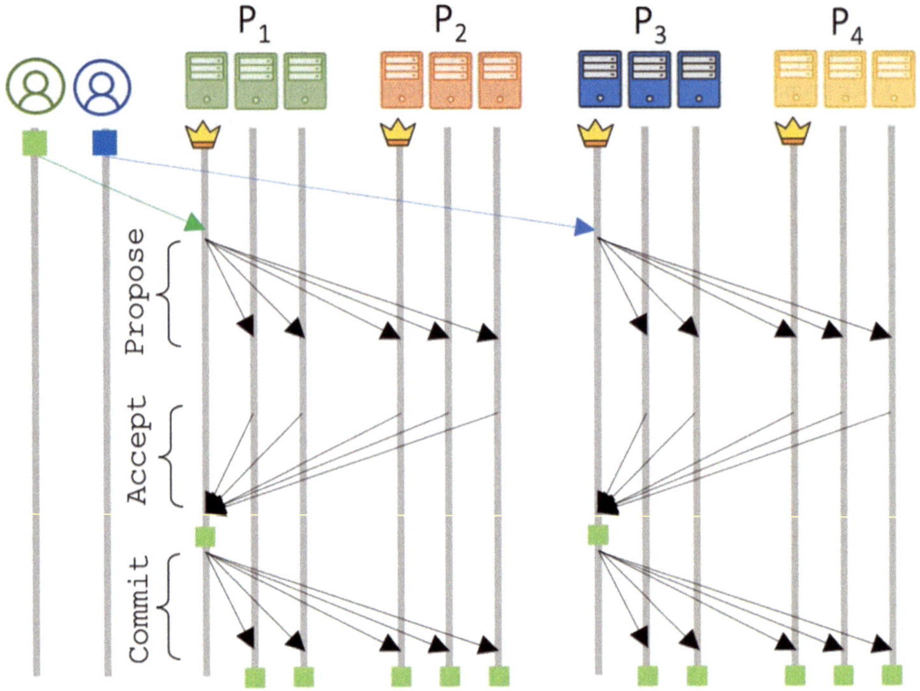

Fig. 4.3 The flow of two *concurrent* cross-shard transactions in SharPer with crash-only nodes

Conflicting Messages. Algorithm 4 demonstrates an optimization to deal with conflicting messages. In case of non-matching accept messages, as indicated in lines 1–3 of Algorithm 4, the initiator primary $\pi(p_i)$ needs to re-initiate the request in *only* the *conflicting clusters*, i.e., clusters that have not sent $f + 1$ matching accept messages to the initiator primary. However, to prevent any further conflicts, the initiator primary $\pi(p_i)$ multicasts a prepare message with the same structure as propose messages to every node of the conflicting clusters. Once the initiator primary $\pi(p_i)$ sends a prepare message for request m to the node of a cluster, $\pi(p_i)$ does not accept any further accept messages for request m from that cluster. As shown in lines 4–6, the *primary node* of each conflicting cluster then assigns a sequence number and multicasts a super-accept message (with the same structure as accept messages) to the nodes of its cluster and also the initiator primary $\pi(p_i)$. Note that the initiator multicasts the prepare message to every node (and not only the primary node) of each conflicting cluster to enable other nodes to detect a possible failure of their cluster's primary node. Upon receiving a super-accept message from the primary of its cluster, as presented in lines 7–9, each node logs the message and sends a super-accept message with the same sequence number to $\pi(p_i)$. Nodes also remove the previous sent accept messages for m from their logs. Once $\pi(p_i)$ receives matching super-accept messages from $f + 1$

Algorithm 4 Dealing with Conflicting ACCEPT Messages

*** The configuration is the same as Algorithm 3***

if $r == \pi(p_i)$ and not receiving matching accept messages from cluster p_j **then**
  multicast $\langle$PREPARE, $h_i, d, m\rangle$ to every node in p_j
end if
if $r == \pi(p_j)$ and receiving $\langle$PREPARE, $h_i, d, m\rangle$ from $\pi(p_i)$ **then**
  multicast $\langle$SUPER-ACCEPT, $h_i, h_j, d, r\rangle$ to $\pi(p_i)$ and every node in p_j
end if
if $r \in p_j$ and receiving $\langle$SUPER-ACCEPT, $h_i, h_j, d, \pi(p_j)\rangle$ from $\pi(p_j)$ **then**
  send $\langle$SUPER-ACCEPT, $h_i, h_j, d, r\rangle$ to $\pi(p_i)$
end if

nodes of *every* conflicting cluster, it returns to its normal operation, as presented in lines 13–16 of Algorithm 3, and multicasts commit messages.

Well-designed distributed systems aim to minimize cross-shard transactions and evenly distribute the load across geographically dispersed nodes. However, shared systems, particularly SharPer, may still experience heavy workloads characterized by a high proportion of cross-shard transactions, increasing the likelihood of receiving conflicting accept messages. In such scenarios, rather than multicasting propose messages and waiting for potentially conflicting accept messages and then re-initiating the transaction with prepare messages, the primary initiator node initially multicasts prepare messages to the nodes of the involved clusters. Upon receiving prepare messages, the primary node of each cluster assigns a sequence number to the request and multicasts propose messages in its cluster. This approach ensures that each cluster's primary node manages all sequence numbers for both intra-shard and cross-shard transactions, thereby preventing conflicts. It's important to note that this solution introduces an additional intra-cluster message passing. Figure 4.4 illustrates how SharPer handles transactions under heavy workloads. Depending on workload characteristics and the percentage of cross-shard transactions, SharPer can dynamically switch between these two techniques to effectively manage conflicting messages.

Deadlock Situations. If different overlapping clusters receive propose messages for concurrent cross-shard transactions in conflicting orders, the system might face a deadlock situation. This could happen even if a prepare phase is added to the system.

Figure 4.5 demonstrates a deadlock scenario where two cross-shard transactions t (green) and t' (yellow) are initiated concurrently. Transaction t accesses data shards maintained by clusters p_1, p_2, and p_3 while transaction t' accesses data shards maintained by clusters p_2, p_3, and p_4. As can be seen, the primary nodes of clusters p_2 and p_3 receive prepare messages in conflicting orders, i.e., the primary node of p_2 receives t before t' while the primary node of p_3 receives t' before t. To maintain the consistency property (as detailed in Algorithm 3, line 9), clusters must ensure that the second transaction does not begin processing until the first one has been committed. Specifically, p_2 will wait for the commit message of t,

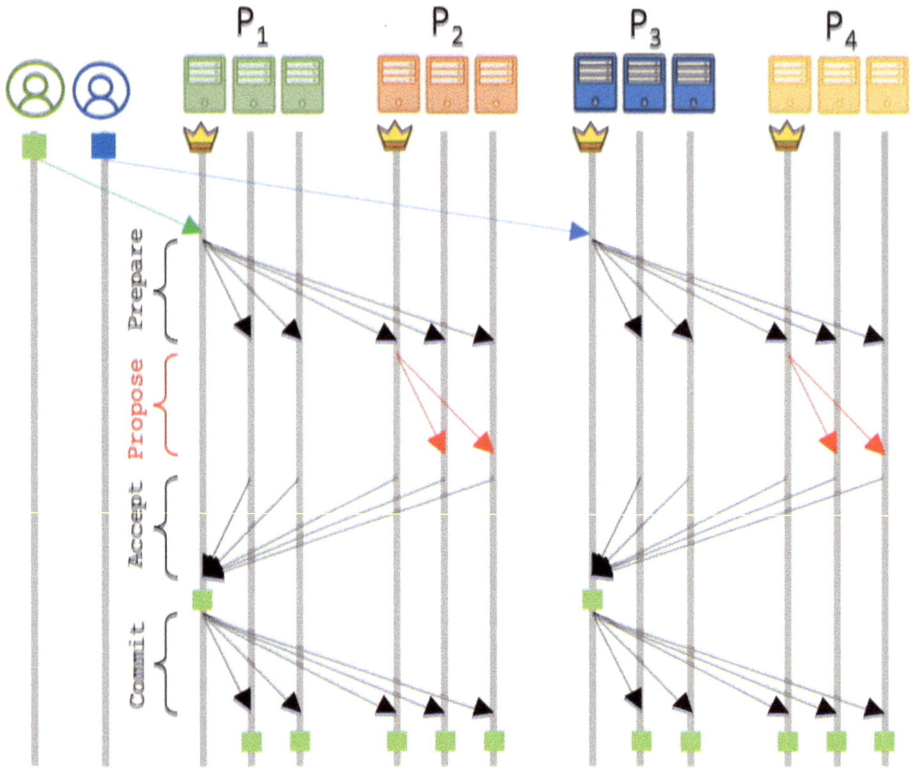

Fig. 4.4 Cross-shard transactions in SharPer in the presence of heavy workloads

while p_3 will wait for the commit message of t'. However, because committing a cross-shard transaction requires receiving $f + 1$ accept messages from each involved cluster, neither transaction t nor transaction t' can be committed, resulting in a deadlock situation. While there are scenarios where it is feasible to establish a unique order among deadlocked transactions, doing so may require multiple communication phases and consequently lead to increased latency. To manage this issue, SharPer, like many other distributed systems, utilizes timers for detecting and aborting these transactions.

4.3.4 Primary Failure Handling

The goal of the primary failure handling routine is to improve liveness by allowing the system to make progress when a primary node fails. The routine is triggered by timeout. When node r of some cluster p_j receives a valid propose message from a primary for either an intra-shard or a cross-shard transaction, it starts a timer that expires after some predefined time τ_f. Time τ_f for cross-shard transactions is longer than τ_f of intra-shard transactions

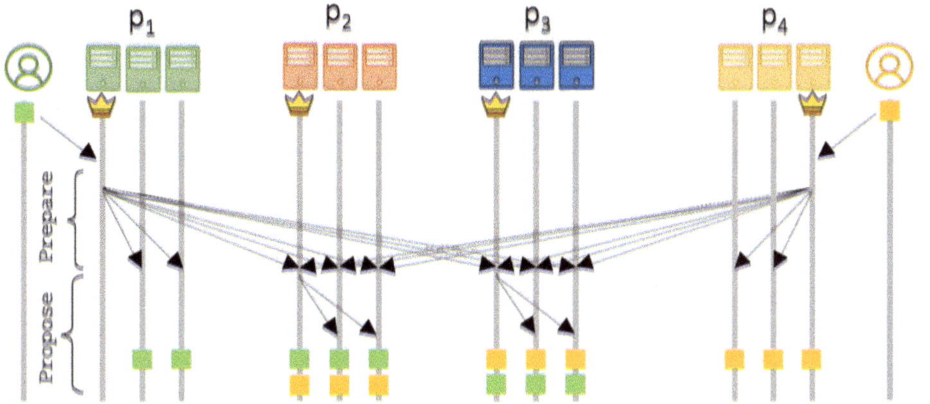

Fig. 4.5 Deadlock situation in SharPer with crash-only nodes

because processing cross-shard transactions usually takes more time. Moreover, time τ_f for cross-shard transactions is much longer than τ_a (i.e., the timeout for resolving conflicting messages) to allow primary nodes to resolve conflicts and deal with deadlock situations. If the timer expires and node r has not committed the request, the node suspects that the primary might be faulty. We need to address three cases. First, a cross-shard transaction where node r (of cluster p_j) and the initiator primary $\pi(p_i)$, which is suspected to be faulty, i.e., it has not sent prepare (if accept messages are conflicting) or commit messages, are in different clusters (i.e., $i \neq j$). Second, a cross-shard transaction where node r is not in the initiator cluster (i.e., $i \neq j$), however, $\pi(p_j)$ is suspected to be faulty, i.e., it has not sent super-accept messages (if accept messages are conflicting or if the system uses the optimization discussed for heavy workloads), and third, an intra- or a cross-shard transaction where node r and the initiator primary, which is suspected to be faulty, i.e., it has not sent propose, prepare, super-accept, or commit messages, are in the same cluster (i.e., $i = j$).

In the first case, node r multicasts a $\langle$COMMIT − QUERY, $h_i, h_j, d, r\rangle$ message to every node of the initiator cluster p_i where h_i and h_j are the sequence numbers assigned to the transaction by clusters p_i and p_j (in the corresponding propose and accept (or super-accept) messages). There are three possible situations: (1) The request has already been committed, thus the corresponding commit message will be sent back to node r by the initiator primary. (2) The initiator primary is still waiting for super-accept messages of some involved cluster. (3) The initiator primary itself has failed, hence the nodes of p_i need to elect a new primary. The nodes of p_i can easily distinguish between cases 2 and 3 (waited or failed initiator primary) by exchanging messages and electing a new primary only if the primary has failed. The primary failure handling routine is performed by the nodes of the same cluster as the faulty primary.

In the second case, when $\pi(p_j)$ has failed, if node r has not detected that $\pi(p_j)$ is failed, similar to the first case, r multicasts a commit-query message to every node of the initiator cluster p_i (assuming that the initiator primary has failed). Upon receiving a commit-query message, the initiator primary multicasts prepare messages to every node of p_j, hence nodes of p_j become suspect that $\pi(p_j)$ might be faulty. Note that, this case is very unlikely to happen because, on one hand, node r usually is able to detect that the $\pi(p_j)$ is faulty (from intra-shard messages) and, on the other hand, the timer τ_a of $\pi(p_i)$ will expire much earlier than the timer τ_f of node r, hence $\pi(p_i)$ will send prepare messages to nodes of cluster p_j earlier (the first time τ_a expires, $\pi(p_i)$ multicasts prepare messages to the primary nodes of the conflicting clusters; the second time, it multicasts prepare to every node; and for heavy workloads, however, it multicasts prepare to every node from the beginning).

Third, when node r and the initiator primary are in the same cluster, node r initiates the leader election phase of multi-Paxos to elect the new primary, and the new primary handles all the uncommitted intra- and cross-shard transactions, and takes care of new client requests.

4.3.5 Correctness Arguments

Consensus protocols have to satisfy *safety* and *liveness* properties. Safety means all correct nodes receive the same requests in the same order whereas liveness means all correct requests are eventually ordered. In this section, the safety (agreement, validity, and consistency) and liveness (termination) properties of SharPer in the presence of crash-only nodes are demonstrated. Since intra-shard transactions follow Paxos, we mainly focus on cross-shard transactions.

Lemma 4.1 (Agreement) *If node r commits request m with sequence number h, no other correct node commits request m' ($m \neq m'$) with the same sequence number h.*

Proof Let m and m' ($m \neq m'$) be two committed requests with sequence numbers $h = [h_i, h_j, h_k, ...]$ and $h' = [h'_k, h'_l, h'_m, ..]$, respectively. Committing a request requires matching accept messages from $f+1$ different nodes of *every* involved cluster. Therefore, if the involved clusters of m and m' intersect in cluster p_k, at least $f+1$ nodes of cluster p_k have sent matching accept messages for m, and similarly, at least $f+1$ nodes of cluster p_k have sent matching accept messages for m'. Since each cluster includes $2f+1$ nodes and nodes are non-malicious, $h_k \neq h'_k$. Note that the same proof logic applies in special cases where m or m' is an intra-shard transaction (i.e., $h = h_k$ or $h' = h'_k$).

If the primary fails, since each committed request has been replicated on a quorum Q_1 of $f+1$ nodes and to become elected primary agreement from a quorum Q_2 of $f+1$ nodes is needed, Q_1 and Q_2 must intersect in at least one node that is aware of the latest committed request. Hence, SharPer guarantees the agreement property for both intra-shard and cross-shard transactions. □

Lemma 4.2 (Validity) *If a correct node r commits m, then m must have been proposed by some correct node π.*

Proof In cross-shard consensus with crash-only nodes, validity is ensured since crash-only nodes do not send fictitious messages. □

Lemma 4.3 (Consistency) *Let P_μ denote the set of involved clusters for a request μ. For any two committed requests m and m' and any two nodes r_1 and r_2 such that $r_1 \in p_i, r_2 \in p_j$, and $\{p_i, p_j\} \in P_m \cap P_{m'}$, if m is committed before m' in r_1, then m is committed before m' in r_2.*

Proof As mentioned in Sect. 4.3.2, once a node r_1 of some cluster p_i receives a propose message for some cross-shard transaction m, if the node is involved in another uncommitted cross-shard transaction m' where $|P_m \cap P_{m'}| > 1$, i.e., some other cluster p_j is also involved in both transactions, node r_1 does not send an accept message for transaction m before m' gets committed. In this way, since committing request m requires $f + 1$ accept messages from *every* involved cluster, m cannot be committed until m' is committed. As a result, the order of committing messages is the same on all involved nodes. In the special case where $i = j$ (both nodes r_1 and r_2 belong to the same cluster), if the primary of the cluster assigns the sequence number, there will be no inconsistency among nodes. Otherwise, when the nodes assign sequence numbers and even if r_1 and r_2 initially assign inconsistent sequence numbers, since at least $f + 1$ matching accept messages from different nodes of the cluster are needed to commit a request and the cluster includes $2f + 1$ nodes, the order of committing transactions on nodes r_1 and r_2 must be consistent. □

Note that ensuring consistency might result in deadlock situations which can be resolved as explained in Sect. 4.3.3.

Lemma 4.4 (Termination) *A request m issued by a correct client eventually completes.*

Proof SharPer, as mentioned earlier and due to the FLP impossibility result [26], guarantees liveness only during periods of synchrony. To show that a request issued by a correct client is eventually completed, we need to address three scenarios. First, if the primary is non-faulty and accept messages are non-conflicting, as shown in Algorithm 3, the protocol ensures that the correct client receives reply from the primary. Second, if a non-faulty primary has multicast propose messages but not received matching accept messages from $f + 1$ nodes of every involved cluster, as explained in Sect. 4.3.3, the initiator primary re-initiates the transaction by multicasting prepare messages. In this case, since the primary node of each cluster assigns the sequence number (in its super-accept message), super-accept messages that are received from each cluster will match, thus increasing the chances of termination. Third, if the (initiator) primary fails, as explained in Sect. 4.3.4, nodes involved in an uncommitted transaction (initiated by the faulty primary) detect its failure (using timeouts) and trigger the primary failure handling. The new primary then will handle all uncommitted transactions. □

4.4 Consensus with Byzantine Nodes

This section discusses intra- and cross-shard consensus in the presence of Byzantine nodes, the view-change routine and the correctness of SharPer.

4.4.1 Intra-shard Consensus

Byzantine fault-tolerant protocols, e.g., PBFT [18], usually rely on $3f+1$ nodes to guarantee safety in the presence of at most f *malicious* nodes. PBFT, as discussed in Sect. 2.6, consists of an agreement routine that orders requests for execution by the nodes, and a view-change routine that coordinates the election of a new primary when the current primary is faulty. The nodes move through a succession of configurations called *views* [27, 28] where, in each view, one node, called *the primary*, initiates the protocol and the others are *backups*.

We briefly review the agreement routine. To establish consensus on the order of intra-shard transactions during a normal case execution of PBFT, a client c requests an intra-shard transaction by sending a signed request message to the primary. When the primary receives a valid request from an authorized client, it initiates the consensus protocol by assigning a sequence number and multicasting a propose (called pre-prepare in the original PBFT) message including the requested transaction to all nodes within the cluster. Once a node receives a valid propose message from the primary, it multicasts an accept (called prepare in the original PBFT) message to every node within the cluster. Each node then waits for $2f$ valid accept messages from different nodes (including itself) that match the propose message and then multicasts a commit message to all the nodes within the cluster. Once a node receives $2f + 1$ valid commit messages from different nodes that match the corresponding propose message, it appends the transaction block including all $2f + 1$ commit messages to the ledger (to ensure immutability), executes the transaction, and sends a reply to the client. Finally, the client waits for $f + 1$ valid matching responses from different nodes to make sure at least one correct replica executed its request.

4.4.2 Cross-Shard Consensus with Byzantine Nodes

In the presence of Byzantine failures, a Byzantine fault-tolerant protocol is needed to order cross-shard transactions where for each cross-shard transaction, similar to the crash-only case, agreement from all involved clusters is needed. Unlike in the case of crash failure where the quorum size is $f + 1$, in consensus with Byzantine nodes, the quorum size is $2f + 1$. Moreover, due to the potential malicious behavior of the primary node, all nodes of every involved cluster multicast both accept and commit messages to each other. The normal case operation for SharPer to process a cross-shard transaction in the presence of Byzantine nodes is presented in Algorithm 5. Similar to Algorithm 3 and as shown in lines

Algorithm 5 Cross-shard Consensus with Byzantine Nodes

1: **init():**
2: $r := node\_id$
3: $p_i :=$ the cluster that initiates the consensus instance
4: $\pi(p) :=$ the primary node of cluster p
5: $P :=$ set of all nodes in the involved clusters
6: **if** $r == \pi(p_i)$ and receiving valid request $m = \langle \text{REQUEST}, op, ts, c \rangle_{\sigma_c}$ **then**
7: multicast $\langle \langle \text{PROPOSE}, h_i, v_i, d \rangle_{\sigma_{\pi(p_i)}}, m \rangle$ to P
8: **end if**
9: **if** $r \in P$ and receiving valid $\langle \text{PROPOSE}, h_i, v_i, d \rangle_{\sigma_{\pi(p_i)}}, m \rangle$ and r is not waiting for commit message of request m' where m and m' intersect in some other cluster p_k **then**
10: assign sequence number h_j to m ▷ assuming r is a member of cluster p_j
11: send $\langle \text{ACCEPT}, h_i, h_j, v_i, v_j, d, r \rangle_{\sigma_r}$ to P
12: **end if**
13: **if** $r \in P$ and receiving $2f+1$ valid matching $\langle \text{ACCEPT}, h_i, h_j, v_i, v_j, d, r \rangle_{\sigma_r}$ from different nodes of every cluster p_j in P **then**
14: multicast $\langle \text{COMMIT}, h_i, h_j, ..., h_k, v_i, v_j, ..., v_k, d, r \rangle_{\sigma_r}$ to P
15: **end if**
16: **if** $r \in P$ and receiving $2f+1$ valid matching $\langle \text{COMMIT}, h_i, h_j, ..., h_k, v_i, v_j, ..., v_k, d, r \rangle_{\sigma_r}$ from different nodes of every cluster in P **then**
17: append the transaction and commit message to the ledger
18: **end if**

1–5, p_i is the initiator cluster, $\pi(p)$ indicates the primary node of cluster p, and P is the set of involved clusters.

Once the initiator primary $\pi(p_i)$ receives a valid signed request m to execute a cross-shard transaction op from an authorized client c with timestamp ts as presented in lines 6–78, the primary assigns sequence number h_i to the request and multicasts a *signed* propose message including sequence number h_i, view number v_i (that indicates the view of cluster p_i in which the message is being sent), and digest d of the request to every node of all involved clusters. As before, sequence number h_i is used to ensure that the new transaction block is ordered correctly with respect to the blocks that the cluster has been involved in. Requests are piggybacked in propose messages to keep propose messages small. Since the network might include malicious nodes, the primary signs its message.

Once a node r of an involved cluster p_j receives a propose message for a request m, as indicated in lines 9–12, it validates the signature and message digest. If the node belongs to the initiator cluster ($i = j$), it also checks h_i to be valid (within a certain range) since a malicious primary might multicast a request with an invalid sequence number. Furthermore, if the node is currently involved in an uncommitted cross-shard request m' where the involved clusters of two requests m and m' overlap in some other cluster, as explained in the crash-only case, the node does not process the new request m before the earlier request m' is processed. This is needed to ensure requests are committed in the same order on different clusters. The node then multicasts a signed accept message including the corresponding sequence number h_j (that represents the order of request m in cluster p_j), the view number v_j of cluster p_j as well as the digest d of request m to *every* node of *all* involved clusters.

Each node then waits for valid accept messages with matching sequence and view numbers from $2f + 1$ nodes of *every* involved cluster with h_i, and d that match the propose message which is sent by primary $\pi(p_i)$. Since the primary node of the initiator cluster p_i does not send accept message (similar to the prepare phase of PBFT), $2f$ matching accept messages from the initiator cluster that match the corresponding propose message sent by $\pi(p_i)$ is sufficient when checking the matching accept messages of cluster p_i. We define the predicate accepted-local$_{p_j}(m, h_i, h_j, v_i, v_j, r)$ to be true if and only if node r has received the request m, a propose for m with sequence number h_i in view v_i of the initiator cluster p_i and $2f + 1$ (or $2f$ in the case of initiator cluster) singed accept messages form different nodes of an involved cluster p_j that match the propose message. The predicate accepted(m, h, v, r) where $h = [h_i, h_j, ..., h_k]$ and $v = [v_i, v_j, ..., v_k]$ is then defined to be true on node r if and only if accepted-local$_{p_j}$ is true for *every* involved cluster p_j in cross-shard request m. The order of sequence numbers and view numbers in the predicate is an ascending order determined by their cluster IDs. Here, since nodes might behave maliciously, each cluster includes $3f + 1$ nodes and $2f + 1$ matching messages from *all* involved clusters for each step of the protocol are needed. The propose and accept phases of the algorithm basically guarantee that non-faulty nodes agree on a total order of transactions. When accepted(m, h, v, r) becomes true, as presented in lines 13–15, node r multicasts a signed commit message to every node of all involved clusters.

Finally, as shown in lines 16–18, each node waits for valid matching signed commit messages from $2f + 1$ nodes of *every* involved cluster that match the corresponding propose message. The predicate committed-local$_{p_j}(m, h, v, r)$ is defined to be true on node r if and only if accepted(m, h, v, r) is true and node r has accepted $2f + 1$ valid matching commit messages from different nodes of cluster p_j that match the propose message for cross-shard request m. The predicate committed(m, h, v, r) is then defined to be true on node r if and only if committed-local$_{p_i}$ is true for *every* involved cluster p_j in cross-shard request m. The committed predicate indeed shows that at least $2f + 1$ nodes of each involved cluster have multicast valid commit messages. When the committed predicate becomes true, the node considers the transaction as committed. If node r of cluster p_j has executed all transactions with lower sequence numbers than h_j, it appends the transaction as well as the corresponding commit message to the ledger and executes it.

Figure 4.6 demonstrates the normal case operation of two concurrent cross-shard transactions in the presence of Byzantine nodes where each transaction accesses two disjoint data shards. The network consists of four clusters, each including four nodes ($f = 1$).

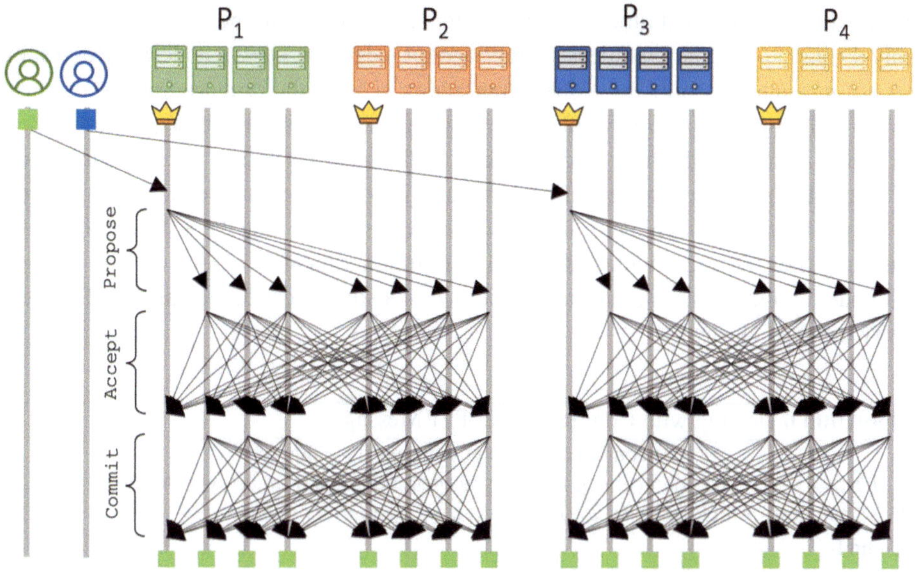

Fig. 4.6 The flow of two *concurrent* cross-shard transactions in SharPer with Byzantine nodes

4.4.3 Dealing with Conflicting Messages

In the consensus protocol with Byzantine nodes, similar to the crash-only case, a quorum of $2f+1$ *matching* accept messages from every cluster might not be received due to conflicting propose messages coming from different primary nodes in parallel. The $\langle \text{ACCEPT}, h_i, h_j, v_i, v_j, d, r\rangle_{\sigma_{\pi(p_i)}}$ messages might be non-matching for two reasons. First, the initiator primary $\pi(p_i)$ is malicious and sends inconsistent messages, i.e., assigns inconsistent sequence numbers, to different nodes, hence, there is no quorum of $2f+1$ nodes from a cluster with the same sequence number h_i for the same request. Note that a malicious initiator primary might also assign invalid digest d or sign its message incorrectly; however, it will be easily detected by all nodes as an *invalid* message. The primary malicious behavior that is not detected by nodes alone and requires communication among them (i.e., sending accept messages) is when the initiator primary node assigns inconsistent sequence numbers to the same request. Second, when different nodes of the same cluster, similar to the crash-only case, assign an inconsistent sequence number h_j (due to slowness of the network or some nodes or due to the maliciousness of some nodes). We address the first case, in the primary failure handling routine. In the second case, as presented in lines 1–3 of Algorithm 6, the primary node of each conflicting cluster p_j, i.e., a cluster where at least $2f+1$ of accept messages have matching h_i and d (to ensure that the initiator primary is non-faulty) but less than $2f+1$ of accept messages have matching h_j, multicasts a super-accept message (with the same structure as accept messages) to the nodes of its own cluster after a predefined time τ_a. Note that this is in contrast to the crash-only case where only the initiator primary multicasts super-accept messages. Once a node receives a super-accept message for some cross-shard transaction m from the primary node of its cluster, as shown in lines 4–6, it first validates the message, the digest, and its sequence number to be within a predefined range. Node also checks the received accept messages from nodes of its cluster to ensure that the initiator primary is non-malicious, i.e., less than f accept messages have non-matching h_i. If the node has received less than $2f + 1$ matching accept messages (i.e., messages with matching h_j) for transaction m from the nodes of its cluster, the node (including the primary node) multicasts a super-accept message to all nodes of every involved cluster.

Algorithm 6 Dealing with Conflicting ACCEPT Messages

*** The configuration is the same as Algorithm 5***

1: **if** $r == \pi(p_j)$ and not receiving matching accept messages from its own cluster p_j **then**
2: multicast $\langle$SUPER-ACCEPT, $h_i, h_j, v_i, v_j, d\rangle_{\sigma_{\pi(p_j)}}$ to every node in p_j
3: **end if**
4: **if** $r \in p_j$, receiving $\langle$SUPER-ACCEPT, $h_i, h_j, v_i, v_j, d\rangle_{\sigma_{\pi(p_j)}}$ from $\pi(p_i)$ **then** and less than $2f + 1$ valid accept messages from p_j for m is logged
5: multicast $\langle$SUPER-ACCEPT, $h_i, h_j, v_i, v_j, d, r\rangle_{\sigma_r}$ to P
6: **end if**

In heavy workloads with a high percentage of cross-shard transactions where the probability of receiving conflicting accept messages is high, similar to the crash-only case, the initiator primary node initially multicasts prepare messages to all nodes of other involved clusters. The primary of each involved cluster then multicasts a propose message to the nodes of its cluster.

4.4.4 View-Change

The primary failure handling routine, similar to the crash-only case, is triggered by timeout. If the timer of some node r of cluster p_j expires (after some predefined time τ_f) node r suspects that the primary might be faulty. There are three cases. First, a cross-shard transaction where $\pi(p_i)$ (the initiator primary node) is suspected to be faulty (i.e., it has not sent valid propose or prepare messages) and $i \neq j$ (node r and $\pi(p_i)$ are in *different* clusters). Second, a cross-shard transaction where $\pi(p_j)$ (the primary node of the cluster hosting r) is suspected to be faulty (i.e., it has not sent valid super-accept messages) and $i \neq j$. Third, an intra- or a cross-shard transaction where $\pi(p_j)$ (the primary node of the cluster hosting r) is suspected to be faulty (i.e., it has not sent valid propose, prepare or super-accept messages) and $i = j$.

In the first case, if the propose message has an incorrect digest or signature, node r discards it. However, if propose messages are valid but more than f of accept messages that node r receives from nodes of an involved cluster p_j have non-matching h_i, then initiator primary $\pi(p_i)$ is suspected to be faulty (i.e., by sending conflicting propose messages to the nodes of cluster p_j). Therefore, node r multicasts an $\langle$ACCEPT-QUERY, $h_i, d, r\rangle_{\sigma_{\pi(r)}}$ messages to every node of initiator cluster p_i. Note that, node r still processes all intra-shard transactions as well as all transactions initiated by other clusters. If a node receives accept-query messages from $2f + 1$ different nodes of another cluster with matching d, the node suspects that the primary of its cluster is faulty and initiates the primary failure handling routine.

Second, when primary $\pi(p_j)$ is malicious and multicasts super-accept messages with (consistent sequence number h_i but) inconsistent sequence numbers h_j to the nodes of its cluster. In this case, node r will receive inconsistent super-accept messages from different nodes of p_j, suspects that $\pi(p_j)$ is faulty, and initiates the primary failure handling routine. Note that, this case happens when either accept messages are conflicting or the optimization presented for heavy workloads is used. Third, when node r and the faulty primary are in the same cluster, inspired by PBFT, node r initiates the primary failure handling routine by multicasting a view-change message including all received valid accept, accept-query, and commit messages for all intra-shard as well as cross-shard transactions to every node of the cluster. To decrease the size of view-change messages, SharPer uses the checkpointing mechanism of PBFT [18] where each node sends the last stable checkpoint that it knows, proof of its correctness, and messages with a sequence number higher than the checkpoint sequence number. An accept-query message is valid if it is received from at least $2f + 1$ different nodes of a cluster. Upon receiving view-change valid messages from $2f + 1$ different nodes (including itself), the next primary (determined in a round-robin manner based on node IDs) handles the uncommitted transactions by multicasting a new-view message including $2f + 1$ view-change messages and a propose message for every uncommitted request (either intra-shard or cross-shard) to every node within the cluster. For uncommitted cross-shard requests where the cluster has initiated the requests, the new primary multicasts a new-view message including $2f + 1$ view-change messages and the related propose messages to every node of all involved clusters. If other clusters have already accepted the request, they simply send back their accept (or super-accept) messages. Once node r multicasts a view-change message, it starts a timer that expires after some time τ_v. If the timer expires before it receives a valid new-view message, it starts the routine again. In the worst case, the system might incur f consecutive faulty primary nodes.

4.4.5 Correctness Arguments

We demonstrate how SharPer satisfies the safety and liveness properties in the presence of Byzantine nodes.

Lemma 4.5 (Agreement) *If node r commits request m with sequence number h, no other correct node commits request m′ ($m \neq m'$) with the same sequence number h.*

Proof The propose and accept phases of the BFT cross-shard consensus protocol guarantee that correct nodes agree on a total order of all requests. If the accepted(m, h, v, r) predicate where $h = [h_i, h_j, ..., h_k]$ is true, then accepted(m', h, v, q) is false for any non-faulty node q (including $r = q$) and any m' such that $m \neq m'$. This is true because (m, h, v, r) implies that accepted-local$_{p_j}(m, h_i, v_i, h_j, v_j)$ is true for each involved cluster p_j and since each cluster includes $3f + 1$ nodes, at least $2f + 1$ nodes within the cluster (from which at least $f + 1$ nodes are non-faulty) have sent accept (or propose) messages for request m with sequence number h_j. As a result, for accepted(m', h, v, q) to be true, at least one of those non-faulty nodes needs to have sent two conflicting accept messages with the same sequence number but different message digest. This condition guarantees that, first, a malicious primary cannot violate safety and, second, at most one of the concurrent *conflicting* transactions can collect the required number of messages $(2f + 1)$ from each overlapping cluster.

The primary failure handling routine of SharPer guarantees that the non-faulty nodes of any cluster p_j agree on the sequence number of requests that are committed-local at different nodes. The committed-local$_{p_j}$ predicate becomes correct on node r if r has received a quorum Q_1 of matching commit messages from $2f + 1$ nodes of cluster p_j. To change the primary node of cluster p_j, a quorum Q_2 of $2f + 1$ valid view-change messages is needed. Since there are $3f + 1$ nodes in each cluster, Q_1 and Q_2 intersect on $f + 1$ nodes, which includes at least one correct node, thus if a request is accepted by the previous primary node, it is propagated to subsequent primary nodes. □

Lemma 4.6 (Validity) *If a correct node r commits m, then m must have been proposed by some correct node π.*

Proof In the presence of Byzantine nodes, validity is guaranteed mainly based on standard cryptographic assumptions about collision-resistant hashes, encryption, and signatures that the adversary cannot subvert (as explained in Sect. 4.2). Since the request as well as all messages are signed and either the request or its digest is included in each message (to prevent changes and alterations to any part of the message), and in each step, $2f + 1$ matching messages (from each cluster) are required, if a request is committed, the same request must have been proposed earlier. □

Lemma 4.7 (Consistency) *Let P_μ denote the set of involved clusters for a request μ. For any two committed requests m and m′ and any two nodes r_1 and r_2 such that $r_1 \in p_i, r_2 \in p_j$, and $\{p_i, p_j\} \in P_m \cap P_{m'}$, if m is committed before m′ in r_1, then m is committed before m′ in r_2.*

Proof Consistency is guaranteed similar to crash-only nodes (Lemma 4.3) except that committing request m requires $2f + 1$ matching commit messages (out of $3f + 1$) from each cluster. □

Lemma 4.8 (Termination) *A request m issued by a correct client eventually completes.*

To provide termination during periods of synchrony, similar to the crash-only case, several scenarios need to be addressed. If the primary is non-faulty and accept messages are non-conflicting, following Algorithm 5, request m completes. Next, if the primary is non-faulty, but more than f accept messages of some involved cluster p_j have inconsistent sequence number h_j, as explained in Sect. 4.4.3, $\pi(p_j)$ multicasts a super-accept message including h_j to the nodes of its own cluster. Finally, the primary failure handling routine (Sect. 4.4.4) handles primary failures in several cases where (1) an initiator primary multicasts invalid propose or prepare messages to other clusters; (2) the primary of an involved cluster multicasts invalid super-accept messages for a cross-shard transaction to nodes of its cluster; and (3) a primary node multicasts invalid propose, prepare, or super-accept messages to the nodes of its cluster.

Note that in the optimization explained in Sect. 4.4.3 for heavy workload where the initiator primary multicasts prepare messages to the nodes of all other involved clusters, assigning an inconsistent sequence number, h_j, will be detected in the accept phase. Furthermore, if the initiator primary does not multicast the prepare message to an involved primary (or cluster) or the primary node of an involved cluster does not multicast the super-accept message to the nodes of its cluster, since all nodes of all involved clusters multicast super-accept messages to each other, as long as nodes of one involved cluster multicast super-accept messages, other involved clusters will be informed (i.e., no liveness issue will happen). If a node receives valid super-accept messages from nodes of other clusters without receiving a super-accept message from the primary of its cluster (and prepare message from the initiator primary), it multicasts a query message to all nodes of the initiator cluster. The primary of an involved cluster multicasts the query message to the nodes of its cluster as well in case they have already received the message and can retransmit it to the primary node (since nodes of a cluster are in proximity, it reduces the latency of processing a request). If nodes of the initiator cluster receive such queries from $2f + 1$ nodes of an involved cluster for a request, they suspect that the initiator primary is faulty. If nodes of an involved cluster do not receive the super-accept message from their primary after some predefined time, they suspect that their primary is faulty. In the worst case, a faulty initiator primary node might continue to operate maliciously by not sending prepare messages to the primary nodes of the involved clusters. However, in this case, the primary node of each involved cluster can obtain the actual request probably from a node in its cluster, since these nodes are in closer proximity, hence the safety and liveness are not affected.

4.5 Summary

Scalability is one of the main obstacles to business adoption of blockchain systems, especially in financial and large-scale database systems. Permissioned blockchain systems mainly use clustering to improve scalability. In clustering approaches, nodes are partitioned into fault-tolerant clusters where each cluster processes a disjoint set of transactions. Permissioned blockchain systems use single-ledger or sharded-ledger techniques to enhance scalability. In the single-ledger technique, the entire ledger is replicated on all clusters and all nodes execute every transaction. In the sharded-ledger technique, on the other hand, the ledger is partitioned into multiple shards that are maintained by different clusters. Sharded-ledger permissioned blockchain systems process two types of intra-shard and cross-shard transactions. Cross-shard transactions can be processed either in a centralized manner using the coordinator-based approach or in a decentralized manner using the flattened approach.

Sharded-ledger approaches mainly differ in how they process cross-shard transactions. Centralized processing of cross-shard transactions is simpler and closer to the traditional two-phase commit, i.e., instead of a single coordinator node, a coordinator cluster is needed to tolerate Byzantine failure; however, a large number of intra- and cross-cluster communication phases is needed. On the other hand, the decentralized approach does not require an extra set of nodes, processes transactions in less number of phases among the involved clusters, and is able to process cross-shard transactions with non-overlapping clusters in parallel. However, if the involved clusters are distant, establishing cross-shard consensus among involved clusters that needs multiple rounds of message passing results in high latency. Single-ledger approaches, on the other hand, do not suffer from the latency of processing cross-shard transactions by replicating the entire data on every cluster. However, exchanging messages between all clusters for every single transaction still results in high latency.

In this chapter, we presented SharPer, a permissioned blockchain system designed specifically for networks with a very high percentage of non-faulty nodes. SharPer consists of a set of fault-tolerant clusters and each maintains a view of the blockchain ledger. SharPer provides deterministic safety guarantees by considering pre-determined fault-tolerant clusters. SharPer processes cross-shard transactions in a decentralized manner among the involved clusters (without requiring a reference committee) using decentralized flattened consensus protocols.

References

1. Miller, A., Bentov, I., Bakshi, S., Kumaresan, R., McCorry, P.: Sprites and state channels: payment networks that go faster than lightning. In: International Conference on Financial Cryptography and Data Security (FC), pp. 508–526. Springer (2019)
2. Poon, J., Dryja, T.: The bitcoin lightning network: scalable off-chain instant payments (2016). https://lightning.network/lightning-network-paper.pdf

3. Croman, K., Decker, C., Eyal, I., Gencer, A.E., Juels, A., Kosba, A., Miller, A., Saxena, P., Shi, E., Sirer, E.G., et al.: On scaling decentralized blockchains. In: International Conference on Financial Cryptography and Data Security (FC), pp. 106–125. Springer (2016)
4. Seres, I.A., Gulyás, L., Nagy, D.A., Burcsi, P.: Topological analysis of bitcoin's lightning network (2019). arXiv preprint arXiv:1901.04972
5. Corbett, J.C., Dean, J., Epstein, M., Fikes, A., Frost, C., Furman, J.J., Ghemawat, S., Gubarev, A., Heiser, C., Hochschild, P.: Spanner: Google's globally distributed database. Trans. Comput. Syst. (TOCS) **31**(3), 8 (2013)
6. Luu, L., Narayanan, V., Zheng, C., Baweja, K., Gilbert, S., Saxena, P.: A secure sharding protocol for open blockchains. In: SIGSAC Conference on Computer and Communications Security (CCS), pp. 17–30. ACM (2016)
7. Kokoris-Kogias, E., Jovanovic, P., Gasser, L., Gailly, N., Syta, E., Ford, B.: Omniledger: a secure, scale-out, decentralized ledger via sharding. In: Symposium on Security and Privacy (SP), pp. 583–598. IEEE (2018)
8. Zamani, M., Movahedi, M., Raykova, M.: Rapidchain: Scaling blockchain via full sharding. In: SIGSAC Conference on Computer and Communications Security, pp. 931–948. ACM (2018)
9. Androulaki, E., Barger, A., Bortnikov, V., Cachin, C., Christidis, K., De Caro, A., Enyeart, D., Ferris, C., Laventman, G., Manevich, Y.: Hyperledger fabric: a distributed operating system for permissioned blockchains. In: European Conference on Computer Systems (EuroSys), pp. 30:1–30:15. ACM (2018)
10. Frey, E., Goes, C.: Cosmos inter-blockchain communication (IBC) protocol (2018). https://cosmos.network
11. George, D., Meiklejohn, S.: Centrally banked cryptocurrencies. In: Network and Distributed System Security Symposium (NDSS) (2016)
12. Dang, H., Dinh, T.T.A., Loghin, D., Chang, E.C., Lin, Q., Ooi, B.C.: Towards scaling blockchain systems via sharding. In: SIGMOD International Conference on Management of Data, pp. 123–140. ACM (2019)
13. Androulaki, E., Cachin, C., De Caro, A., Kokoris-Kogias, E.: Channels: horizontal scaling and confidentiality on permissioned blockchains. In: European Symposium on Research in Computer Security (ESORICS), pp. 111–131. Springer (2018)
14. Gupta, S., Rahnama, S., Hellings, J., Sadoghi, M.: Resilientdb: global scale resilient blockchain fabric. Proceed. VLDB Endowment **13**(6), 868–883 (2020)
15. Nawab, F., Sadoghi, M.: Blockplane: A global-scale Byzantizing middleware. In: International Conference on Data Engineering (ICDE), pp. 124–135. IEEE (2019)
16. Amiri, M.J., Agrawal, D., El Abbadi, A.: SharPer: Sharding permissioned blockchains over network clusters. In: SIGMOD International Conference on Management of Data, pp. 76–88. ACM (2021)
17. Amiri, M.J., Agrawal, D., El Abbadi, A.: On sharding permissioned blockchains. In: International Conference on Blockchain, pp. 282–285. IEEE (2019)
18. Castro, M., Liskov, B.: Practical byzantine fault tolerance. In: Symposium on Operating Systems Design and Implementation (OSDI), pp. 173–186. USENIX Association (1999)
19. Curino, C., Jones, E.P.C., Zhang, Y., Madden, S.R.: Schism: a workload-driven approach to database replication and partitioning. Proceed. VLDB Endowment **3**(1) (2010)
20. Pavlo, A., Curino, C., Zdonik, S.: Skew-aware automatic database partitioning in shared-nothing, parallel OLTP systems. In: SIGMOD International Conference on Management of Data, pp. 61–72. ACM (2012)
21. Mehta, B., Iyer, P., Amiri, M.J., Loo, B.T., Marcus, R.: Towards adaptive fault-tolerant sharded databases (extended abstracts) (2023)
22. Lamport, L.: Time, clocks, and the ordering of events in a distributed system. Commun. ACM **21**(7), 558–565 (1978)

23. Cachin, C., Guerraoui, R., Rodrigues, L.: Introduction to Reliable and Secure Distributed Programming. Springer Science & Business Media (2011)
24. Ongaro, D., Ousterhout, J.K.: In search of an understandable consensus algorithm. In: Annual Technical Conference (ATC), pp. 305–319. USENIX Association (2014)
25. Lamport, L.: Paxos made simple. ACM Sigact News **32**(4), 18–25 (2001)
26. Fischer, M.J., Lynch, N.A., Paterson, M.S.: Impossibility of distributed consensus with one faulty process. J. ACM (JACM) **32**(2), 374–382 (1985)
27. El Abbadi, A., Skeen, D., Cristian, F.: An efficient, fault-tolerant protocol for replicated data management. In: SIGACT-SIGMOD Symposium on Principles of Database Systems, pp. 215–229. ACM (1985)
28. El Abbadi, A., Toueg, S.: Availability in partitioned replicated databases. In: SIGACT-SIGMOD Symposium on Principles of Database Systems, pp. 240–251. ACM (1986)

Confidentiality 5

5.1 Introduction

Confidentiality of data is required in many collaborative distributed applications, e.g., supply chain management, where multiple enterprises collaborate following Service Level Agreements (SLAs), which are agreed upon by all involved enterprises, to provide different services. SLAs can be written as self-executing computer programs, called *smart contracts* [1]. The collaboration is realized by means of cross-enterprise transactions that are *visible* to every enterprise. During the execution of cross-enterprise transactions, agreement on the shared state of the collaborating enterprises is needed without trusting a central authority or any particular participant. While cross-enterprise collaborations and the involved data are *visible* to every enterprise, the internal data of each enterprise, i.e., the enterprise logic, internal transactions, and their data, might be *confidential*. Hence, it is desirable to restrict access to such data. Although cryptographic techniques can be used to achieve confidentiality, the high overhead of such techniques makes them impractical [2].

The unique features of blockchain such as transparency, provenance, and authenticity have been used by many systems to deploy a wide range of large-scale data management applications such as supply chain management [3] and healthcare [4] in a permissioned setting. Existing permissioned blockchains, however, mostly suffer from confidentiality issues since a single blockchain ledger with all transactions is maintained at every node. While Hyperledger Fabric [2] addresses the confidentiality issue by restricting access to the blockchain state (using private data collections) and *smart contracts*, which include the enterprise logic, the blockchain ledger is still maintained by every node. To provide confidentiality, different enterprises could have independent disjoint blockchains. However, to support collaboration between enterprises on distinct blockchains, techniques such as atomic cross-chain transaction [5, 6] and interledger protocol [7] are needed to exchange (transfer) assets or information between the blockchains (*Interoperability*). Such techniques

M. J. Amiri et al., *Blockchain-Enabled Large-Scale Transaction Management*,
Synthesis Lectures on Data Management,
https://doi.org/10.1007/978-3-031-91058-6_5

are often costly, complex, and mainly designed for permissionless blockchains. Techniques that support collaborating enterprises on a single blockchain either do not support internal transactions of enterprises [8] (results in data integration issues), or suffer from confidentiality issues since the entire ledger is visible to all enterprises, e.g., single-channel Fabric [2] or require a trusted channel among participants, e.g., multi-channel Fabric [9].

This chapter presents *Caper* [10]: a permissioned blockchain system that supports both internal and cross-enterprise transactions of collaborating distributed enterprises. In Caper, each enterprise orders and executes its internal transactions locally while cross-enterprise transactions are public and visible to every enterprise. In addition, the blockchain ledger of Caper is a directed acyclic graph that includes the internal transactions of every enterprise and all cross-enterprise transactions. Nonetheless, for the sake of confidentiality, the blockchain ledger is *not maintained* by any node. In fact, each enterprise maintains its own *local view* of the ledger including its internal and all cross-enterprise transactions. Since ordering cross-enterprise transactions requires *global* agreement among all enterprises, Caper introduces different consensus protocols to globally order cross-enterprise transactions.

Lack of trust is an important problem in collaboration between enterprises. Lack of trust has two main origins: first, a *physical node* (server) might fail, thus behave maliciously, and second, an *enterprise* could behave maliciously in communication with other enterprises for its benefit. To address both types of behavior, Caper distinguishes between trust at the node level and trust at the enterprise level, e.g., while the nodes of an enterprise might behave non-maliciously within the enterprise, the enterprise (as a collection of nodes) might still behave maliciously in communication with other enterprises.

The primary goal of this chapter is to illustrate how a blockchain system can efficiently handle internal and cross-enterprise transactions among a group of collaborating but untrustworthy enterprises, ensuring that the confidentiality of internal transactions is maintained while also providing transparency for cross-enterprise transactions.

The rest of this chapter is organized as follows: Section 5.2 briefly describes the limitations of existing blockchain systems and motivates the problem. The Caper model and its architecture are introduced in Sects. 5.3 and 5.4. Section 5.5 presents consensus in Caper and Sect. 5.6 concludes the chapter.

5.2 Background and Motivation

In this section, we discuss the confidentiality limitations of permissioned blockchain systems and provide a motivating example to explain the limitations.

5.2.1 Confidentiality Limitations of Permissioned Blockchain

Data confidentiality is essential in many permissioned blockchain systems. These systems may require restrictions on access to smart contracts, which contain enterprise logic, the blockchain ledger, or transaction data. Although cryptographic techniques can provide confidentiality, their significant overhead often renders them impractical [2]. Hyperledger Fabric [2] addresses this challenge by utilizing private data collections that allow two or more enterprises within a single channel to manage and keep certain confidential data hidden from others on that channel.

Fabric also ensures the confidentiality of smart contracts by storing each enterprise's contracts on distinct sets of endorsers (as discussed in Chapter 3). The endorsers for each enterprise independently execute its transactions without interference from other enterprises. However, the blockchain ledger remains accessible to agents from all enterprises involved in a channel. Collaboration among these enterprises is necessary for providing diverse services, and distributed applications are frequently designed and implemented across different blockchain systems that process and store data separately [11].

To facilitate cross-enterprise collaboration under these circumstances, atomic cross-chain transactions [5, 6] or Interledger protocols [7] can be employed, allowing two parties to exchange assets or information across their respective blockchains. In Fabric specifically, atomic cross-chain transactions between permissioned blockchains (or channels) can be processed using a trusted third channel or an atomic commit protocol [9].

Overall, supporting cross-enterprise transactions presents significant challenges and costs. However, when collaborating enterprises operate within a single permissioned blockchain—where participants in cross-enterprise transactions are pre-identified and agreements adhere to service-level terms—it may be feasible to devise solutions that balance both confidentiality and performance effectively.

5.2.2 A Motivating Example: Supply Chain

We now examine collaborative workflows as a practical use case to highlight the limitations previously discussed. In these workflows, various parties must communicate across enterprises to provide services, but the inherent lack of trust among them poses significant challenges.

Figure 5.1 illustrates a Supply Chain scenario (as reported in [8]). This workflow involves five participants: supplier, manufacturer, bulk buyer, transportation company, and middleman. Each participant may have multiple trusted or untrusted servers (nodes) engaged in different internal tasks (transactions). For instance, within the manufacturer's production process, several departments, such as finance, marketing, and purchasing, are involved in various internal activities including assembly, painting, drying, testing, and packaging.

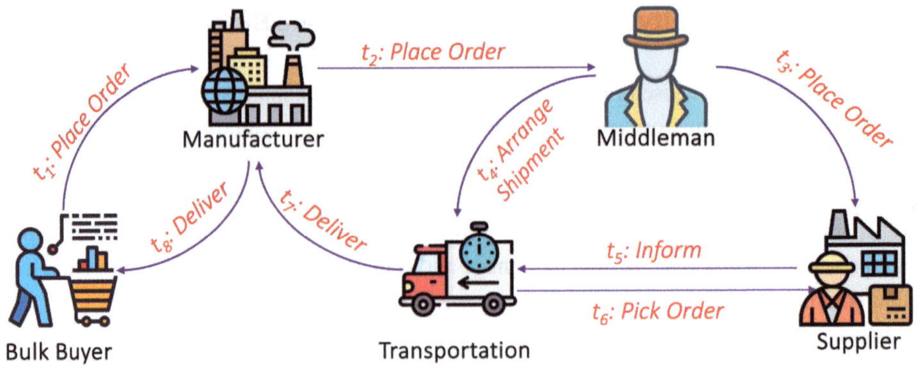

Fig. 5.1 A supply chain scenario consisting of five different enterprises

Participants need to coordinate with one another to fulfill their service obligations. The bulk buyer communicates with the manufacturer to place an order; subsequently, the manufacturer orders materials through the middleman. The middleman then forwards this order to the supplier while also arranging transportation with a transportation company. Upon acquiring the materials from the supplier's location, the transportation company picks them up for delivery to the manufacturer. Once ready for shipment, the manufacturer sends goods over to the bulk buyer. Such collaborations are governed by service level agreements (SLAs) established by all participants.

However, issues can arise if materials are received later than expected or differ from what was agreed upon. In such cases of dispute between parties, the supplier may claim that they delivered exactly what was ordered by the middleman while blaming shifts occur, the transportation company faces additional complications if delivery is rejected by the manufacturer due to discrepancies in expectations. Consequently, the transportation company becomes entitled to compensation depending on which party is deemed responsible for any fault.

To address these challenges effectively, permissioned blockchain systems can be utilized among all participating entities ensuring consensus on shared states without relying on a central authority or any individual participant [8]. A blockchain would effectively monitor collaborative processes and verify compliance with SLAs throughout execution.

Any blockchain-based solution must consider several key concerns:

1. **Support for Cross-Enterprise and Internal Transactions**: The system should accommodate both types of transactions seamlessly. The manufacturer might wish to leverage blockchain technology for its own internal operations, like calculating material demands or product testing, to take advantage of unique features offered by blockchains.
2. **Confidentiality Preservation**: While cross-enterprise transactions remain public and accessible by all relevant participants; each enterprise's internal transactions should be

restricted solely within their nodes' access rights, safeguarding sensitive data that could reveal proprietary operational details.
3. **Performance Considerations**: Efficient performance is crucial when implementing solutions across diverse enterprises.

One potential resolution involves consolidating all enterprises onto a single blockchain where every transaction updates a unified ledger replicated across every node involved. This method facilitates efficient handling of cross-enterprise transactions since access extends universally among participants. However, it compromises confidentiality as all transaction data is visible across parties.

An alternative approach could involve establishing separate blockchains per enterprise whereby internal transactions run concurrently leading to potentially better performance outcomes while preserving confidentiality since data resides within distinct blockchains. To enable communication among different entities under this framework, atomic cross-chain operations could be employed. However, they tend toward higher costs.

As an alternative strategy, one might utilize an additional public blockchain to maintain public interactions. However, since public transactions often use data that is provided by internal transactions, e.g., to place an order, the manufacturer needs to calculate demand internally, and these two types of transactions are stored in different blockchains, *data integration* becomes an expensive and challenging task.

In this chapter, we present an approach aimed at addressing both performance optimization alongside maintaining confidentiality while also handling cross-enterprise transactions efficiently.

5.3 The Caper Model

This section presents the Caper model. We first present distributed applications and the blockchain ledger and then show how the distributed applications are deployed in the blockchain.

5.3.1 Distributed Applications

Caper is a blockchain system designed to support distributed applications consisting of a set of collaborating enterprises that might not trust each other. Each enterprise maintains two sets of *private* and *public* records. The private records of an enterprise are accessible only to the enterprise whereas the public records are replicated on all enterprises.

Caper supports internal and cross-enterprise transactions. *Internal* transactions are performed within an enterprise following the logic of the enterprise, e.g., in the supply chain scenario, the manufacturer calculates materials demand internally. Internal transactions of an enterprise can read and write its private records. They can also read (and not write on) the public records. *Cross-enterprise (public)* transactions, on the other hand, involve multiple enterprises and are visible to all enterprises, e.g., the manufacturer places an order for materials via a middleman. Cross-enterprise transactions follow the service level agreements (SLAs) between the involved enterprises. SLAs present the flow of communication between the enterprises and indicate different aspects of the services, e.g., quality, availability, and responsibilities, that should be provided by different enterprises. For example, in the supply chain scenario, the transportation company is responsible for delivering requested materials to the manufacturer in 2 business days from the date it is informed by the supplier. Public records can only be updated via cross-enterprise transactions.

5.3.2 Blockchain Ledger

The blockchain ledger in Caper consists of internal transactions of all enterprises and all cross-enterprise transactions in the system where each block consists of a single transaction. To support both types of transactions, similar to SharPer [12], the ledger is formed as a *directed acyclic graph* where nodes of the graph are transactions and edges enforce the order of transactions.

Within an enterprise, since transactions have access to the same datastore, a total order between the transactions that are initiated by the enterprise is enforced to ensure consistency. To present the total order of transactions in the blockchain ledger, transactions are *chained*, i.e., each transaction includes the cryptographic hash of the previous transaction. In addition, since cross-enterprise transactions update data that is replicated on all the enterprises, cross-enterprise transactions are ordered to ensure consistency. Furthermore, internal transactions of enterprises might use data that is provided by cross-enterprise transactions, e.g., the manufacturer calculates material's demand based on the place-order cross-enterprise transaction of the bulk buyer. To show such data dependencies, an internal transaction might include the cryptographic hash of a cross-enterprise transaction in the ledger.

In summary, the blockchain ledger has three properties: (1) There is a total order between all transactions (internal as well as cross-enterprise) that are initiated by an enterprise. (2) There is a total order between cross-enterprise transactions. (3) An internal transaction of an enterprise might include the cryptographic hash of a cross-enterprise transaction (that is initiated by another enterprise).

In addition to internal and cross-enterprise transactions, a unique initialization transaction (block), called the genesis transaction, is considered for the blockchain. Function $H(.)$ denotes the cryptographic hash function. For simplicity and in order to show that transaction t includes $H(t')$, an edge from t to t' is included in the DAG representation of the blockchain ledger, which represents that either t is ordered immediately after t' as explained in properties 1 and 2 or t has data dependency to t', as explained in property 3.

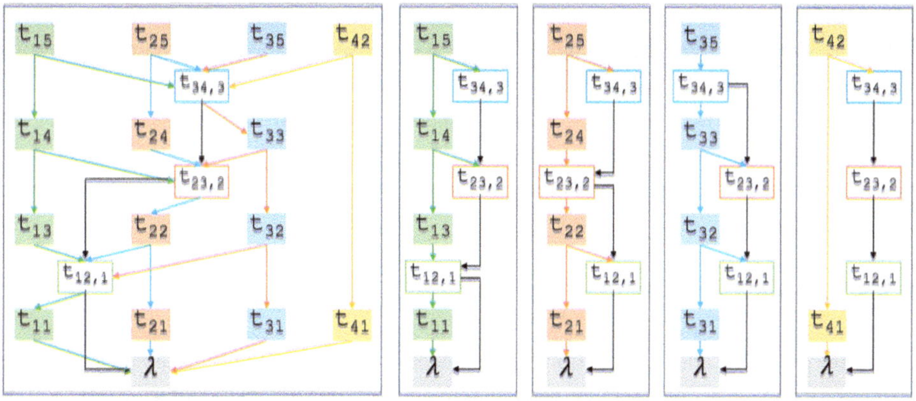

Fig. 5.2 **a** A blockchain ledger, **b–e** Different views of the blockchain

Figure 5.2a shows a Caper blockchain ledger consisting of four enterprises α_1, α_2, α_3, and α_4. In this figure, λ is the genesis transaction. Internal and cross-enterprise transactions of each enterprise are also specified. For example, t_{11}, t_{13}, t_{14}, and t_{15} are the internal transactions of enterprise α_1, and $t_{12,1}$, $t_{23,2}$, and $t_{34,3}$ are the cross-enterprise transactions initiated by α_1, α_2, and α_3, respectively. Note that each cross-enterprise transaction is labeled with $t_{i,j}$ where i indicates the order of the transaction among the transactions that are initiated by its initiator enterprise and j presents the order of the transaction among all cross-enterprise transactions. As can be seen, transactions (both internal and cross-enterprise) that are initiated by an enterprise are chained together (property 1), e.g., t_{31}, t_{32}, t_{33}, $t_{34,3}$, and t_{35}. In addition, cross-enterprise transactions are chained together (property 2), i.e., $t_{12,1}$, $t_{23,2}$, and $t_{34,3}$. Finally, an internal transaction includes the hash of a cross-enterprise transaction that shows the data dependency of the internal transaction to the cross-enterprise transaction (property 3), e.g., internal transaction t_{22} of α_2 has an edge to cross-enterprise transaction $t_{12,1}$.

Note that, since an edge from transaction t to transaction t' indicates that t occurs after t' (t includes the hash of t', thus t' has to be appended to the ledger earlier), it is easy to show that the resulting graph is acyclic.

In contrast to the cross-enterprise transactions that are visible to and maintained by all enterprises, the internal transactions of an enterprise present confidential data about the enterprise, e.g., its business logic. For example, in the supply chain scenario, the internal transactions of the manufacturer show its internal process for producing a product which the manufacturer might intend to keep as a secret. The presented blockchain ledger, however, is at odds with confidentiality because every enterprise has access to every transaction. For the sake of confidentiality, we need to prohibit an enterprise from observing the internal transactions of other enterprises. To achieve this, in Caper, the entire blockchain ledger is *not maintained* by any enterprise. In fact, each enterprise only maintains its own *view* of the blockchain ledger that includes its internal transactions and all the cross-enterprise transactions. The blockchain ledger is indeed the union of all these physical views.

Figure 5.2b–e shows the views of the blockchain ledger for enterprises α_1, α_2, α_3, and α_4, respectively, where each enterprise maintains only the part of the ledger consisting of its own internal and all the cross-enterprise transactions.

5.3.3 Application Deployment on a Blockchain

Each enterprise in Caper, in addition to the datastore and its view of the blockchain ledger, maintains its own *private smart contract* which includes the logic of the internal transactions. In addition, a *public smart contract* is maintained, which implements the logic of cross-enterprise transactions, determined by the service level agreements between the enterprises. As discussed in Sect. 5.2, to execute a collaborative process, participants agree on SLAs which are then written in the public smart contracts. The public smart contract runs on every enterprise to check if the cross-enterprise transactions are *conforming* to the SLAs, and enforce the conditions defined in the cross-enterprise transactions. In Caper, each private smart contract runs only on its enterprise to preserve confidentiality. However, the public smart contract runs on every enterprise to support cross-enterprise transactions.

In the supply chain scenario in Fig. 5.1, each of the five involved enterprises, i.e., supplier, manufacturer, bulk buyer, transportation company, and middleman, executes its internal transactions following the enterprise logic implemented in its private smart contract. Once a cross-enterprise transaction is requested, e.g., the bulk buyer places an order with the manufacturer, every enterprise executes and appends the transaction to its view of the ledger. To execute cross-enterprise transactions, the public smart contract is used which includes the SLAs (that are agreed upon by all enterprises). Hence, if the requested transaction does not conform to the SLAs, it will be detected. For each cross-enterprise transaction, the SLA defines several conditions to check. SLAs also include actions for non-conforming transactions, e.g., if the transportation company delivers the materials later than agreed upon, it will be penalized as specified in the SLA or if the delivered materials are different from what was agreed on, the transaction will be aborted.

5.4 The Caper Architecture

Caper consists of a set of nodes in an asynchronous distributed system where each enterprise runs on a (non-empty) disjoint subset of nodes called the *agents* of the enterprise. We use N and A to denote the set of agent nodes and enterprises. In addition, N_α indicates the set of agents of enterprise $\alpha \in A$ where for each pair of enterprises α_1 and α_2 in A, $N_{\alpha_1} \cap N_{\alpha_2} = \varnothing$.

Nodes in Caper might crash, behave maliciously, or be reliable. In addition, we assume that enterprises do not trust each other, thus we model enterprise failures as Byzantine failures. In fact, we define two levels of behavior in the system. First, at the node level, each agent might be a crash-only, a Byzantine, or a reliable node. In a crash failure model, nodes operate at arbitrary speed, may fail by stopping, and may restart. Whereas, in a Byzantine failure model, faulty nodes may exhibit arbitrary, potentially malicious, behavior. A reliable node, on the other hand, never fails. Second, at the enterprise level, an enterprise (as a group of agents) follows the Byzantine failure model and might behave maliciously. Note that these two levels of behavior are independent of each other. Thus, even if the agents of an enterprise are crash-only nodes, the enterprise might still behave maliciously.

Ordering transactions within each enterprise needs consensus among the agents of the enterprise. To establish consensus for cross-enterprise transactions, a Byzantine fault-tolerant protocol among enterprises is needed (as enterprises may not trust each other). To provide both safety and liveness for consensus at the enterprise level, we assume that at most $\lfloor\frac{|A|-1}{3}\rfloor$ enterprises might be malicious. As a result, to commit a cross-enterprise transaction, by a similar argument as in PBFT [13], at least *two-thirds* ($\lfloor\frac{2|A|}{3}\rfloor + 1$) of the enterprises *including* the initiator enterprise of each cross-enterprise transaction must agree on the order of the transaction. We need agreement from agents of the initiator enterprise to ensure that the cross-enterprise transaction is consistent with the internal transactions of the initiator enterprise. The conformance of a cross-enterprise transaction and the SLAs is checked by every enterprise during the execution of the transaction, thus, if the initiator enterprise initiates a transaction that does not conform to the SLAs, it will be detected by other enterprises during the execution.

5.5 Consensus

Caper supports both local and global consensus. In a local consensus, the agents of an enterprise, *independent* of other nodes in the network, agree on the order of transactions within the enterprise. The local consensus protocols in Caper are pluggable. Depending on the failure model of nodes (agents), the enterprise can use a crash fault-tolerant protocol, e.g., Paxos [14], or a Byzantine fault-tolerant protocol, e.g., PBFT [15], as the local consensus protocol. The number of required agents is determined by the protocol and the maximum number of simultaneous failures, f, in the network.

In this section, we mainly focus on global consensus and demonstrate how cross-enterprise transactions are ordered and executed in Caper using global consensus among enterprises. We discuss three ordering approaches for achieving global consensus in Caper.

Ordering transactions using a disjoint set of nodes was utilized by Hyperledger [2] to enhance the scalability of the system and to add flexibility for implementing the consensus protocol, i.e., different protocols can be used to establish consensus. Similarly, in the first approach of Caper, a disjoint set of nodes, called *orderers*, which are not the agents of any enterprise, are used to globally order cross-enterprise transactions. The global consensus protocol among orderers is pluggable and depending on the specifications of the system, a crash or a Byzantine fault-tolerant protocol can be used.

In the absence of such orderer nodes, and in the second approach, Caper relies on the enterprises to order cross-enterprise transactions in a hierarchical way. To distinguish between trust at the node level and trust at the enterprise level, agreement is established in two levels: a local level among the agents of each enterprise, and a global level among the enterprises of the system.

Although the second approach does not require a separate set of orderers to order transactions, the hierarchical nature of the algorithm, which needs local consensus within each enterprise for each step of global ordering, makes the protocol expensive. In the third approach, similar to the second approach, the agents of all enterprises order cross-enterprise transactions; however, agreement is established in a single communication step.

In all three approaches, when agreement is achieved, the agents execute the transaction and append it to their local views of the ledger. Note that if the transaction does not follow the service level agreements implemented in the public smart contract, it will be detected during the execution of the transaction (as discussed in Sect. 5.3.3).

5.5.1 Global Consensus Using a Separate Set of Orderers

Using a separate set of nodes to order transactions adds flexibility to the system by allowing the global consensus implementation to be tailored to the trust assumption of a particular deployment. In addition, since the orderers are decoupled from the agents that execute transactions and maintain the blockchain ledger, using orderers enhances the scalability of the system.

In the first approach, Caper orders the cross-enterprise transactions using a disjoint set of *orderers* O where for each enterprise α in A, $O \cap N_\alpha = \varnothing$. As discussed earlier, each cross-enterprise transaction is ordered first *locally* among the transactions that are initiated by the initiator enterprise and then *globally* among all cross-enterprise transactions, thus both local and global orderings are needed. Since orderers are not involved in the local consensus and enterprise agents do not participate in the global consensus, these two ordering stages are separated from each other. As a result, cross-enterprise transactions are first, similar to the internal transactions, ordered locally within each enterprise using the enterprise consensus protocol and then ordered globally among all cross-enterprise transactions using orderers. Note that the cross-enterprise transactions are first ordered locally to prevent the case where the agents of the initiator enterprise do not agree on the local order of a transaction that has already been ordered globally. Once orderers agree on the global order of the transaction, they multicast the transaction to all the enterprises, thus, every agent of all enterprises executes and appends the transaction to its ledger.

Algorithm 7 Global Consensus using Orderers

1: **init():**
2: $r := node\_id$
3: $\alpha_i :=$ the enterprise that initiates consensus
4: $\pi(p) :=$ the primary node of cluster (enterprise) p
5: $O :=$ the set of orderer nodes
6: **if** $r == \pi(\alpha_i)$ and receiving valid request $m = \langle \text{REQUEST}, op, ts, c\rangle_{\sigma_c}$ **then**
7: initiate local consensus
8: **if** local consensus achieved **then**
9: send $\langle\langle \text{ORDER}, h_L, d, r\rangle_{\sigma_{\pi(\alpha_i)}}, C^o_{\alpha_i}, m\rangle$ to every node in O
10: **end if**
11: **end if**
12: **if** $r == \pi(O)$ and receiving valid $\langle\langle \text{ORDER}, h_L, d, r\rangle_{\sigma_{\pi(\alpha_i)}}, C^o_{\alpha_i}, m\rangle$ **then**
13: initiate a global consensus among orderers O
14: **if** global consensus achieved **then**
15: multicast $\langle \text{SYNC}, h_L, h_G, d, o\rangle_{\sigma_{\pi(O)}}, C^s_O, m\rangle$ to the agents of all enterprises (N)
16: **end if**
17: **end if**
18: **if** $r \in N$ and receiving $\langle \text{SYNC}, h_L, h_G, d, o\rangle_{\sigma_{\pi(O)}}, C^s_O, m\rangle$ from $\pi(O)$ **then**
19: execute and append the transaction to the ledger
20: **end if**

The normal case operation of *global consensus using orderers* to execute a cross-enterprise transaction is presented in Algorithm 7. Although not explicitly mentioned, every sent and received message is logged by the nodes. As indicated in lines 1–5 of the algorithm, α_i is the enterprise that initiates consensus, O is the set of ordered nodes, and we use π to refer to the primary node of each cluster, e.g., $\pi(\alpha_1)$ refers to the primary node of enterprise α_1.

As shown in lines 6–11 of the algorithm, when primary agent $\pi(\alpha_i)$ of the initiator enterprise α_i receives a valid request $\langle \text{REQUEST}, op, ts, c\rangle_{\sigma_c}$ from an authorized client c (with timestamp ts) to execute a cross-enterprise transaction op, it initiates the local consensus protocol to establish agreement on the local order of the cross-enterprise transaction within the enterprise. Once agreement is achieved, the primary agent $\pi(\alpha_i)$ sends a signed order message $\langle\langle \text{ORDER}, h_L, d, r\rangle_{\sigma_{\pi(\alpha_i)}}, C^o_{\alpha_i}, m\rangle$ including the client's request message m to all orderer nodes. Here, d represents the digest of request m and h_L denotes the local sequence number of the transaction. If the enterprise operates under the Byzantine failure model, a certificate $C^o_{\alpha_i}$ composed of a set of commit messages is included as evidence to help orderers validate the order message. It's important to note that instead of having only the primary node send order messages, all nodes can transmit order messages to the orderers. Although this approach eliminates the need for a certificate, it requires a greater number of messages to be exchanged. The order message is disseminated to all orderer nodes to ensure receipt of the message and to mitigate any potential malicious actions from either of the primary nodes.

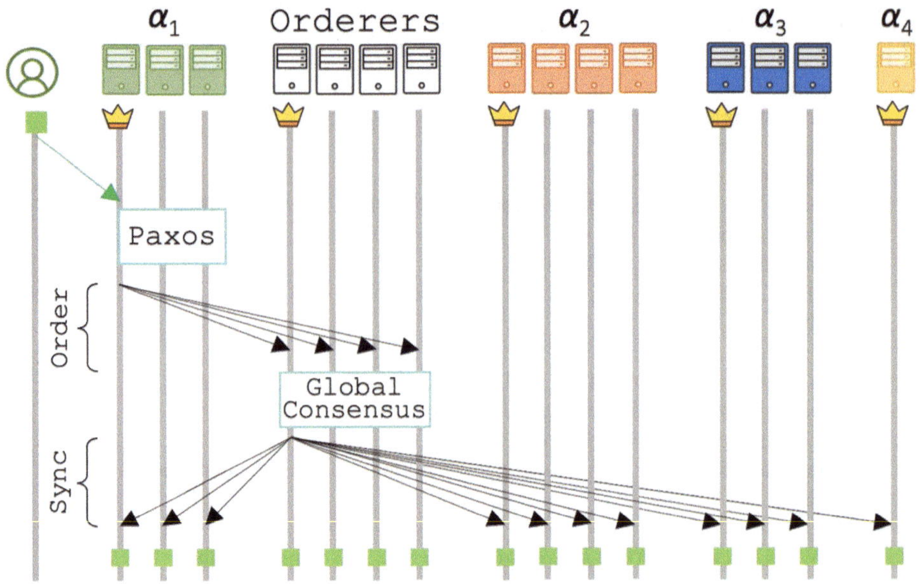

Fig. 5.3 Global consensus using a set of orderers

When the order message is sent, the primary of the initiator enterprise waits for the corresponding sync message before initiating any other transactions. Agents of the enterprise also wait for global agreement when local agreement is established before appending the transaction to the blockchain ledger.

As presented in lines 12–17, once primary node of the ordered cluster, $\pi(O)$, receives a valid order message, it initiates the (global) consensus protocol by multicasting the transaction to other orderers to establish a total order on the cross-enterprise transaction. Once consensus is achieved, the primary node of the ordered cluster multicasts a sync message $\langle \text{SYNC}, h_L, h_G, d, o\rangle_{\sigma_{\pi(O)}}, \mathcal{C}^s_O, m\rangle$ to all agents of every enterprise where d is the digest of m, h_L is copied from order message of the initiator enterprise, h_G is the global sequence number of the transaction, and certificate $\mathcal{C}^s_O$ composed of a set of commit messages is proof to help nodes validate the sync message.

Upon receiving a sync message, the agents of each enterprise log the message, execute the transaction, and append the transaction to its blockchain ledger (as shown in lines 18–20). Finally, depending on the utilized local consensus protocol, either the primary or every agent node r of the initiator enterprise sends a reply message $\langle \text{REPLY}, , u, r\rangle_{\sigma_r}$ to client c where ts is the timestamp of the corresponding request and u is the result of executing the request. The message might include other parameters such as view number (depending on the employed consensus protocol).

Figure 5.3 presents the flow of cross-enterprise transactions using a set of orderers with four enterprises α_1 (initiator), α_2, α_3, and α_4 and a set of ordered nodes.

Correctness. Since the global ordering protocol is pluggable, its correctness is guaranteed by Paxos [14] and PBFT [13]. The ordering of cross-enterprise transactions is distinct, as these transactions are sequentially arranged by the orderers, and the agents within each enterprise adhere to the order established by the orderers. It is important to highlight that if an enterprise's agents fail to follow the prescribed order, it could jeopardize their ability to initiate cross-enterprise transactions in the future, as these transactions may no longer align with the agreed-upon SLAs. To maintain a total order among transactions initiated by the same enterprise, once the primary node of an enterprise submits a cross-enterprise transaction for ordering, it stops initiating any subsequent transactions and awaits a response from the orderers.

5.5.2 Hierarchical Global Consensus

Utilizing a separate set of orderer nodes simplifies and modularizes the agreement process, but it also incurs the additional cost of incorporating these orderers into the system. Without dedicated orderer nodes, achieving consensus on the ordering of cross-enterprise transactions requires the involvement of all enterprises. To differentiate between trust at the node level and trust at the enterprise level, Caper, inspired by the coordinator-based atomic commit protocols, e.g., two-phase commit, employs an asynchronous Byzantine fault-tolerant protocol for global consensus. In this framework, for each cross-enterprise transaction, every enterprise executes its local consensus protocol among its agents to determine the enterprise vote during each phase of the global consensus.

Moreover, since the agents of the initiating enterprise are involved in the global consensus, the local and global orderings are consolidated, unlike in the previous approach. Nonetheless, the protocol guarantees that the initiating enterprise agrees with the ordering at every step of the global process, ensuring that each transaction is correctly ordered concerning those initiated by the enterprise.

In each phase of the global ordering process, after reaching consensus within each enterprise, the manner in which votes are communicated to other enterprises depends on the local consensus protocol in use. For instance, if the local consensus protocol is Paxos, the primary node's message would be sufficient; in contrast, if PBFT is used, votes from $2f + 1$ agents are needed. If an enterprise employs a crash fault-tolerant protocol, the primary's response is accepted as the enterprise vote by the other enterprises. However, if a Byzantine fault-tolerant protocol is in place, other enterprises require a certificate showing that the agents of the initiator enterprise have committed the request. This additional verification is necessary because, in a crash fault-tolerant context, the primary is assumed to be non-malicious, whereas, in a Byzantine fault-tolerant scenario, the primary node might be malicious.

Algorithm 8 presents the *hierarchical global consensus*. Same as before, every sent and received message is logged by the agents. As presented in lines 1–4 of the algorithm, α_i is the enterprise that initiates consensus and $\pi(\alpha)$ refers to the primary agent of an enterprise α.

Algorithm 8 Hierarchical Global Consensus

1: **init()**:
2: $r := node\_id$
3: α_i := the enterprise that initiates consensus
4: $\pi(\alpha)$:= the primary node of enterprise α
5: **if** $r == \pi(\alpha_i)$ and receiving valid request $m = \langle \mathsf{REQUEST}, op, ts, c\rangle_{\sigma_c}$ **then**
6: multicast $\langle\langle \mathsf{PROPOSE}, h_L, h_G, d\rangle_{\sigma_{\pi(\alpha_i)}}, m\rangle$ to all nodes
7: **end if**
8: **if** $r == \pi(\alpha)$ for an enterprise α and receiving $\langle\langle \mathsf{PROPOSE}, h_L, h_G, d\rangle_{\sigma_{\pi(\alpha_i)}}, m\rangle$ **then**
9: initiate local consensus
10: **if** local consensus achieved **then**
11: multicast $\langle\langle \mathsf{ACCEPT}, h_L, h_G, d, \pi(\alpha)\rangle, C^{a}_{\alpha}\rangle_{\sigma_{\pi(\alpha)}}$ to every agent of all enterprises
12: **end if**
13: **end if**
14: **if** $r == \pi(\alpha)$ for an enterprise α and receiving $\langle\langle \mathsf{ACCEPT}, h_L, h_G, d, \pi(\alpha_j)\rangle, C^{a}_{\alpha_j}\rangle_{\sigma_{\pi(\alpha_j)}}$ from **two-thirds** of the enterprises including α_i **then**
15: initiate local consensus
16: **if** local consensus achieved **then**
17: multicast $\langle\langle \mathsf{COMMIT}, h_L, h_G, d, \pi(\alpha)\rangle, C^{c}_{\alpha}\rangle_{\sigma_{\pi(\alpha)}}$ to every agent of all enterprises
18: **end if**
19: **end if**
20: **if** $r \in N$ and receiving $\langle\langle \mathsf{COMMIT}, h_L, h_G, d, \pi(\alpha_j)\rangle, C^{c}_{\alpha_j}\rangle_{\sigma_{\pi(\alpha_j)}}$ from **two-thirds** of the enterprises including α_i **then**
21: execute and append the transaction to the ledger
22: **end if**

When $\pi(\alpha)$, the primary node of the initiator enterprise receives a valid cross-enterprise request (lines 5–7), it multicasts a signed $\langle\langle \mathsf{PROPOSE}, h_L, h_G, d\rangle_{\sigma_{\pi(\alpha_i)}}, m\rangle$ message to all agents of every enterprise where d is the digest of m, h_L is the local sequence number, and h_G is the global sequence number of the transaction. Note that h_L is only used by the agents of the initiator enterprise to ensure that the new transaction is ordered correctly with respect to the transactions that are initiated by the enterprise.

Upon receiving a propose message (lines 8–13), the primary agent of each enterprise validates the message by checking the signature, h_G, and the message digest to confirm its authenticity. Subsequently, all primary agents, including the primary agent of the initiator enterprise, initiate the local consensus protocol internally to reach an agreement on the transaction order. Once consensus is achieved, the primary node of each enterprise multicasts an accept message to all agents across every enterprise. The certificate C^{α}_{a} within the accept message from enterprise α contains the commit messages collected during the internal consensus and serves to validate the accept message.

As detailed in lines 14–19, each enterprise awaits valid accept messages from *two-thirds* of the enterprises, including the initiator, matching the accept message it sent. It's important to note that a valid accept message from the initiator enterprise is necessary to confirm that the transaction aligns with previous transactions initiated by that enterprise. Upon receiving enough accept messages, the primary agent of each enterprise initiates the local consensus protocol to agree on the received accept messages. Once consensus is reached, the primary agent multicasts a commit message to all agents in the other enterprises.

The propose and accept phases of the global consensus, akin to the pre-prepare and prepare phases of PBFT [13], ensure that non-malicious enterprises agree on a total order for transactions. They guarantee that no forks occur in the blockchain, meaning it is impossible to have two different transactions sharing the same sequence number h_G. This is because at least *two-thirds* ($\lfloor \frac{2|A|}{3} \rfloor + 1$) of enterprises agree on the order of each transaction, ensuring that any two quorums of enterprises intersect in at least $\lfloor \frac{|A|-1}{3} \rfloor + 1$ enterprises. Given that at most $\lfloor \frac{|A|-1}{3} \rfloor$ enterprises can be malicious, there will always be at least *one non-malicious* enterprise within the intersection of any two quorums.

Lastly, similar to the previous phase, if an agent of an enterprise receives matching commit messages from *two-thirds* of the enterprises, including the initiator, the agents execute the transaction and append it to their ledger (lines 20–22).

Figure 5.4 illustrates the hierarchical consensus involving four enterprises, similar to Fig. 5.3. In this scenario, the nodes of enterprises α_1 and α_3 operate under the crash failure

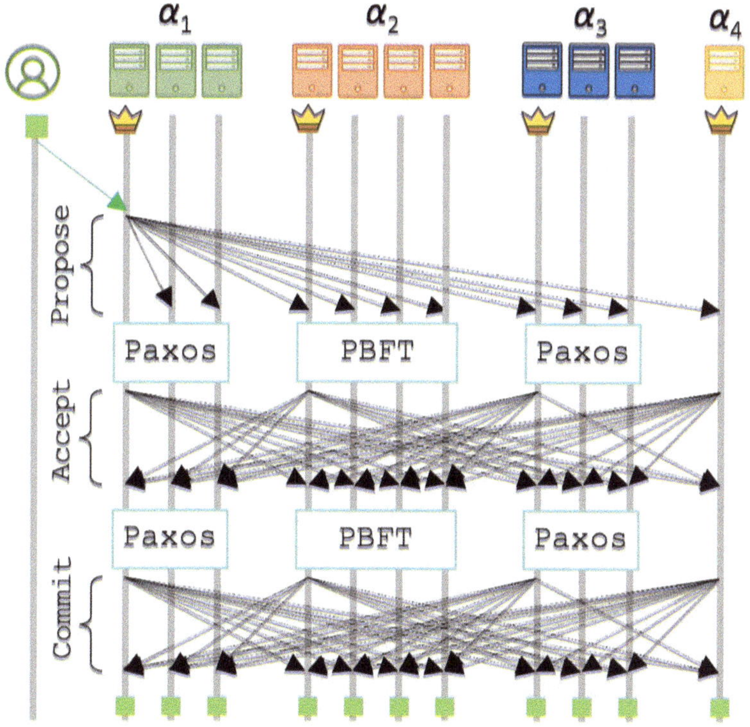

Fig. 5.4 Hierarchical global consensus

model and employ Paxos, while the nodes of enterprise α_2 follow the Byzantine failure model and use PBFT for the local consensus protocol. Here, the primary node of enterprise α_1 initiates the consensus process.

To optimize the system in scenarios with a high volume of cross-enterprise transactions and to avoid the initiation of concurrent transactions, one primary node from the enterprises can be designated as a *super primary* to initiate consensus for all cross-enterprise transactions.

Correctness. In the hierarchical consensus, as previously mentioned, safety is guaranteed because at least $\lfloor \frac{2|A|}{3} \rfloor + 1$ enterprises must agree on the transaction order, while at most $\lfloor \frac{|A|-1}{3} \rfloor$ enterprises may be malicious. Consequently, if two or more concurrent transactions are initiated, only one can gather the required number of messages (two-thirds of the enterprises), meaning it is not possible for more than one transaction to be assigned the same sequence number h_G. If none of the concurrent transactions secures enough votes, these transactions are aborted, and the initiating enterprises will attempt to re-initiate them. To ensure liveness during this process, Caper introduces a random delay before re-initiating the transactions, thus minimizing the chances of concurrent initiations.

5.5.3 One-Level Global Consensus

While hierarchical consensus eliminates the necessity of an additional set of orderer nodes and differentiates between trust at the node level and trust at the enterprise level, it imposes the requirement of a costly two-level consensus protocol. This means that each step of the global consensus must execute the entire local consensus protocol within each enterprise. In this section, drawing inspiration from the flattened protocol of SharPer discussed in Chapter 4, we discuss a *one-level* global consensus protocol. In this protocol, agents from all enterprises collaborate to reach a consensus on the order of each cross-enterprise transaction.

The number of agents per enterprise varies based on the consensus protocol employed within that enterprise, leading to different requirements for the number of matching replies needed to ensure that a majority of an enterprise's agents agree on the transaction order. We define *local-majority* as the required number of matching messages from an enterprise's agents. For enterprises utilizing crash-only nodes, the local-majority is defined as $f + 1$ (from a total of $2f + 1$ agents). In contrast, for enterprises following the Byzantine failure model, the local-majority is set at $2f + 1$ (from a total of $3f + 1$ agents). Additionally, for an enterprise with only a single reliable agent, the local-majority is simply one.

Algorithm 9 outlines the procedure for achieving *one-level global consensus*. In lines 5–7, the primary of the initiator enterprise sends a signed propose message that includes the request m, the local sequence number h_L, and the global sequence number h_G to the agents of each enterprise. As before, h_L is utilized exclusively by the agents of the initiator enterprise.

Algorithm 9 One-Level Global Consensus

1: **init():**
2: $r := node\_id$
3: α_i := the enterprise that initiates consensus
4: $\pi(\alpha)$:= the primary node of enterprise α
5: **if** $r == \pi(\alpha_i)$ and receiving valid request $m = \langle \mathsf{REQUEST}, op, ts, c\rangle_{\sigma_c}$ **then**
6: multicast $\langle\langle \mathsf{PROPOSE}, h_L, h_G, d\rangle_{\sigma_{\pi(\alpha_i)}}, m\rangle$ to all nodes
7: **end if**
8: **if** $r \in N$ and receiving $\langle \mathsf{PROPOSE}, h_L, h_G, d\rangle_{\sigma_{\pi(\alpha_i)}}, m\rangle$ **then**
9: multicast $\langle \mathsf{ACCEPT}, h_L, h_G, d, r\rangle_{\sigma_r}$ to every agent of all enterprises
10: **end if**
11: **if** $r \in N$ and receiving $\langle \mathsf{ACCEPT}, h_L, h_G, d, q\rangle_{\sigma_q}$ from **local-majority** of **two-thirds** of the enterprises including α_i **then**
12: multicast $\langle \mathsf{COMMIT}, h_L, h_G, d, r\rangle_{\sigma_r}$ to every agent of all enterprises
13: **end if**
14: **if** $r \in N$ and receiving $\langle \mathsf{COMMIT}, h_L, h_G, d, q\rangle_{\sigma_q}$ from **local-majority** of **two-thirds** of the enterprises including α_i **then**
15: execute and append the transaction to the ledger
16: **end if**

Upon receiving a propose message, an agent verifies the signature, message digest, and h_G to confirm the message's validity. If the agent belongs to the initiator enterprise, it additionally checks the value of h_L. After successful validation, the agent broadcasts an accept message to all agents across every enterprise, as detailed in lines 8–10.

Lines 11–13 illustrate that when an agent receives valid accept messages from a local-majority of two-thirds of the enterprises, including the initiator enterprise, and these messages match the accept message sent by the agent, the agent will then broadcast a commit message to every agent in every enterprise. The propose and accept phases of this algorithm, similar to the pre-prepare and prepare phases in PBFT [13], ensure that non-faulty agents reach a consensus on the order of the transactions.

Finally, as depicted in lines 14–16, when an agent receives valid commit messages from a local-majority of two-thirds of the enterprises, including the initiator enterprise, matching its commit message, the agent determines that the transaction is committed. Consequently, it executes the transaction and appends it to the ledger.

Figure 5.5 shows the one-level consensus in Caper for four enterprises with different failure models.

Correctness. To ensure safety in one-level consensus, it is necessary for messages from a local-majority of two-thirds of the enterprises to be matched during both the accept and commit phases. This requirement guarantees that any two quorums overlap in at least one non-faulty node within the enterprise. Additionally, the involvement of two-thirds of the enterprises ensures that any two quorums also intersect in at least one non-malicious enterprise, considering that a maximum of $\lfloor \frac{|A|-1}{3} \rfloor$ enterprises may be malicious.

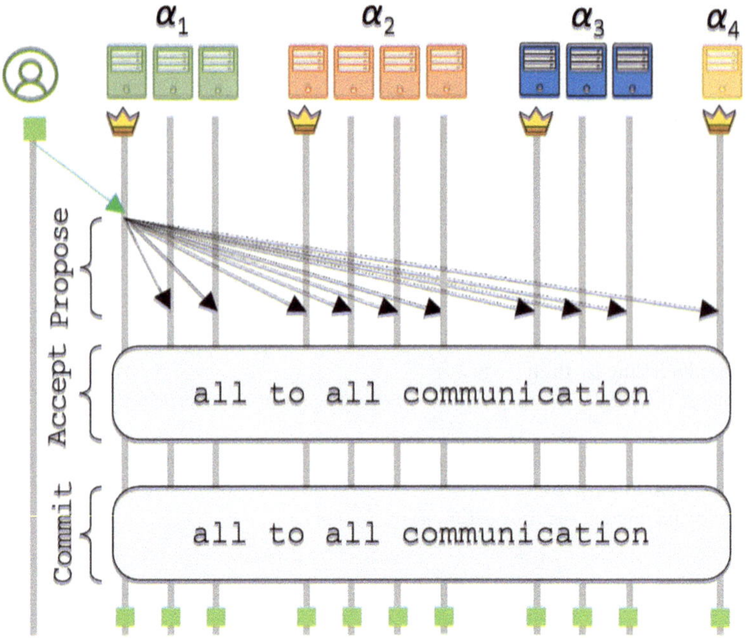

Fig. 5.5 One-level global consensus

Consequently, similar to hierarchical consensus, even in scenarios where two or more concurrent transactions are initiated, only one transaction can gather the requisite number of matching accept and commit messages. To improve liveness, Caper assigns timers to manage concurrent transactions and employs a super primary as an optimization for systems with a high volume of cross-enterprise transactions.

5.6 Summary

In this chapter, we tackled the confidentiality requirement of permissioned blockchain systems by presenting Caper, a permissioned blockchain system that supports both internal and cross-enterprise transactions of collaborating enterprises. Caper targets both the performance and confidentiality aspects of blockchain systems. To achieve better performance, Caper orders and executes internal transactions of different enterprises simultaneously. In addition, to achieve confidentiality, the blockchain ledger is *not maintained* by any node and each enterprise maintains its own local view of the ledger including its internal and all cross-enterprise transactions. Caper also distinguishes between trust at the node level and trust at the enterprise level and allows an enterprise to behave maliciously for its benefit while its nodes are non-malicious. Furthermore, Caper introduces three consensus protocols to globally order cross-enterprise transactions: using a separate set of orderers, hierarchical consensus, and one-level consensus.

References

1. Ethereum blockchain app platform (2017). https://www.ethereum.org
2. Androulaki, E., Barger, A., Bortnikov, V., Cachin, C., Christidis, K., De Caro, A., Enyeart, D., Ferris, C., Laventman, G., Manevich, Y.: Hyperledger fabric: a distributed operating system for permissioned blockchains. In: European Conference on Computer Systems (EuroSys), pp. 30:1–30:15. ACM (2018)
3. Korpela, K., Hallikas, J., Dahlberg, T.: Digital supply chain transformation toward blockchain integration. In: Hawaii International Conference on System Sciences (HICSS) (2017)
4. Azaria, A., Ekblaw, A., Vieira, T., Lippman, A.: Medrec: Using blockchain for medical data access and permission management. In: International Conference on Open and Big Data (OBD), pp. 25–30. IEEE (2016)
5. Herlihy, M.: Atomic cross-chain swaps. In: Symposium on Principles of Distributed Computing (PODC), pp. 245–254. ACM (2018)
6. Zakhary, V., Agrawal, D., El Abbadi, A.: Atomic commitment across blockchains. Proc. VLDB Endowment **13**, 1319–1331 (2020)
7. Thomas, S., Schwartz, E.: A protocol for interledger payments (2015). https://interledger.org/interledger.pdf
8. Weber, I., Xu, X., Riveret, R., Governatori, G., Ponomarev, A., Mendling, J.: Untrusted business process monitoring and execution using blockchain. In: International Conference on Business Process Management (BPM), pp. 329–347. Springer (2016)
9. Androulaki, E., Cachin, C., De Caro, A., Kokoris-Kogias, E.: Channels: horizontal scaling and confidentiality on permissioned blockchains. In: European Symposium on Research in Computer Security (ESORICS), pp. 111–131. Springer (2018)
10. Amiri, M.J., Agrawal, D., El Abbadi, A.: CAPER: a cross-application permissioned blockchain. Proc. VLDB Endowment **12**(11), 1385–1398 (2019)
11. Jin, H., Dai, X., Xiao, J.: Towards a novel architecture for enabling interoperability amongst multiple blockchains. In: International Conference on Distributed Computing Systems (ICDCS), pp. 1203–1211. IEEE (2018)
12. Amiri, M.J., Agrawal, D., El Abbadi, A.: SharPer: sharding permissioned blockchains over network clusters. In: SIGMOD International Conference on Management of Data, pp. 76–88. ACM (2021)
13. Castro, M., Liskov, B.: Practical byzantine fault tolerance. In: Symposium on Operating Systems Design and Implementation (OSDI), pp. 173–186. USENIX Association (1999)
14. Lamport, L.: Paxos made simple. ACM SIGACT News **32**(4), 18–25 (2001)
15. Castro, M., Liskov, B.: Practical byzantine fault tolerance and proactive recovery. Trans. Comput. Syst. (TOCS) **20**(4), 398–461 (2002)

Generalized Confidentiality 6

6.1 Introduction

Emerging multi-enterprise applications, e.g., supply chain management [1], multi-platform crowdworking [2], and healthcare [3], require extensive use of *collaboration workflows* where multiple mutually distrustful distributed enterprises collaboratively process a mix of public and private transactions. Despite years of research in distributed transaction processing, data management systems today have not yet achieved a good balance between the *confidentiality* and *scalability* requirements of these applications.

One of the main requirements of multi-enterprise applications is confidentiality with respect to *data sharing* and *data leakage*. First, while public collaboration among all enterprises is visible to everyone, specific subsets of the data may need to be shared only with specific subsets of involved enterprises. For example, in a product trading situation, the distributor may want to keep collaboration with a farmer and a shipper involving terms of the trades *confidential* from the wholesaler and the retailer, so as not to expose the premium they are charging [4]. Second, enterprises must prevent malicious nodes from leaking confidential data, e.g., requests, replies, and stored data.

Multi-enterprise applications also need to scalably process a large number of transactions within or across enterprises. Although sharding has been used in single-enterprise applications to address scalability, it is challenging to use sharding in multi-enterprise applications where data confidentiality is paramount.

In multi-enterprise applications, furthermore, data *provenance* is needed to provide a detailed picture of how the data was collected, where it was stored, and how it was used. The information should be stored in a *transparent* and *immutable* manner which is *verifiable* by all participants, e.g., transparent end-to-end tracking of goods to detect possible fraud in a supply chain collaboration workflow.

M. J. Amiri et al., *Blockchain-Enabled Large-Scale Transaction Management*,
Synthesis Lectures on Data Management,
https://doi.org/10.1007/978-3-031-91058-6_6

In recent years, as discussed in the previous chapter, various permissioned blockchain systems have been proposed to address the confidentiality and/or scalability of multi-enterprise applications. Hyperledger Fabric [5] and its variants [6–9] support multi-enterprise applications and provide scalability using channels [10] managed by subsets of enterprises. However, all transactions of a channel are sequentially ordered, resulting in reduced performance. Fabric also uses private data collections [4] to manage confidential collaboration among a subset of enterprises. However, appending a hash of all private transactions to a global ledger replicated on every enterprise increases computational overhead and hence reduces throughput. Furthermore, Fabric does not address confidential data leakage by malicious nodes.

In the previous chapter, we presented Caper [11] and showed how it supports collaborative enterprises and provides confidentiality by maintaining a partial view of the global ledger on each enterprise. Caper, however, does not support (1) confidential collaboration among subsets of enterprises (i.e., it only supports internal or public transactions), (2) data consistency across collaboration workflows that an enterprise is involved in, (3) data confidentiality in the presence of malicious nodes, and (4) multi-shard enterprises.

Scalability has also been studied in the context of applications that are used within a single enterprise, e.g., AHL [12], SharPer [13], and ResilientDB [14]. However, since these systems are restricted to single-enterprise applications, they do not address the confidentiality requirement of multi-enterprise applications.

To address the above scalability and confidentiality challenges of multi-enterprise applications, we present *Qanaat* [1] [15], a permissioned blockchain system that supports collaboration workflows across enterprises. In Qanaat, each enterprise partitions its data into multiple *shards* to improve scalability. Each shard's transactions are processed by a disjoint *cluster* of nodes.

To support confidential collaboration (i.e., data sharing), in addition to public transactions among all enterprises and internal transactions within each enterprise, any subset of enterprises might process transactions *confidentially* from other enterprises. As a result, Qanaat uses a novel hierarchical data model consisting of a set of *data collections* where each transaction is executed on a data collection. The root data collection consists of the public records from executing public transactions replicated on all enterprises. Each local data collection includes the private records of a single enterprise. Intermediate data collections, which are optional and are needed in case of *confidential* collaborations among subsets of enterprises, maintain private records shared among subsets of collaborating enterprises. Qanaat replicates such shared data collections on the involved enterprises to facilitate the use of shared data by enterprises in their internal transactions. For example, a supplier in a supply chain collaboration workflow requires the order data stored in the shared data collection with a consumer to perform its internal transactions that produce the products.

[1] Qanaat is a scalable underground network consisting of private channels to transport water from an aquifer to the surface (i.e., an underground aqueduct).

To support this collaborative yet confidential data model, Qanaat proposes a transaction ordering scheme to preserve the data consistency of transactions. In Qanaat, an enterprise might be involved in multiple data collections. Hence, the traditional transaction ordering schemes used in fault-tolerant protocols where each cluster orders transactions on a single data store do not work. In fact, while ordering transactions, Qanaat needs to capture the state of all data collections that might affect the execution of a transaction.

Finally, to prevent confidential data leakage despite the Byzantine failure of nodes, Qanaat utilizes the privacy firewall technique [16, 17] and (1) separates ordering nodes that agree on the order of transactions from execution nodes that execute transactions and maintain the ledger, and (2) uses a *privacy firewall* between execution nodes and ordering nodes. The privacy firewall restricts communication from execution nodes in order to filter out incorrect messages, possibly including confidential data.

The main contributions of this chapter are

- An infrastructure consisting of ordering nodes, execution nodes, a privacy firewall, and a data model consisting of data collections to preserve confidentiality, followed by a transaction ordering scheme that enforces only the *necessary* and *sufficient* constraints to guarantee data consistency.
- A suite of consensus protocols to process transactions that access single or multiple data shards within or across enterprises in a *scalable* manner.
- Qanaat is a scalable multi-enterprise permissioned blockchain system that guarantees confidentiality.

The rest of this chapter is organized as follows. Section 6.2 motivates Qanaat by discussing the vaccine supply chain. The Qanaat model is introduced in Sect. 6.3. Section 6.4 presents transaction processing in Qanaat, and Sect. 6.5 concludes the chapter.

6.2 Motivation

Qanaat is designed to support multi-enterprise applications such as supply chain management [1], multi-platform crowdworking [2], and healthcare [3] in a scalable and confidentiality-preserving manner. To motivate Qanaat, we consider an example application based on the COVID-19 vaccine supply chain, given that it is a demanding application. The COVID-19 outbreak has demonstrated diverse challenges that supply chains face [18]. While the vaccine supply chain seems to work fine on the surface, it suffers from several crucial challenges. First, existing vaccine supply chains are subjected to different types of vulnerabilities, e.g., attacks on 44 companies involved in the COVID-19 vaccine distribution in 14 countries [19], rapidly growth of the black market for COVID-19 vaccines [20], issuing fake vaccine cards [21], and loss of 400 millions of vaccine doses [22]. Moreover, while vaccines are well distributed in most developed countries, getting them to developing countries and accounting for them remains a challenge, e.g., fake vaccines [23, 24] and falsified CoviShield vaccines [25]. Currently, the COVID-19 vaccine supply chains have been overstretched given the global supply chain challenges and the possibility of abuse and fraud stated above. At the same time, other supply chains were under unprecedented pressure [26, 27]. Even in a developed country, supply chains can be subjected to attacks that can potentially disrupt the distribution [19]. Vaccines are vulnerable to counterfeiting [28, 29], tampering, and theft [30] especially since products and components often pass through multiple locations and even countries and it has become difficult to trace the source of vaccines, creating space for substandard and falsified vaccines [31].

Multiple enterprises collaborate in a vaccine supply chain to get vaccines from manufacturers to citizens. Enterprises involved in the vaccine ecosystem need to collaborate and share data based on agreed-upon service level agreements. Vaccines, on the one hand, need to be tracked and monitored throughout the process to ensure that they are stable and not tampered with, and, on the other hand, this data should be accessible to the public to increase their trust in the vaccines. While distributed databases can be used to address these challenges, they lack mechanisms to first prevent any malicious entity from altering data and second enable enterprises to verify the data and the state of collaboration. Qanaat uses blockchains to provide verifiability, provenance, transparency, and assurances to end-users of the vaccines' safety and efficacy. In particular, blockchains enable pharmaceutical manufacturers to easily track on-time shipment and delivery of vaccines, provide efficient delivery tracking for transportation companies, and help hospitals manage their stocks and mitigate supply and demand constraints.

Figure 6.1 shows a simplified vaccine supply chain collaboration workflow consisting of the pharmaceutical manufacturer (M), a supplier (S), a logistics provider (L), a transportation company (T), and hospitals (H). Using Qanaat, the public transactions of the collaboration workflow (t_1 to t_8) are executed on *data collection* d_{MSLTH} maintained by all enterprises. In particular, the pharmaceutical manufacturer `places orders` (t_1 and t_2) of materials via the supplier and logistics provider. The logistics provider `arranges shipment` (t_3) by the transportation company. Once the materials are ready, the supplier `informs` (t_4) the trans-

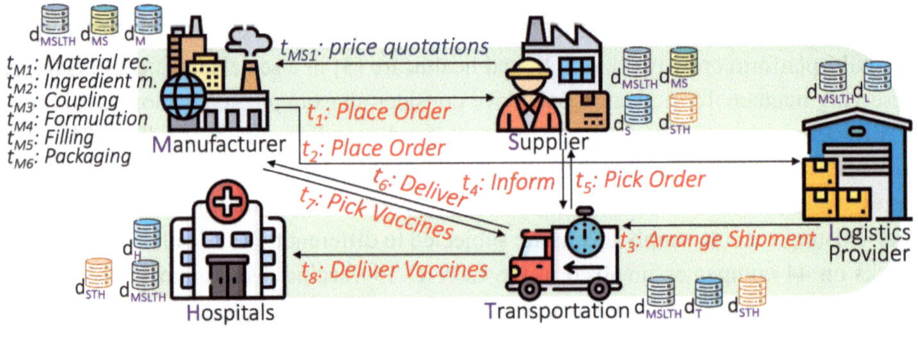

Fig. 6.1 A vaccine supply chain collaboration workflow

portation company to `pick order` (t_5) and `deliver order` (t_6) to the manufacturer. Once the vaccines become available, the transportation company `pick vaccines` (t_7) and `deliver` (t_8) them to hospitals. These transactions are public and are executed on data collection d_{MSLTH}.

In addition, the collaboration workflow includes the internal transactions of each enterprise. Internal transactions are executed on the enterprise's *private* data collection and might reflect patented and copyrighted formulas and information. For example, producing vaccines in a pharmaceutical manufacturer consists of `material reception` (t_{M1}) (some vaccines requiring ∼160 consumables), `ingredient manufacturing` (t_{M2}), `coupling` (t_{M3}), `formulation` (t_{M4}), `filling` (t_{M5}), and `packaging` (t_{M6}) [32]. The pharmaceutical manufacturer executes these transactions on its private data collection d_M. The supplier, logistics provider, transportation company, and hospitals also execute their internal transactions on private data collections d_S, d_L, d_T, and d_H, respectively.

A blockchain-enabled multi-enterprise application, e.g., a vaccine supply chain, needs to support the following requirements:

R1. Confidential collaborations across enterprises. Any subset of enterprises involved in a collaboration workflow might want to keep their collaboration private from other enterprises. For example, the supplier might want to make private transactions with the pharmaceutical manufacturer to keep some terms of trade confidential from other enterprises, e.g., `price quotation` (t_{MS1}) transaction. Such private transactions need to be executed on a data collection shared between *only* the involved enterprises, e.g., d_{MS} between the pharmaceutical manufacturer and the supplier.

R2. Consistency across collaboration workflows. An enterprise might be involved in multiple collaboration workflows with different sets of enterprises. For example, a transportation company that distributes both Pfizer and Moderna vaccines needs to assign trucks based on the total number of vaccine packages and correctly manage the interleaving of transactions. In case of data dependency among transactions that span collaboration workflows, data integrity and consistency must be maintained.

R3. Confidential data leakage prevention. An enterprise needs to ensure that even if its infrastructure includes malicious nodes (i.e., an attacker manages to compromise some nodes), the malicious nodes cannot leak any confidential data, e.g., requests, replies, processed data, and stored data.

R4. Scaling multi-shard enterprises. Every day, millions of people get vaccinated, thousands of shipments take place, and many other transactions are executed. All these activities need to be immediately processed by the system and specifically by all involved enterprises. A transportation company that distributes vaccines across the world might maintain its data in multiple data shards. This highlights the need for a system that can scale as demand increases and efficiently process distributed transactions that access multiple data shards across multiple enterprises.

Existing blockchain solutions, however, are not able to meet all requirements of multi-enterprise collaboration workflows. While Caper [11] enables enterprises to keep their local data confidential, it does not address any of the **R1** to **R4** requirements. Fabric [5] addresses confidential collaboration using private data collection (although with a high overhead) and scalability using channels. However, Fabric does not support requirements **R2** and **R3**. Several variants of Fabric, such as Fast Fabric [6], Fabric++ [8], FabricSharp [9], and XOX Fabric [7], try to address the performance shortcomings of Fabric, especially when dealing with contentious workloads. However, these permissioned blockchain systems, similar to Fabric, suffer from the overhead of confidential collaboration and also do not support requirements **R2** and **R3**.

6.3 Qanaat Model

Qanaat is a permissioned blockchain system designed to support multi-enterprise applications. This section introduces the Qanaat model and demonstrates how it supports different requirements of multi-enterprise applications.

6.3.1 The Model Assumptions

Qanaat consists of a set of collaborative *enterprises*. Each enterprise owns a set of *nodes* (i.e., servers) that are grouped into different *clusters*. Each enterprise further partitions its data into multiple *data shards*. Each cluster of nodes maintains a *shard* of the enterprise data and processes transactions on that data shard.

Qanaat assumes the partially synchronous communication model [33, 34]. In the partial synchrony model, there exists an unknown global stabilization time (GST), after which all messages between correct nodes are received within some bound Δ. Qanaat inherits the standard assumptions of previous permissioned blockchain systems, including a strong computationally bounded adversary that can coordinate malicious nodes and delay communication to compromise service, as well as an unreliable network that connects nodes that might drop, corrupt, or delay messages, and the existence of pairwise authenticated communication channels, standard digital signatures, and public-key infrastructure (PKI). A message m signed by node i is denoted as $\langle m \rangle_{\sigma_i}$. Qanaat further uses threshold signatures where each node i holds a distinct private key that is used to create a signature share $\sigma\langle m \rangle_i$ for message m. A node can generate a valid threshold signature $\sigma\langle m \rangle$ for m given $n - f$ signature shares from distinct nodes, where f is the maximum number of faulty nodes. A collision-resistant hash function $D(.)$ is also used to map a message m to a constant-sized digest $D(m)$.

We next present the data model (Sect. 6.3.2) and the blockchain ledger (Sect. 6.3.3) of Qanaat, which together address the collaboration confidentiality (**R1**) and data consistency (**R2**) requirements and then demonstrate the Qanaat infrastructure (Sect. 6.3.4) that addresses the confidential data leakage prevention requirement (**R3**). For simplicity of presentation, we first consider single-shard enterprises and then show how the model and the ledger are extended to support multi-shard enterprises (Sect. 6.3.6), which addresses the scalability requirement (**R4**).

6.3.2 Data Model

Qanaat constructs a hierarchical data model consisting of a set of *data collections* for each collaboration workflow. Each data collection can be seen as a separate datastore where the execution of transactions updates its data. Each data collection further has its own (business) logic to execute transactions. *Public* transactions of a collaboration workflow, e.g., `place order` or `arrange shipment` in the vaccine supply chain, are executed on the *root* data collection. All enterprises maintain the root data collection. This is needed because enterprises use the data maintained in the root data collection in other transactions. For example, the `order` data stored in the root data collection is used by the supplier in its private transactions to provide raw materials.

Internal private transactions of each enterprise, on the other hand, are executed on its local data collection. Internal transactions are performed within an enterprise following the logic of the enterprise, e.g., `develop formulation` and `package vaccines` take place within the pharmaceutical manufacturer.

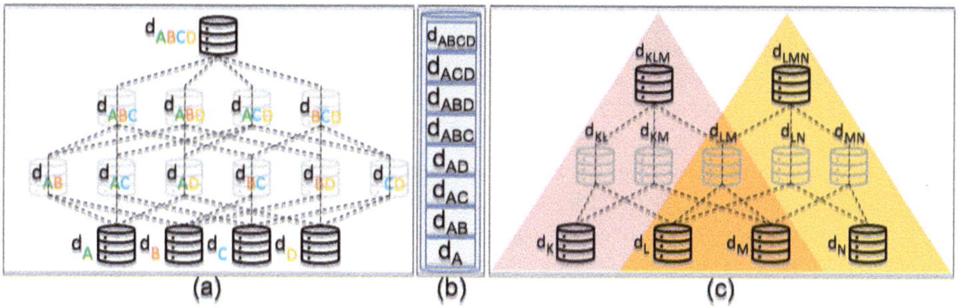

Fig. 6.2 **a** A data model for a 4-enterprise collaboration workflow. Intermediate data collections are optional and needed only if there is a collaboration among a specific subset of enterprises, **b** data maintained by enterprise A, **c** data models for 3-enterprise workflows

Any subset of enterprises might also execute private transactions among themselves and confidentially from other enterprises. Such transactions are executed on a data collection shared among and maintained by *only* the involved enterprises. For example, to supply the requested material, the supplier executes private transactions with the pharmaceutical company a data collection that is maintained only by the supplier and pharmaceutical company.

It should be noted that a data collection is not a physically separated datastore, rather a logical partition of the data records of an enterprise that might be shared with a set of enterprises. Hence, creating a data collection causes no overhead, e.g., configuration cost.

Figure 6.2a presents a data model for a collaboration workflow with enterprises A, B, C, and D. At the top level, a public data collection d_{ABCD} is stored on all four enterprises. At the bottom level, there are four private data collections d_A, d_B, d_C, and d_D stored on the servers of the corresponding enterprises. The figure also includes all possible private data collections with different subsets of enterprises at the intermediate levels, e.g., d_{AB} or d_{ACD}. When a subset of enterprises, e.g., A and B, creates a data collection, e.g., d_{AB}, to execute private transactions, the shared data collection maintains the execution results of transactions that are executed on the data collection. Such data records are different from the records maintained in the data collection of each individual enterprise, e.g., d_A and d_B. In contrast to the root and the local data collections that are needed in every collaboration workflow, intermediate data collections are *optional* and needed only if there is a collaboration among a specific subset of enterprises.

Qanaat defines operational primitives necessarily to capture data consistency and data dependency across data collections.

Write. The execution results of transactions executed on a data collection are written on the records of the same data collection. This is needed to guarantee collaboration confidentiality as (intermediate) data collections are created for private collaboration, e.g., private lobbying, among a subset of enterprises while preventing other enterprises from accessing the data. In particular, if enterprises A and B make a confidential collaboration, the resulting data should not be written on a data collection that is either shared with some other enterprise C or not shared with one of the involved enterprises, e.g., d_A. Note that d_{AB} is maintained by both enterprises A and B and they have access to its record. This captures the confidential collaborations in real-world cross-enterprise applications.

Read. When a transaction is being executed on a data collection d_X, it might read records of a data collection d_Y if enterprises sharing d_X are a subset of the enterprises sharing d_Y. For example, the internal transactions of the supplier can read the records of all data collections that the supplier is involved in with other enterprises. This is needed because those records might affect the internal transactions of the supplier, e.g., the number of vaccines that the supplier supplies depends on the orders it receives from other enterprises.

More formally, given a data collection d_X where X is the set of enterprises sharing d_X. For each data collection d_Y where $X \subseteq Y$, we define d_X as *order dependent* of d_Y. We say transactions executed on d_X can read the records of d_Y if data collection d_X is order dependent on d_Y. The dashed lines between data collections in Fig. 6.2a present order dependency among data collections; the transactions executed on the lower level data collections can read the records of the higher level data collections, e.g., d_{AB} can read d_{ABC}, d_{ABD}, and d_{ABCD}.

In some applications, transactions that are executed on data collection d_X might also need to verify the records of another data collection d_Y in a *privacy-preserving* manner (i.e., without reading the exact records) revealing any information about the content of the records if enterprises sharing d_X are a *superset* of the enterprises sharing d_Y, i.e., $Y \subset X$. In particular, for intangible assets, e.g., cryptocurrencies, if enterprise A initiates a transaction in data collection d_{AB} that consumes some coins, enterprise B needs to verify the existence of the coins in data collection d_A. In supply chain workflows, however, since transactions are usually placed as a result of physical actions, verifying the records of order-dependent data collections is unnecessary. Qanaat can be extended to support privacy-preserving verifiability using advanced cryptographic primitives like secure multiparty computation [35, 36] and zero-knowledge proofs [37–39].

Every enterprise maintains all data collections that the enterprise is involved in, i.e., the root, a local, and perhaps several intermediate data collections. Qanaat replicates shared data collections on all involved enterprises to facilitate the use of shared data by the transactions on order-dependent data collections. Note that such shared data collections can be maintained by a third party, e.g., a cloud provider, trusted by all enterprises. However, this is a centralized solution that contradicts the decentralized nature of blockchains. Moreover, the data maintained in a shared data collection might be used (i.e., read) in transactions on all order-dependent data collections. Hence, enterprises would need to query the third party for every simple read operation to access the data.

As shown in Fig. 6.2b, enterprise A maintains local data collection d_A, root data collection d_{ABCD}, and all intermediate data collections (if exist), e.g., d_{AB} and d_{ACD}.

A data model represents data processed by each collaboration workflow among a set of enterprises. However, an enterprise (or a group of enterprises) might be involved in multiple collaboration workflows (instances of Qanaat) with different sets of enterprises. The transactions of the same enterprise in different collaboration workflows might be data dependent. Creating an independent data collection for each enterprise in each collaboration workflow might result in *data consistency* issues. For example, a supplier that provides raw materials for both Pfizer and Moderna vaccines in two different supply chain collaboration workflows needs to know the total number of the requested materials in order to provision for them correctly. As a result, Qanaat creates a single data collection for each enterprise and if an enterprise is involved in multiple possibly data-dependent collaboration workflows, the transactions of the enterprise in different collaboration workflows are executed on the same data collection. An enterprise might also collaborate with enterprises outside Qanaat and require to access its data. Such data operations can be performed on the enterprise's local data collection without violating data consistency enabling the enterprise to use such data in its collaboration workflows within Qanaat.

Figure 6.2c presents two data models for two collaboration workflows where enterprises K, L, and M are involved in the first and enterprises L, M, and N are involved in the second collaboration workflow. Since L and M are involved in both workflows, the local data collections d_L and d_M and the intermediate data collection d_{LM} are shared in both collaboration workflows.

6.3.3 Blockchain Ledger

The blockchain ledger is an append-only data structure that maintains transaction records. The blockchain ledger provides immutability and verifiability that prevents any malicious enterprise from altering data and enables enterprises to verify the state of the data. When several enterprises execute transactions across different data collections, maintaining consistency and preserving confidentiality in a scalable manner is challenging. Before describing the Qanaat ledger, we discuss three possible solutions for ordering transactions in cross-enterprise collaborations.

1. A single, global ledger. One possibility is to construct a linear blockchain ledger for each collaboration workflow where all transactions on all data collections are totally ordered and appended to a single global ledger. To preserve the confidentiality of private transactions, the cryptographic hash of such transactions (instead of the actual transaction) can be maintained in the blockchain ledger. This technique, which has been used in Hyperledger Fabric [5], suffers from two main shortcomings. First, forcing *all* transactions into a single, sequential order unnecessarily degrades performance, especially in the large-scale collaborations targeted by Qanaat. To see this, note that while total ordering is needed for data-dependent transactions, e.g., transactions executed on the same data collection to preserve data consistency, total ordering among transactions of independent data collections, e.g., d_A and d_B, is clearly not needed. Second, since this solution requires a single, global blockchain ledger to be maintained by every enterprise, each enterprise needs to maintain (the hash of) transactions that the enterprise was not involved in, e.g., internal transactions of other enterprises, which increases bandwidth and storage costs.

2. One ledger for each data collection. A second possibility is to maintain a separate transaction ordering (i.e., linear blockchain ledger) for each data collection. The blockchain ledger of each enterprise then consists of multiple parallel linear ledgers (one per each data collection that the enterprise is involved in). This solution, however, does not consider dependencies across order-dependent data collections where the execution of a transaction might require reading records from other data collections. Such dependencies need to be captured during the *ordering phase* to ensure that all replicas read the same state in the execution phase. Note that the read-set and write-set of transactions might not be known before execution. As a result, writing the read values into the block is not possible in the ordering phase.

For example, consider an internal transaction of the supplier that reads the order record of the root data collection and based on that computes and stores the results. In the meantime (during the period from the initiation to the execution of the transaction), the value of the order record might change. As a result, if the state of the root data collection has not been captured, different nodes (i.e., replicas) of the supplier, might read different values (old or new) of the order in the execution phase resulting in inconsistency. Alternatively, the system would need to support atomic cross-chain transactions [40, 41].

3. One ledger for each enterprise. A third solution is to maintain a total order among all transactions in which an enterprise is involved. This solution, in contrast to the second solution, guarantees data consistency. However, similar to the first solution, this solution prevents order-independent transactions from being appended to the ledger in parallel. For example, transactions on data collections d_{AB} have no data dependency with transactions on d_{AC} and can append to the ledger of enterprise A in parallel.

Qanaat addresses the shortcomings of the existing solutions in guaranteeing data consistency and preserving collaboration confidentiality while creating a ledger in an efficient and scalable manner. In Qanaat, the blockchain ledger guarantees two main properties:

- **Local consistency.** A total order on the transactions of each data collection is enforced due to data dependency among transactions executed on a data collection.
- **Global consistency.** The order of the transactions of data collection d_X with respect to the transactions of all data collections that d_X is order dependent on is determined by capturing the state of such data collections. Moreover, transactions are ordered across the enterprises consistently.

Qanaat constructs a single DAG-structured ledger for each enterprise consisting of transaction records of the data collections that are maintained by the enterprise. The first rule guarantees data consistency within each single data collection and the second rule ensures global data consistency across all order-dependent data collections maintained by an enterprise. Given the above rules, each transaction t initiated on data collection d_X has an identifier, `ID` = $\langle \alpha, \gamma \rangle$, composed of a *local* part α and possibly a *global* part γ where the `ID` is assigned during the ordering phase. The local part α is $[X{:}n]$ where X is a *label* representing the involved enterprises in d_X and n is a *sequence number* representing the order of transaction t on d_X. In the global part γ, for *every* data collection d_Y where d_X is order dependent on d_Y, $Y{:}m$ is added to the γ of t to capture the state of data collection d_Y. Here, $Y{:}m$ is the local part of the `ID` of the last transaction that is committed on data collection d_Y. When t is executed, it might read the state of a subset of data collections that are captured in the global part of its `ID`.

Given two transactions t and t' on data collection d_X. Let $\texttt{ID}(t) = \langle \alpha, \gamma \rangle$ where $\alpha = [X{:}n]$, $\gamma = [..., Y_p{:}m_p, Y_q{:}m_q, ...]$ and $\texttt{ID}(t') = \langle \alpha', \gamma' \rangle$ where $\alpha' = [X{:}n']$, and $\gamma = [..., Y_q{:}m'_q, Y_r{:}m'_r, ...]$. If t is ordered before t' ($t \rightarrow t'$) then

- $n < n'$ (local consistency) and
- $\forall$ data collection $d_{Y_q} \in \gamma \cap \gamma', m_q \leq m'_q$ (global consistency).

Figure 6.3a–d shows the blockchain ledger of four enterprises A, B, C, and D created in the Qanaat model (following Fig. 6.2a) for a collaboration workflow. The collaboration workflow includes two public transactions on root data collection d_{ABCD}, several internal transactions on local data collec-

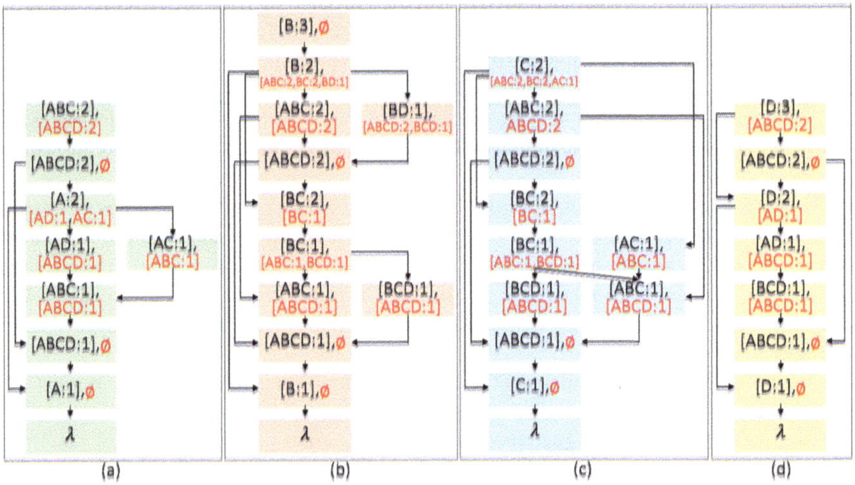

Fig. 6.3 a–d The blockchain ledger for enterprises A, B, C, and D in a collaboration workflow

tions, and multiple transactions among subsets of enterprises. In this figure, $\langle[A{:}1], \varnothing\rangle$ is an internal transaction on data collections d_A (with $\gamma = \varnothing$ because no transactions has been processed yet). $\langle[ABCD{:}1], \varnothing\rangle$ is a public transaction on d_{ABCD} (with $\gamma = \varnothing$ because the root data collection is not order dependent on any data collections). As shown, two transactions $\langle[ABC{:}1], [ABCD{:}1]\rangle$ (on d_{ABC}) and $\langle[BCD{:}1], [ABCD{:}1]\rangle$ (on d_{BCD}) are appended to the ledger of enterprise B (as well as C) in parallel because d_{ABC} and d_{BCD} are not order dependent. Both transactions include global part $\gamma = [ABCD{:}1]$ because both d_{ABC} and d_{BCD} are order dependent on d_{ABCD}. Transactions of each non-local data collection, e.g., $\langle[ABC{:}1], [ABCD{:}1]\rangle$, which is shared between multiple enterprises, e.g., A, B, and C, is *replicated* on all involved enterprises in the same order. $\langle[BC{:}1], [ABC{:}1, BCD{:}1]\rangle$ (on d_{BC}) has $\gamma = [ABC{:}1, BCD{:}1]$ as the global part of its `ID`. Note that d_{BC} in addition to d_{ABC} and d_{BCD} is order dependent on d_{ABCD}. However, since the state of d_{ABCD} is captured in the global part of transaction $\langle[ABC{:}1], [ABCD{:}1]\rangle$ (and $\langle[BCD{:}1], [ABCD{:}1]\rangle$) and it has not been changed, there is no need to add $ABCD{:}1$ to the global part of $\langle[BC{:}1], [ABC{:}1, BCD{:}1]\rangle$. Dashed lines, e.g., between $\langle[B{:}1], \varnothing\rangle$ and $\langle[ABCD{:}1], \varnothing\rangle$, are only used to show the order of appending entries to the ledger, i.e., does not imply any data or ordering dependencies. Note that while in this example, most transactions are cross-enterprise (to help illustrate how a blockchain ledger is created), in practical collaboration workflows, a significant percentage of transactions are internal.

6.3.4 Qanaat Infrastructure

In Qanaat, nodes follow either the crash failure model or the Byzantine failure model. To guarantee fault tolerance, clusters with crash-only nodes include $2f{+}1$ nodes. In the presence of Byzantine nodes, $3f{+}1$ nodes are needed to provide fault tolerance [42]. The malicious nodes, however, can violate data confidentiality by leaking requests, replies, and data stored and processed at the nodes. To prevent confidential data leakage (known as *intrusion tolerance* [43, 44]), Qanaat can use either of the following two techniques: (1) restricting the data that nodes can access [44–48] using secret sharing schemes or (2) adding a privacy firewall between the ordering nodes and the execution nodes [16, 17].

In the secret sharing scheme, clients encode data using an $(f+1, n)$-threshold secret sharing scheme, where $f+1$ shares out of n total shares are needed to reconstruct the confidential data [43]. Secret sharing schemes only perform basic store and retrieve operations (Belisarius [45] also supports addition) and do not support general transactions that require nodes to manipulate the contents of stored data. As a result, this technique is not suitable for blockchain systems that need to support complex transactions.

In the privacy firewall mechanism [16], the infrastructure consists of $3f+1$ ordering nodes (where f is the maximum number of malicious ordering nodes) that run a BFT protocol to order client requests, $2g+1$ execution nodes (where g is the maximum number of malicious execution nodes) that maintain data and deterministically execute arbitrary transactions following the order assigned by the ordering nodes, and a privacy firewall consisting of a set of $h+1$ rows of $h+1$ filters (where h is the maximum number of malicious filter nodes) between the ordering nodes and execution nodes. The privacy firewall architecture assumes a network configuration that physically restricts communication paths between ordering nodes, filters, and execution nodes, i.e., clients can only communicate with ordering (and not execution) nodes and each filter has a physical network connection only to all (filter) nodes in the rows above and below itself. As a result, a malicious node can *either* access confidential data (an execution node or a filter) *or* communicate freely with clients (an ordering node) *but not both*. The $h+1$ rows of $h+1$ filters guarantee that, first, there is at least one path between execution nodes and ordering nodes which only consists of non-faulty filters (liveness) and, second, since there are $h + 1$ rows and maximum h malicious filters, there exist a row consisting of only non-faulty filters that filters any malicious message (possibly including confidential data). As a result, the rows below of non-faulty filters have no access to any confidential data leaked by malicious execution nodes. Note that if $h \leq 3f$, ordering nodes can be merged with the bottom row of filters by placing a filter on each ordering node. In most applications, request and reply bodies must also be encrypted, thus, ordering nodes cannot read them (while clients and execution nodes can).

By separating ordering nodes from execution nodes, a simple majority of non-faulty nodes is sufficient to mask Byzantine failure among execution nodes, i.e., $2g + 1$ execution nodes can tolerate g Byzantine faults. This is important because, compared to ordering, executing transactions and maintaining the application logic (e.g., smart contracts) and data require more powerful computation, storage, and I/O resources. The overhead of the privacy firewall mechanism can be reduced by adding h filters to each row while providing a higher degree of confidentiality [17].

Separating ordering nodes from execution nodes and using a privacy firewall comes with extra resource costs because ordering nodes and execution nodes need to be physically separated. However, if a cluster is deployed in a cloud platform, ordering nodes and execution nodes can match the control layer and computing nodes, respectively. Similarly, tools such as internal authorization services, node auditors, and load balancers deployed in existing cloud platforms can be used as privacy firewalls [17].

Qanaat prevents confidential data leakage despite Byzantine failure using the privacy firewall mechanism presented in [16].

Figure 6.4 presents a cluster in Qanaat and shows the flow of reply messages in different settings where different types of nodes follow different failure models. When nodes are crash-only, as shown in Fig. 6.4a, a cluster consisting of $2f + 1$ nodes can order *and* execute transactions while confidential data leakage is prevented. If ordering nodes follow the Byzantine failure model, the ordering nodes and execution nodes need to be separated to prevent data leakage. However, if execution nodes are

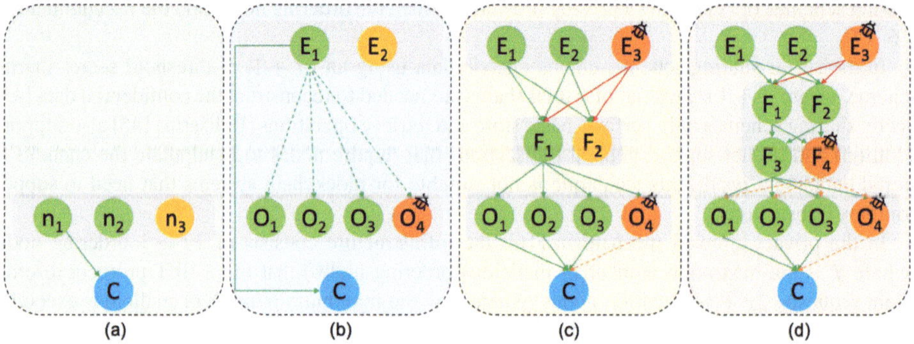

[●: non-faulty, ●: malicious, ●: crashed, and ●: clients]

Fig. 6.4 The flow of reply messages in an instance of Qanaat with **a** $2f + 1$ crash-only nodes, **b** $3f + 1$ Byzantine ordering nodes and $g + 1$ crash-only execution nodes, **c** $3f + 1$ Byzantine ordering and $2g + 1$ Byzantine execution nodes, and a privacy firewall consisting of $h + 1$ crash-only filter nodes, and **d** $3f + 1$ Byzantine ordering nodes, $2g + 1$ Byzantine execution nodes and $h + 1$ rows of $h + 1$ Byzantine filter nodes crash-only, as shown in Fig. 6.4b, there is no need to add a privacy firewall and execution nodes can directly send the reply to the client and inform ordering nodes about the execution. Since execution nodes are crash-only, $g + 1$ nodes are sufficient to execute transactions. When both ordering and execution nodes might behave maliciously, a privacy firewall consisting of a set of filters is needed. The firewall physically restricts communication from execution nodes, hence, a malicious execution node cannot send confidential data to a malicious ordering node that might share the data with clients. If filters are crash-only (Fig. 6.4c), a row of $h + 1$ filters is sufficient to filter incorrect messages (data leakage) where h is the maximum number of crashed filters.

The general case, as shown in Fig. 6.4d, is when all ordering nodes, execution nodes, and filters follow the Byzantine failure model. In this case, a privacy firewall with $h + 1$ rows of $h + 1$ filters per row is needed. Communication is restricted so that each filter has a physical network connection only to all (filter) nodes in the row above and all (filter) nodes in the row below.

6.3.5 Confidentiality Guarantees

Qanaat provides collaboration confidentiality through its hierarchical data model, which segregates data into "data collections" that are only maintained by authorized enterprises. Qanaat also prevents confidential data leakage by separating ordering nodes from execution nodes and using a privacy firewall in between. Confidentiality is mainly preserved based on three main rules:

1. Data collections are completely separated. For example, d_{AC} captures transactions that are executed in a shared collaboration between A and C. This is different from the data records of d_A or d_C (internal transactions of A or C). Moreover, each data collection is maintained *only* by its involved enterprises. Similarly, each transaction record in the blockchain ledger, as shown in Fig. 6.3, is only maintained by the involved enterprises.

2. Transactions of a data collection d_X can read transactions of another data collection d_Y *if and only if* $X \subseteq Y$. For example, transactions of d_{AB} can read records of d_{ABC} because both A and B are involved in d_{ABC}. However, transactions of d_{ABC} cannot read records of d_{AB} because enterprise C is not involved in d_{AB}.

3. A malicious node can *either* access confidential data (an execution node or a filter) *or* communicate freely with clients (an ordering node) *but not both.* This is guaranteed by separating ordering nodes from execution nodes using a privacy firewall.

Note that a compromised client may leak its own state or updates. Qanaat, similar to all other confidential fault-tolerant systems (that we are aware of), does not prevent this. Moreover, an enterprise might share the data resulting from its cross-enterprise collaborations with some external entity or even grant its access to the external entity. Qanaat cannot restrict such external data leakage.

6.3.6 Multi-shard Enterprises

We now show how the data model and the blockchain ledger can be extended to support multi-shard enterprises. With single-shard enterprises, every execution node of each enterprise maintains all data collections that the enterprise is involved in. Enterprises, however, partition their data into different shards. Each data shard is then assigned to a cluster of nodes where the ordering nodes of the cluster order the transactions and the execution nodes maintain the data shard and execute transactions on the data shard. A shard of the enterprise data might not include a shard of every data collection that the enterprise is involved in. For example, consider a private collaboration between the logistic provider and the pharmaceutical manufacturer maintained on a shared data collection. While the logistic provider might partition its data into multiple shards, it maintains this shared data collection in only one of its data shards on a cluster that is placed in Michigan (close to the Pfizer manufacturing site), e.g., a local collaboration.

We assume that enterprises use the same sharding schema for each shared data collection to facilitate transaction processing across different enterprises. The schema is agreed upon by all involved enterprises when a data collection is created, i.e., the sharding schema is part of the configuration metadata. Using the same sharding schema leads to a more efficient ordering phase for cross-enterprise transactions because there is no need for all involved enterprises to run a consensus protocol to agree on the order of every transaction. For each cross-enterprise transaction, one enterprise orders the transaction and other involved enterprises only validate the order (details in Sects. 6.4.3 and 6.4.4). Furthermore, different data shards of an enterprise are processed by different clusters. Using the same sharding schema, enterprises can easily communicate with the right cluster that processes the data records of transactions. If enterprises use different sharding schema for a shared data collection, Qanaat could still process cross-enterprise transactions but with the overhead required to execute a consensus protocol with every transaction on each cluster.

The blockchain ledger of a single-shard enterprise maintains all transactions that are executed on the enterprise data. In a multi-shard enterprise, the enterprise data is partitioned into different shards where each shard is replicated on a cluster of execution nodes. Since each cluster maintains a separate data shard, it executes a different set of transactions. As a result, each cluster in a multi-shard enterprise needs to maintain a different ledger. The ledger of each cluster of a multi-shard enterprise, however, is constructed in the same way as a single-shard enterprise. Moreover, the notion of global consistency is extended to guarantee that each cross-shard transaction is ordered across participating shards consistently.

6.4 Transaction Processing in Qanaat

Processing transactions requires establishing consensus on a unique order of requests. Qanaat, similar to most other permissioned blockchain systems, guarantees safety in an asynchronous network; however, it considers a synchrony assumption to ensure liveness (due to FLP results [49]).

A transaction might be executed on a single shard or on multiple shards of a data collection where the data collection belongs to a single enterprise (i.e., a local data collection) or is shared among multiple enterprises (i.e., a root or an intermediate data collection). As a result, as shown in Table 6.1,

Table 6.1 Processing transactions in Qanaat

Transaction type		Example	Consensus protocol	
Shard	Enterprise	Clusters-shards	Coordinator based	Flattened
Intra	Intra	$A_1 - d_A^1$	Pluggable	Pluggable
Intra	Cross	$C_3, D_3 - d_{CD}^3$	Fig. 6.5a	Fig. 6.6a
Cross	Intra	$A_2, A_3 - d_A^2, d_A^3$	Fig. 6.5b	Fig. 6.6b
Cross	Cross	$B_1, C_1, B_2, C_2 - d_{BC}^1, d_{BC}^2$	Fig. 6.5c	Fig. 6.6c

Qanaat needs to support four different types of transactions. In Table 6.1, the network consists of four enterprises where each enterprise $\psi \in \{A, B, C, D\}$ owns three clusters of nodes, e.g., ψ_1, ψ_2, and ψ_3 and processes shard d^i_ψ by nodes of cluster ψ_i.

An *intra-shard* transaction is executed on the same shard of a data collection either *intra-enterprise*, e.g., on shard d^1_A of a local data collection d_A by cluster A_1, or *cross-enterprise*, e.g., on shard d^3_{CD} of a shared data collection d_{CD} by clusters C_3 and D_3. A *cross-shard transaction* is executed on multiple shards of a data collection either *intra-enterprise*, e.g., on shards d^2_A and d^3_A of a data collection d_A by clusters A_2, A_3, or *cross-enterprise*, e.g., on shards d^1_{BC} and d^2_{BC} of a shared data collection d_{BC} by clusters B_1, C_1, B_2, and C_2.

A transaction can be executed on multiple shards of the same data collection (i.e., a cross-shard transaction) or the same data shard that is maintained by multiple enterprises (i.e., a cross-enterprise transaction). However, as mentioned earlier, a transaction cannot be executed or write data records on multiple data collections for two main reasons. First, the data of each (non-root) data collection is confidentially shared with only its involved enterprises. For example, transactions of d_{AB} should not write data on d_{AC} as C is not involved in d_{AB}. Note that transactions among enterprises A, B, and C are executed on d_{ABC}. Moreover, there is no need to write the transaction results of d_{AB} on d_A or d_B as both enterprises A and B store d_{AB} (see Fig. 6.2b) and can read its data record in their local data collections d_A and d_B. Second, each data collection might have its own business logic to execute transactions.

In Qanaat, cross-shard intra-enterprise transactions and intra-shard cross-enterprise transactions are handled differently. In a cross-shard intra-enterprise transaction, different clusters maintain separate data shards. As a result, each cluster needs to separately reach agreement on the transaction order among transactions of its shard. However, in an intra-shard cross-enterprise transaction, since the involved enterprises use the same sharding schema for each shared data collection, the cluster that initiates the transaction and all the involved clusters process the transaction on the same shard of data. Hence, the order of transactions on different clusters is the same. As a result, it is sufficient that one (initiator) cluster determines the order and other clusters only validate the suggested order. Note that while the involved clusters belong to different distrustful enterprises, all clusters can detect any malicious behavior of the initiator cluster. We will discuss how Qanaat addresses all possible malicious behaviors, e.g., assigning invalid `ID` (order) or even not sending the transaction to other clusters. In cross-enterprise collaboration, enterprises cannot trust that the other enterprise nodes might not be compromised. As a result, independent of the declared failure model of nodes, Qanaat uses a BFT protocol to order cross-enterprise transactions. Furthermore, as it is suggested in Caper [11], we can assume that less than a *one-third* of enterprises might be malicious. Hence, by a similar argument as in PBFT [50], with agreement from at least *two-thirds* of the enterprises, a cross-enterprise transaction can be committed. For cross-shard intra-enterprise transactions, on the other hand, the involved clusters belong to the same enterprise and trust each other. As a result, if all nodes are crash-only, cross-shard consensus can be achieved using a crash fault-tolerant protocol.

To process transactions across clusters *coordinator-based* and *flattened* approaches are used. In the coordinator-based approach, inspired by existing permissioned blockchains such as AHL [12], Saguaro [51], and Blockplane [52], a cluster coordinates transaction ordering, whereas, in the flattened approach, transactions are ordered across the clusters without requiring a coordinator.

Nodes in Qanaat follow different failure models, i.e., crash or Byzantine. We mainly focus on two common cases. First, when nodes follow the crash failure, a cluster contains $2f + 1$ nodes that perform both ordering and execution. Second, when nodes follow the Byzantine failure and each cluster includes $3f+1$ ordering nodes, $2g+1$ execution nodes, and a privacy firewall consisting of $h+1$ rows of $h + 1$ filters. The number of required matching votes to ensure that a quorum of ordering nodes within a cluster agrees with the order of a transaction is different in different settings. We define *local-majority* as the number of required matching votes from a cluster. For crash-only clusters, local-majority is $f + 1$ (from $2f + 1$ nodes), and for clusters with Byzantine ordering nodes, local-majority is $2f + 1$ (from $3f + 1$ ordering nodes).

6.4.1 Intra-cluster Consensus

In the internal (intra-cluster) consensus protocol, the ordering nodes of a cluster, *independently* of other clusters, agree on the order of a transaction. The internal consensus protocol is pluggable and depending on the failure model of nodes of the cluster a crash fault-tolerant (CFT) protocol, e.g., (Multi-)Paxos [53] or a Byzantine fault-tolerant (BFT) protocol, e.g., PBFT [50], can be used. If nodes follow the Byzantine failure model, as discussed before, Qanaat separates ordering nodes from execution nodes and uses a privacy firewall to prevent confidential data leakage.

The protocol is initiated by a pre-elected ordering node of the cluster, called *the primary*. When the primary node $\pi(P_i)$ of cluster P_i receives a valid signed request message $\langle \text{REQUEST}, op, t_c, c\rangle_{\sigma_c}$ from an authorized client c (with timestamp t_c) to execute (encrypted) operation op on local data collection d_{P_i}, it initiates the protocol by multicasting a message, e.g., accept message in Multi-Paxos (assuming the primary is elected) or pre-prepare message in PBFT, including the req and its digest to other ordering nodes of the cluster.

To provide a total order among transaction blocks and preserve data consistency, the primary also assigns an `ID`, as discussed in Sect. 6.3.3, to the request. The `ID` consists of a local part, e.g., $[P_i{:}n]$, and a global part including the state of all data collections that d_{P_i} is order dependent on. The global part includes the state of *all* data collections that d_{P_i} is order dependent on because the read-set of the transaction is not known (will be known during the execution time). The primary includes the current state (i.e., the local sequence number of the last committed transaction) of such data collections in the global part. The ordering nodes of the cluster then agree on the order of the transaction using the utilized protocol.

6.4.2 Transaction Execution Routine

The next step after ordering is to execute a transaction and inform the client. If nodes follow the Byzantine failure model, ordering and execution are performed by distinct sets of nodes that are separated by a privacy firewall. Once a transaction is ordered, the ordering nodes generate a commit certificate consisting of signatures from $2f + 1$ different nodes and multicast both the request and the commit certificate to the lowest row of filters. The filters check the request and the commit certificate to be valid and multicast them to the next row. Filters also track the requests that they have seen in a commit or a reply certificate and their `ID`s.

Upon receiving both a valid request and a valid commit certificate, execution nodes append the transaction and the corresponding commit certificate to the ledger. Note that the execution nodes store the last reply certificate sent to client c to check if the current request is new (i.e., has a larger timestamp) that needs to be executed and committed to the ledger or an old request (i.e., has the same or smaller timestamp) where nodes re-send the reply messages. If all transactions accessing on d_{P_i} with lower local sequence numbers ($< n$) have been executed, nodes execute the transaction on data collection d_{P_i} following its application logic. If, during the execution, the execution nodes need to read values from some other data collection d_X where d_{P_i} is order dependent on d_X (i.e., $P_i \subseteq X$), the nodes check the public part of the transaction `ID` to ensure that they read the correct state of d_X.

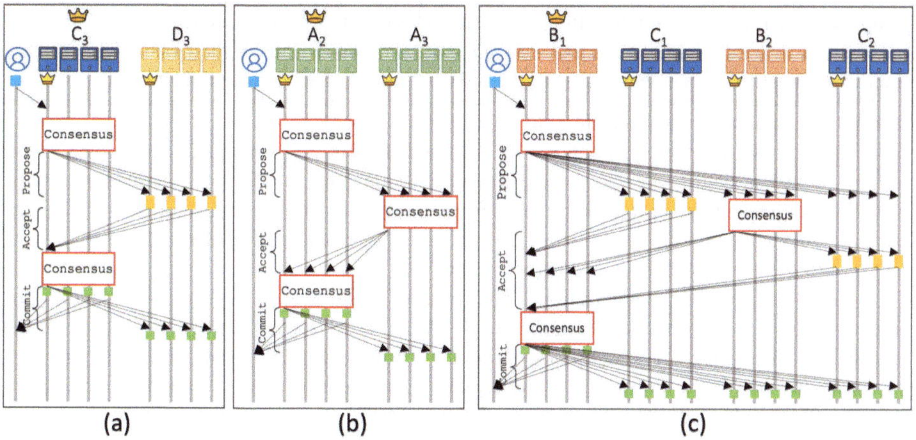

Fig. 6.5 **a** Intra-shard cross-enterprise, **b** cross-shard intra-enterprise, and **c** cross-shard cross-enterprise coordinator-based consensus protocols

Data collections store data in multi-versioned datastores to enable nodes to read the version they need to. This ensures that all execution nodes execute requests in the same order and on the same state.

The commit certificate are appended to the ledger to guarantee immutability. Since commit messages include the digest of transaction blocks, by appending them to the ledger, any attempt to alter the block data can easily be detected.

Execution nodes then multicast a signed reply message including the (encrypted) results to the top row of filters. When a filter node in the top row receives $g + 1$ valid matching reply messages, it generates a reply certificate authenticated by $g + 1$ signature shares from distinct execution nodes and multicasts it to the row below. Each filter then multicasts the reply certificate to the row of filter nodes or ordering nodes below. Finally, client c accepts the result once it receives a valid reply certificate from ordering nodes.

If nodes follow the crash failure model, ordering and execution are performed by the same set of nodes. In this case, nodes append the transaction to the ledger and execute it as explained before and then the primary node sends a reply message to client c.

6.4.3 Coordinator-Based Consensus

The coordinator-based approach has been used in distributed databases to process cross-shard transactions, e.g., two-phase commit. Coordinator-based protocols have also been used in several permissioned blockchain systems, e.g., AHL [12], Blockplane [52], and Saguaro [51]. This section briefly demonstrates how Qanaat can leverage the coordinator-based approach to process cross-cluster transactions. In contrast to the existing coordinator-based databases and blockchains that address multi-shard single-enterprise contexts, Qanaat deals with multi-shard multi-enterprise environments. Moreover, since each transaction might read data from multiple data collections, ordering transactions in Qanaat is more complex. All three coordinator-based protocols (i.e., intra-shard cross-enterprise, cross-shard intra-enterprise, and cross-shard cross-enterprise), as shown in Fig. 6.5, consist of propose, accept and commit phases. We briefly explain the normal case operation of the protocols.

Propose: Upon receiving a transaction, ordering nodes of the *coordinator* cluster establish (internal) consensus on the order of the transaction among the transactions of their shard. The primary then sends a signed propose message to the ordering nodes of all involved clusters.

Accept: This phase is handled differently in different protocols.
Intra-shard cross-enterprise transactions: All involved clusters, e.g., C_3 and D_3 in Fig. 6.5a, maintain the same data shard. As a result, there is no need to run consensus in non-coordinator clusters, e.g., D_3. Upon receiving a propose message from the primary of the coordinator cluster, e.g., C_3, each ordering node of a non-coordinator cluster, e.g., D_3, validates the order and sends a accept message to the primary of the coordinator cluster.
Cross-shard intra-enterprise transactions: The involved clusters, e.g., A_2 and A_3, maintain different shards of a local data collection, e.g., d_A. Upon receiving a propose message from the coordinator cluster, e.g., A_2, each non-coordinator cluster separately establishes (internal) consensus on the order of the transaction in its data shard. The primary of each non-coordinator cluster, e.g., A_3, then sends a accept message to the ordering nodes of the coordinator cluster, e.g., A_2.
Cross-shard cross-enterprise transactions: The involved clusters of the initiator enterprise, e.g., B_1 and B_2 of enterprise B, maintain different shards of a shared data collection, e.g., d_{BC}, while each shard is replicated on clusters of different enterprises, e.g., d^1_{BC} is maintained by B_1 and C_1. Upon receiving a propose message from the coordinator cluster, e.g., B_1, if the cluster belongs to the initiator enterprise, e.g., B_2, it establishes (internal) consensus on the transaction order. Otherwise, the cluster waits for a message from the cluster of the initiator enterprise that maintains the same data shard as they do, e.g., C_1 waits for B_1 and C_2 waits for B_2. Each node then validates the received message and sends a accept message to the primary of the coordinator cluster.

Commit: When the primary of the coordinator cluster receives valid accept messages from every involved cluster, it establishes internal consensus within the coordinator cluster and multicasts a signed commit message to the ordering nodes of all involved clusters.

Intra-shard Cross-Enterprise Consensus

In the intra-shard cross-enterprise protocol, multiple clusters (one from each enterprise) process a transaction on the same shard of a non-local data collection shared between enterprises, e.g., clusters C_3 and D_3 on shard d^3_{CD} of data collection d_{CD} (Fig. 6.5a).

Upon receiving a valid transaction m, the primary of the coordinator cluster P_c, i.e., the cluster that receives the transaction, assigns an ID to the transaction (as discussed in Sect. 6.3.3) and initiates internal consensus on the order of m in the coordinator cluster.

Once consensus is achieved, the primary sends a signed propose message $\langle \text{PROPOSE}, \text{ID}, d, m \rangle_{\sigma_{P_c}}$ to the nodes of all involved clusters where $d = D(m)$ is the digest of request m. The propose messages are signed by local-majority of the clusters (denoted by σ_{P_c}). Upon receiving a propose message with valid ID (following the local and global consistency rules discussed in Sect. 6.3.3), digest, and signature, each node r sends a signed accept message $\langle \text{ACCEPT}, \text{ID}, d, r \rangle_{\sigma_r}$ to the primary node of the coordinator cluster.

Upon receiving valid accept messages from the local-majority of every involved cluster, the primary establishes internal consensus within the coordinator cluster and sends a commit message signed by a local-majority of the cluster to every node of all involved clusters. The commit message includes the transaction ID, its digest, and also accept messages received from the local-majority of every involved cluster as evidence of message validity. When a node receives a valid commit message, the node appends the transaction to the ledger and executes the transaction.

If a node of an involved cluster waits for a message from another cluster, e.g., a node in D_3 does not receive a **commit** message from the coordinator cluster C_3, it sends a query message to all nodes of that cluster resulting in either receiving the message or replacing the faulty primary. The routine is explained in Sect. 6.4.3.

Cross-Shard Intra-Enterprise Consensus

The cross-shard intra-enterprise consensus protocol, inspired by permissioned blockchains AHL [12] and Saguaro [51], processes transactions on different shards of a local data collection within an enterprise, e.g., a transaction on data shards d_A^2 and d_A^3 of data collection d_A processed by clusters A_2 and A_3 (Fig. 6.5b).

After receiving transaction m, the primary of the coordinator cluster P_c assigns an `ID` to the transaction and establishes internal consensus on the order of m in the coordinator cluster. P_c then multicasts a signed **propose** message $\langle \text{PROPOSE}, \text{ID}_c, d, m\rangle_{\sigma_{P_c}}$ to the nodes of all involved clusters. Upon receiving a valid **propose** message, the primary of each involved cluster P_i assigns $\texttt{ID}_i$ to m and establishes consensus on request m in cluster P_i. $\texttt{ID}_c$ and $\texttt{ID}_i$ represent the order of transaction m in clusters P_c and P_i, respectively. Note that the primary of the coordinator and all involved clusters processes the request only if there is no concurrent (uncommitted) request m' where m and m' intersect in at least 2 shards. This is needed to ensure that requests are committed in different shards in the same order (global consistency).

The primary of each involved cluster P_i then multicasts a signed **accept** message $\langle \text{ACCEPT}, \text{ID}_c, \text{ID}_i, d\rangle_{\sigma_{P_i}}$ to all nodes of the coordinator cluster P_c. Otherwise (if consensus is not achieved), it multicasts a signed **abort** message. As before, each message is signed by a local-majority of a cluster. When the primary node of the coordinator cluster receives valid **accept** messages from every involved cluster, e.g., $P_i, P_j, \ldots$, it initiates internal consensus within the coordinator cluster and multicasts a signed **commit** message $\langle \text{COMMIT}, \text{ID}_c, \text{ID}_i, \text{ID}_j, \ldots, d\rangle_{\sigma_{P_c}}$ to every node of all involved clusters.

Otherwise (if some cluster has aborted the transaction), the primary multicasts a signed **abort** message. The `ID` of the **commit** messages is a concatenation of the received `ID`s from all involved clusters. Since the transaction takes place within an enterprise, in contrast to the previous protocol, the primary of the coordinator cluster does not need to include the received **accept** messages in its **commit** message. Upon receiving a valid **commit** message, each node appends the transaction to the ledger and executes it.

Cross-Shard Cross-Enterprise Consensus

The cross-shard cross-enterprise consensus protocol is needed when a transaction is executed on different shards of a non-local data collection shared between different enterprises, e.g., a transaction that is executed on data shards d_{BC}^1 and d_{BC}^2 of shared data collection d_{BC} where d_{BC}^1 is maintained by B_1 and C_1 and d_{BC}^2 is maintained by B_2 and C_2 (Fig. 6.5(c)).

In this case, different clusters of each enterprise maintain different data shards, e.g., B_1 and B_2 maintain d_{BC}^1 and d_{BC}^2; however, each data shard is replicated on only one cluster of each involved enterprise, e.g., d_{BC}^1 is replicated on B_1 and C_1. In Qanaat, in order to improve performance, only the clusters of the initiator enterprise, e.g., B_1 and B_2, establish consensus on the transaction order and clusters of other enterprises, e.g., C_1 and C_2, validate the order.

Upon receiving a valid transaction m, the primary node of the coordinator cluster P_c establishes internal consensus on the order of m in the coordinator cluster and then multicasts a signed **propose** message $\langle \text{PROPOSE}, \text{ID}_c, d, m\rangle_{\sigma_{P_c}}$ to the nodes of all involved clusters. When the primary node of an involved cluster P_i of the *initiator enterprise* receives a valid propose message, it assigns $\texttt{ID}_i$ to m and initiates internal consensus on request m in cluster P_i. Same as cross-shard intra-enterprise consensus, the primary of P_c and every P_i processes the request only if there is no concurrent request m' with shared data shards. Once consensus is achieved, the primary of the involved cluster P_i multicasts a signed accept message $\langle \text{ACCEPT}, \text{ID}_c, \text{ID}_i, d\rangle_{\sigma_{P_i}}$ to every node of P_c and also any other clusters that maintain *the same* data shard as cluster P_i. Otherwise, it multicasts an abort message to those clusters.

A node in a cluster of a non-initiator enterprise either (1) maintains the same shard as the coordinator cluster and receives a valid propose message (with $\texttt{ID}_c$) from the primary of coordinator cluster P_c or (2) maintains some other shard and receives a valid accept message (with $\texttt{ID}_i$) from the primary of cluster P_i. In either case, the node sends a signed accept message including $\texttt{ID}_c$ (and $\texttt{ID}_i$) and the message digest to the primary of the coordinator cluster.

The primary node of the coordinator cluster waits for (1) signed valid accept messages from the primary node of all involved clusters of its enterprise and (2) signed valid accept messages from a local-majority of every involved cluster of other enterprises. The primary then initiates internal consensus within the coordinator cluster and multicasts a signed commit (or abort) message to every node of all involved clusters.

Primary Failure Handling

We use the retransmission routine presented in [16] to handle unreliable communication between ordering nodes and execution nodes. In this section, we focus on the failure of the primary ordering node. If the timer of node r expires before it receives a commit certificate, it suspects that the primary might be faulty.

The timeout mechanism prevents the protocol from blocking and waiting forever by ensuring that eventually (after the global stabilization time) communication between non-faulty ordering nodes is timely and reliable. Ordering nodes use different timers for intra-cluster and cross-cluster transactions because processing transactions across clusters usually takes more time. The timeout value mainly depends on the network latency (within or across clusters). It must be long enough to allow nodes to communicate with each other and establish consensus, i.e., at least three times the WAN round-trip for cross-cluster transactions to allow a view-change routine to complete without replacing the primary node again. The timeouts are adjusted to ensure that this period increases exponentially until some transaction is committed, e.g., in case of consecutive primary failure, the timeout is doubled as in PBFT [50].

When the primary node of a cluster fails, the primary failure handling routine of the internal consensus protocol, e.g., view-change in PBFT, is triggered by timeouts to elect a new primary. For transactions across clusters, if a node of an involved cluster does not receive a commit message from the primary of the coordinator cluster for a prepared request and its timer expires, the node multicasts a signed commit-query message to all nodes of the coordinator cluster including the request $\texttt{ID}$ and its digest. As a result, if the (malicious) primary of the coordinator cluster maliciously has not sent commit messages to other clusters (while the transaction is committed in the coordinator cluster), other nodes of the coordinator cluster will be informed (to prevent any inconsistency between clusters). Similarly, if a node in the coordinator cluster does not receive accept messages from an involved cluster (either from the primary node when it is required to run consensus or from a local-majority of nodes), it multicasts a accept-query to all nodes of the involved cluster. It might also happen between two involved clusters in cross-shard cross-enterprise transactions, where a cluster is waiting for consensus results, e.g., C_2 and B_2 in Fig. 6.5c.

In all such cases, if the message has already been processed, the nodes simply re-send the corresponding response. Nodes also log the query messages to detect denial-of-service attacks initiated by malicious nodes. If the query message is received from a local-majority of a cluster, the primary will be suspected to be faulty, triggering the execution of the failure handling routine. Moreover, since all messages from a primary of a cluster, e.g., propose, accept, or commit, are multicasts to every node of the receiver cluster, if the primary of the receiver cluster does not initiate consensus on the message among the nodes of its cluster, it will eventually be suspected to be faulty by the nodes. Finally, if a client does not receive a reply soon enough, it multicasts the request to all nodes of the cluster that it has already sent its request. If the request has already been processed, the nodes simply send the execution result back to the client. Otherwise, if the node is not the primary, it relays the request to the primary. If the nodes do not receive propose messages, the primary will be suspected to be faulty.

Correctness Argument

We briefly analyze the safety (agreement, validity, and consistency) and liveness properties of the coordinator-based protocols.

Proposition (Agreement) *If node r commits request m with local* $\texttt{ID}\,\alpha$ *in cluster P, no other non-faulty node commits request m' ($m \neq m'$) with the same local* $\texttt{ID}\,\alpha$ *in P.*

Proof We assume that the internal consensus protocols, e.g., Paxos and PBFT, are correct and ensure safety. Let m and m' ($m \neq m'$) be two committed requests where $\texttt{ID}(m) = [\texttt{ID}_i, \texttt{ID}_j, \texttt{ID}_k, ...]$ and $\texttt{ID}(m') = [\texttt{ID}'_k, \texttt{ID}'_l, \texttt{ID}'_m, ..]$, respectively. Note that in intra-shard transactions, the $\texttt{ID}$ includes a single part. Given an involved cluster P_k in the intersection of m and m' where $\texttt{ID}_k(m) = \langle \alpha, \gamma \rangle$ and $\texttt{ID}_k(m') = \langle \alpha', \gamma' \rangle$. To commit m and m', a local-majority Q agreed with m and local-majority Q' agreed with m' (if nodes of P_k are crash-only, local-majority is $f+1$ out of $2f+1$ and if nodes might be Byzantine, local-majority is $2f+1$ out of $3f+1$). Since any two local-majority Q and Q' intersect on at least one non-faulty node and non-faulty nodes do not behave maliciously, if $m \neq m'$ then $\alpha \neq \alpha'$, hence agreement is guaranteed. □

Proposition (Validity) *If a non-faulty node r commits m, then m must have been proposed by some node π.*

Proof For crash-only clusters, validity is guaranteed as crash-only nodes do not send fictitious messages. Since the adversary cannot subvert standard cryptographic assumptions (as explained in Sect. 6.3), validity is guaranteed for Byzantine clusters as well. All messages are signed and include the request or its digest (to prevent changes and alterations to any part of the message). As a result, if request m is committed by non-faulty node r, the same request must have been proposed earlier by some node π. □

Proposition (Consistency) *Let $\mathcal{P}(m)$ denote the set of involved clusters in a request m. For any two committed requests m and m′ and any two nodes r_1 and r_2 such that $r_1 \in P_i$, $r_2 \in P_j$, and $\{P_i, P_j\} \in \mathcal{P}(m) \cap \mathcal{P}(m')$, if m is committed after m′ on r_1, then m is committed after m′ on r_2.*

Proof For intra-shard cross-enterprise transactions, consistency is guaranteed as all clusters in $\mathcal{P}(m)$ maintain the same data shard. For cross-shard transactions, as discussed in Sects. 6.4.3 and 6.4.3, the primary of the coordinator as well as all involved clusters processes the request only if there is no concurrent (uncommitted) request m' where m and m' intersect in at least two shards (to make sure that shards in the intersection commit requests in the same order). Committing request m requires sufficient accept messages from *every* involved cluster, hence, m cannot be committed in any cluster until m' is committed. □

Proposition (Liveness) *A request m issued by a correct client eventually completes.*

Proof Qanaat guarantees liveness *only* during periods of synchrony (FLP result [49]). If the primary of the coordinator cluster is faulty, e.g., does not multicast valid propose or commit messages, or the primary of an involved cluster that needs to run consensus is faulty and does not multicast valid accept messages, as explained in Sect. 6.4.3, its failure will be detected using timeouts. As explained, nodes use different timers for intra-cluster and cross-cluster transactions where the timer for cross-cluster transactions is long enough to allow nodes to communicate with each other and establish consensus, i.e., at least three times the WAN round-trip for cross-cluster transactions to allow a view-change routine to complete without replacing the primary node again. If a newly elected leader is not able to change the view, the timeout is doubled (as in PBFT [50]). This adjustment is needed to ensure that some transactions will be committed, i.e., nodes are synchronized. Qanaat uses the primary failure handling routine of the internal consensus protocol, e.g., view-change in PBFT, to elect a new primary.

Two coordinator clusters might initiate concurrent transactions on the same data shard of the same data collection with inconsistent `ID`s, e.g., both have the same local `ID`, and the involved clusters receive these transactions in a different order. In this case, neither of the concurrent transactions receive accept messages from all involved clusters resulting in a deadlock situation. In such a situation, once the timer of a coordinator cluster for its transaction expires, the coordinator cluster sends a new propose message to the involved clusters to resolve the deadlock. Qanaat assigns different timers to different clusters to prevent parallel and consecutive deadlock situations. To prevent deadlock, Qanaat can consider a designated coordinator cluster for each (shard of a) data collection. An enterprise, however, might not want to consume its resources to coordinate transactions that are initiated by other enterprises. □

6.4.4 Flattened Consensus

The flattened consensus protocols of Qanaat, in contrast to the flattened cross-shard consensus protocols, e.g., SharPer [13], which are designed for single-enterprise environments, support multiple multi-shard collaborative enterprises.

Propose: Upon receiving a transaction, the primary of the coordinator cluster sends a signed propose message to the nodes of all involved clusters.

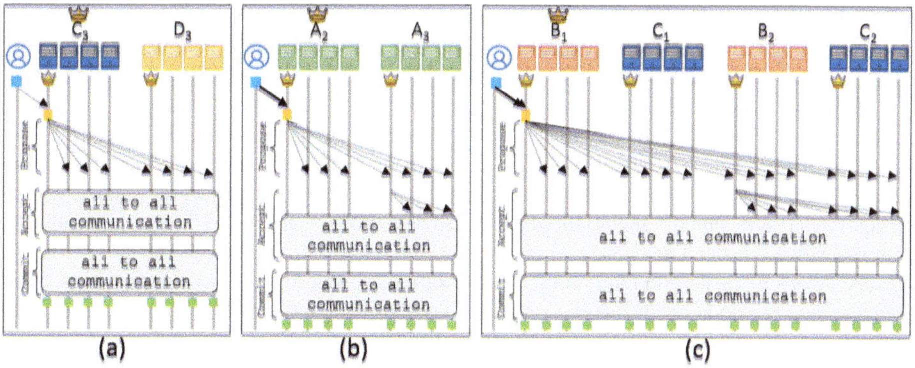

Fig. 6.6 **a** Intra-shard cross-enterprise, **b** cross-shard intra-enterprise, and **c** cross-shard cross-enterprise flattened consensus protocols

Accept: This phase is handled differently in different protocols.
Intra-shard cross-enterprise transactions: All involved clusters, e.g., C_3 and D_3 in Fig. 6.6a, maintain the same data shard. Upon receiving a **propose** message from the primary of the coordinator cluster, each node (in the coordinator, e.g., C_3 or another involved cluster, e.g., D_3) validates the message and its `ID` and multicasts an **accept** message to all nodes of every involved cluster.
Cross-shard intra-enterprise transactions: The involved clusters, e.g., A_2 and A_3, maintain different shards of a local data collection, e.g., d_A. Upon receiving a **propose** message including $\texttt{ID}_i$ from the coordinator cluster, e.g., A_2, the primary of each non-coordinator cluster, e.g., A_3, assigns an $\texttt{ID}_j$ and sends an **accept** message (including both `ID`s) to the nodes of its clusters. Each node then multicasts an **accept** message to all nodes of every involved cluster.
Cross-shard cross-enterprise transactions: While different involved clusters of each enterprise, e.g., B_1 and B_2 of enterprise B, maintain different shards, e.g., d^1_{BC} and d^2_{BC}, of a shared data collection, e.g., d_{BC}, each data shard is replicated on one cluster of each involved enterprise, e.g., d^2_{BC} is maintained by B_2 and C_2. Upon receiving a valid **propose** message from the coordinator cluster, e.g., B_1, if the cluster belongs to the initiator enterprise, e.g., B_2, its primary sends an **accept** message to the nodes of clusters that maintain the same shard, e.g., B_2 and C_2. Each node then sends an **accept** message to all nodes of every involved cluster.

Commit: Upon receiving valid matching **accept** messages from a local-majority of every involved cluster, each node multicasts a **commit** message to every node of all involved clusters. Once a node receives valid matching **commit** messages from the local-majority of every involved cluster, the node commits the transaction.

The flattened protocols of Qanaat enable clusters to commit a transaction in a smaller number of communication phases. For instance, a cross-shard intra-enterprise transaction can be committed using the flattened protocol in 3 cross-cluster communication steps. In contrast, using the coordinator-based protocol, the same transaction requires three cross-cluster and nine intra-cluster communication steps (three runs of PBFT). It also reduces the load on the coordinator cluster. We now discuss the flattened consensus protocols in detail.

Intra-shard Cross-Enterprise Consensus

In the intra-shard cross-enterprise protocol, multiple clusters from different enterprises process a transaction on the same data shard of a shared data collection, e.g., clusters C_3 and D_3 on shard d^3_{CD} of shared data collection d_{CD} (Fig. 6.6a). Upon receiving a valid request message m, the primary ordering node $\pi(P_i)$ of the initiator cluster P_i assigns transaction ID (as discussed in Sect. 6.3.3) and multicasts a signed propose message $\langle \text{PROPOSE}, \text{ID}, d, m\rangle_{\sigma_{\pi(P_i)}}$ to the nodes of all involved clusters where $d = D(m)$ is the digest of request m. Upon receiving a propose message, each node r validates the digest, signature, and ID, and multicasts a signed accept message $\langle \text{ACCEPT}, \text{ID}, d\rangle_{\sigma_r}$ to all nodes of every involved cluster. Each node r waits for valid matching accept messages from a local-majority of every involved cluster and then multicasts a commit message including the transaction ID and its digest to every node of all involved clusters. The propose and accept phases of the protocol, similar to the pre-prepare and prepare phases of PBFT, guarantee that non-faulty nodes agree on an order for the transactions. Finally, once an ordering node receives valid commit messages from the local-majority of all involved clusters that match its commit message, it generates a commit certificate by merging messages from all involved clusters. Each cluster then uses the transaction execution routine to execute the transaction and send reply back to the client.

Cross-Shard Intra-enterprise Consensus

The cross-shard intra-enterprise consensus protocol of Qanaat is inspired by the flattened cross-shard consensus protocols of SharPer [13]. In the cross-shard intra-enterprise consensus protocol, as shown in Fig. 6.6b, the involved clusters, e.g., A_2 and A_3, maintain different shards of a local data collection, e.g., d_A. Upon receiving a valid request message m, the primary $\pi(P_i)$ of the initiator cluster P_i assigns ID_i to the transaction and multicasts a propose message $\mu = \langle \text{PROPOSE}, \text{ID}_i, d, m\rangle_{\sigma_{\pi(P_i)}}$ to all nodes of every involved cluster. Upon receiving a valid propose message, each primary node $\pi(P_j)$ of an involved cluster P_j multicasts $\langle \text{ACCEPT}, \text{ID}_i, \text{ID}_j, d, d_\mu\rangle_{\sigma_{\pi(P_j)}}$ to the nodes of its cluster where ID_j represents the order of m on the data shard of cluster P_j. The digest of the propose message, $d_\mu = D(\mu)$, is added to link the accept message with the corresponding propose message enabling nodes to detect changes and alterations to any part of the message. The primary of the initiator and all involved clusters process the request only if there is no (concurrent) uncommitted request m' where m and m' intersect in at least two shards. This is needed to ensure that requests are committed in different shards in the same order (global consistency) [13].

Each node r (including the primary) of an involved cluster P_j then multicasts a signed accept message $\langle \text{ACCEPT}, \text{ID}_i, \text{ID}_j, d, r\rangle_{\sigma_r}$ to all nodes of every involved cluster. Upon receiving valid matching accept messages from the local-majority of all involved clusters $P_i, P_j, ..., P_k$, each node r multicasts a $\langle \text{COMMIT}, \text{ID}_i, \text{ID}_j, ..., \text{ID}_k, d, r\rangle_{\sigma_r}$ message to every node of all involved clusters.

Upon receiving valid matching commit messages from the local-majority of every involved cluster, the node generates a commit certificate. The transaction execution routine then executes the transaction and appends the transaction to the ledger.

In this protocol, since all clusters belong to the same enterprise, if the nodes of all involved clusters are crash-only, Qanaat processes transactions more efficiently. In that case, and upon receiving $\langle \text{PROPOSE}, \text{ID}_i, d, m\rangle_{\sigma_{\pi(P_i)}}$ from the initiator primary $\pi(P_i)$, the primary node of each involved cluster P_j assigns ID_j to the transaction and multicasts an accept message to the ordering nodes of its cluster. Nodes of each involved cluster then send an accept message to *only* the initiator primary (in contrast to the previous protocol where nodes multicast accept messages to all nodes of every involved cluster). The initiator primary waits for $f + 1$ valid matching accept messages from different nodes of every involved cluster and multicasts a commit message to every node of all involved clusters.

Once an ordering node receives a valid commit message from the initiator primary, it considers the transaction as committed.

Cross-Shard Cross-Enterprise Consensus

The cross-shard cross-enterprise consensus protocol is needed when a transaction is executed on different shards of a non-local data collection shared between different enterprises, e.g., a transaction that is executed on data shards d^1_{BC} and d^2_{BC} of shared data collection d_{BC} where d^1_{BC} is maintained by B_1 and C_1 and d^2_{BC} is maintained by B_2 and C_2 (Fig. 6.6(c)).

In this case, the different clusters of each enterprise maintain different data shards, e.g., B_1 and B_2 maintain d^1_{BC} and d^2_{BC}; however, each data shard is replicated on only one cluster of each involved enterprise, e.g., d^1_{BC} is replicated on B_1 and C_1. In Qanaat, in order to improve performance, only the clusters of the initiator enterprise, e.g., B_1 and B_2, establish consensus on the transaction order and clusters of other enterprises, e.g., C_1 and C_2, validate the order.

The primary node $\pi(P_i)$ of the initiator cluster P_i multicasts a signed propose message $\mu = \langle \text{PROPOSE}, \text{ID}_i, d, m\rangle_{\sigma_{\pi(P_i)}}$ to the nodes of all involved clusters. Upon receiving a valid propose message, each primary node $\pi(P_j)$ of an involved cluster P_j belonging to the initiator enterprise assigns an $\texttt{ID}_j$ to the transaction and multicasts a signed $\langle \text{ACCEPT}, \text{ID}_i, \text{ID}_j, d, d_\mu\rangle_{\sigma_{\pi(P_j)}}$ message to all the nodes of its cluster *and* all other clusters that maintain the same data shard. As before, primary nodes ensure consistency (i.e., no concurrent request with more than one shared shard) before processing a request. The accept and commit phases process the transaction in the same way as cross-shard intra-enterprise protocol.

Primary Failure Handling

We use the retransmission routine presented in [16] to handle unreliable communication between ordering nodes and execution nodes. In this section, we focus on the failure of the primary ordering node. If the timer of node r expires before it receives a commit certificate, it suspects that the primary might be faulty. When the primary node of a cluster fails, the primary failure handling routine of the internal consensus protocol, e.g., view-change in PBFT, is triggered by timeouts to elect a new primary.

While in the intra-shard cross-enterprise consensus, only the failure of the initiator primary node needs to be handled, in the second and third protocols, the primary node of any of the involved clusters that assign an `ID`, i.e., belongs to the initiator enterprise, might fail. In the intra-shard cross-enterprise consensus, if the timer of node r expires and r belongs to the initiator cluster, it initiates the failure handling routine of the internal consensus protocol, e.g., view-change in PBFT. Otherwise, if the node is in some other involved cluster, it multicasts a commit-query message including the request `ID` and its digest to the nodes of the initiator cluster. If nodes of the initiator cluster receive commit-query from the local-majority of an involved cluster for a request, they suspect their primary is faulty and did not send consistent propose messages. Nodes also log the query messages to detect denial-of-service attacks initiated by malicious nodes.

In the second and third protocols, each transaction needs to be ordered by the initiator primary as well as the primary nodes of all clusters belonging to the initiator enterprise (i.e., which maintain different data shards). Suppose a malicious primary node (from the initiator or an involved cluster) sends a request with inconsistent `ID` to different nodes. In that case, nodes detect the failure in all-to-all communication phases of the protocol triggering the primary failure handling routine within the faulty primary cluster. Note that since propose and accept messages need to be multicast to all nodes, and all nodes of all involved clusters multicast accept and commit messages to each other, even if a malicious primary decides not to multicast a request to a group of nodes, it will be easily detected.

Finally, if a client does not receive a reply soon enough, it multicasts its request message to all ordering nodes of the cluster that it has already sent its request. If an ordering node has both the commit certificate (i.e., the request has already been ordered) and the reply certificate (i.e., the request has already been executed), the node simply sends the reply certificate to the client. If the node has not received the reply certificate, it re-sends the commit certificate to the filter nodes. Otherwise, if the node is not the primary, it relays the request to the primary. If the nodes do not receive propose messages, the primary will be suspected to be faulty.

Correctness Argument

We briefly analyze the agreement and liveness properties of the flattened protocols. Validity and consistency are proven in the same way as coordinator-based protocols.

Lemma 6.1 (Agreement) *If node r commits request m with local* $\texttt{ID}\,\alpha$ *in cluster P, no other non-faulty node commits request* m' $(m \neq m')$ *with the same local* $\texttt{ID}\,\alpha$ *in P.*

Proof The propose and accept phases of each presented consensus protocol guarantee that all non-faulty nodes agree on the order of a transaction. To commit a request, matching messages from the local-majority of every involved cluster are needed. Given two requests m with local $\texttt{ID}$ α and m' with local $\texttt{ID}$ α' where local-majority Q agreed with m and local-majority Q' agreed with m'. Let m and m' $(m \neq m')$ be two committed requests where $\texttt{ID}(m) = [\texttt{ID}_i, \texttt{ID}_j, \texttt{ID}_k, ...]$ and $\texttt{ID}(m') = [\texttt{ID}'_k, \texttt{ID}'_l, \texttt{ID}'_m, ..]$, respectively. Note that in intra-shard transactions, the $\texttt{ID}$ includes a single part. Given an involved cluster P_k in the intersection of m and m' where $\texttt{ID}_k(m) = \langle \alpha, \gamma \rangle$ and $\texttt{ID}_k(m') = \langle \alpha', \gamma' \rangle$. To commit m and m', a local-majority Q agreed with m and local-majority Q' agreed with m'. Since Q and Q' intersect on at least one non-faulty node and non-faulty nodes do not behave maliciously, if $m \neq m'$ then $\alpha \neq \alpha'$, hence agreement is guaranteed. □

Lemma 6.2 (Liveness) *A request m issued by a correct client eventually completes.*

Proof Qanaat guarantees liveness *only* during periods of synchrony. If the primary of a cluster that needs to order the request and assign $\texttt{ID}$ is faulty, as explained in Sect. 6.4.4, its failure will be detected using timers and Qanaat uses the primary failure handling routine of the internal consensus protocol to elect a new primary. As explained for the coordinator-based protocols, nodes use different timers for intra-cluster and cross-cluster transactions where the timer for cross-cluster transactions is long enough to allow nodes to communicate with each other and establish consensus, i.e., at least three times the WAN round-trip for cross-cluster transactions to allow a view-change routine to complete without replacing the primary node again. If a newly elected leader is not able to change the view, the timeout is doubled (as in PBFT [50]). This adjustment is needed to ensure that some transactions will be committed, i.e., nodes are synchronized. The deadlock situation is addressed in the same way as the coordinator-based protocols. □

6.5 Summary

In this chapter, we extend the notion of confidentiality presented in Chap. 5 by presenting Qanaat, a permissioned blockchain system to support the scalability and confidentiality requirements of multi-enterprise applications. To guarantee collaboration confidentiality, Qanaat constructs a hierarchical data model consisting of a set of data collections for each collaboration workflow. Every subset of enterprises is able to form a confidential collaboration private from other enterprises and execute transactions on a private data collection shared between only the involved enterprises. To prevent confidential data leakage, Qanaat utilizes the privacy firewall mechanism [16]. To support scalability, each enterprise partitions its data into different data shards. Qanaat further presents a transaction ordering scheme that enforces only the necessary and sufficient constraints to guarantee data consistency. Finally, a suite of consensus protocols is presented to process different types of intra-shard and cross-shard transactions within and across enterprises.

References

1. Korpela, K., Hallikas, J., Dahlberg, T.: Digital supply chain transformation toward blockchain integration. In: Hawaii International Conference on System Sciences (HICSS) (2017)
2. Amiri, M.J., Duguépéroux, J., Allard, T., Agrawal, D., El Abbadi, A.: Separ: Towards regulating future of work multi-platform crowdworking environments with privacy guarantees. In: The Web Conference (WWW), pp. 1891–1903 (2021)
3. Azaria, A., Ekblaw, A., Vieira, T., Lippman, A.: Medrec: using blockchain for medical data access and permission management. In: International Conference on Open and Big Data (OBD), pp. 25–30. IEEE (2016)
4. Hyperledger: Private data collections: a high-level overview. https://www.hyperledger.org/blog/2018/10/23/private-data-collections-a-high-level-overview
5. Androulaki, E., Barger, A., Bortnikov, V., Cachin, C., Christidis, K., De Caro, A., Enyeart, D., Ferris, C., Laventman, G., Manevich, Y.: Hyperledger fabric: a distributed operating system for permissioned blockchains. In: European Conference on Computer Systems (EuroSys), pp. 30:1–30:15. ACM (2018)
6. Gorenflo, C., Lee, S., Golab, L., Keshav, S.: Fastfabric: scaling hyperledger fabric to 20,000 transactions per second. In: International Conference on Blockchain and Cryptocurrency (ICBC), pp. 455–463. IEEE (2019)
7. Gorenflo, C., Golab, L., Keshav, S.: Xox fabric: a hybrid approach to transaction execution. In: International Conference on Blockchain and Cryptocurrency (ICBC), pp. 1–9. IEEE (2020)
8. Sharma, A., Schuhknecht, F.M., Agrawal, D., Dittrich, J.: Blurring the lines between blockchains and database systems: the case of hyperledger fabric. In: SIGMOD International Conference on Management of Data, pp. 105–122. ACM (2019)
9. Ruan, P., Loghin, D., Ta, Q.T., Zhang, M., Chen, G., Ooi, B.C.: A transactional perspective on execute-order-validate blockchains. In: SIGMOD International Conference on Management of Data, pp. 543–557. ACM (2020)
10. Androulaki, E., Cachin, C., De Caro, A., Kokoris-Kogias, E.: Channels: horizontal scaling and confidentiality on permissioned blockchains. In: European Symposium on Research in Computer Security (ESORICS), pp. 111–131. Springer (2018)
11. Amiri, M.J., Agrawal, D., El Abbadi, A.: CAPER: a cross-application permissioned blockchain. Proc. VLDB Endowment **12**(11), 1385–1398 (2019)

12. Dang, H., Dinh, T.T.A., Loghin, D., Chang, E.C., Lin, Q., Ooi, B.C.: Towards scaling blockchain systems via sharding. In: SIGMOD International Conference on Management of Data, pp. 123–140. ACM (2019)
13. Amiri, M.J., Agrawal, D., El Abbadi, A.: SharPer: sharding permissioned blockchains over network clusters. In: SIGMOD International Conference on Management of Data, pp. 76–88. ACM (2021)
14. Gupta, S., Rahnama, S., Hellings, J., Sadoghi, M.: Resilientdb: global scale resilient blockchain fabric. Proc. VLDB Endowment **13**(6), 868–883 (2020)
15. Amiri, M.J., Loo, B.T., Agrawal, D., El Abbadi, A.: Qanaat: a scalable multi-enterprise permissioned blockchain system with confidentiality guarantees. Proc. VLDB Endowment **15**(11), 2839–2852 (2022)
16. Yin, J., Martin, J.P., Venkataramani, A., Alvisi, L., Dahlin, M.: Separating agreement from execution for byzantine fault tolerant services. Oper. Syst. Rev. (OSR) **37**(5), 253–267 (2003)
17. Duan, S., Zhang, H.: Practical state machine replication with confidentiality. In: Symposium on Reliable Distributed Systems (SRDS), pp. 187–196. IEEE (2016)
18. Alam, S.T., Ahmed, S., Ali, S.M., Sarker, S., Kabir, G., et al.: Challenges to covid-19 vaccine supply chain: implications for sustainable development goals. Int. J. Prod. Econ. **239**, 108193 (2021)
19. Patterson, D.: Hackers are attacking the covid-19 vaccine supply chain (2021). https://www.cbsnews.com/news/covid-19-vaccine-hackers-supply-chain/
20. Stone, J.: How counterfeit covid-19 vaccines and vaccination cards endanger us all (2021). https://www.forbes.com/sites/judystone/2021/03/31/how-counterfeit-covid-19-vaccines-and-vaccination-cards-endanger-us-all/?sh=eaddb0e36495
21. Reilly, S., Paladino, J., Lambert, J., Stiles, M.: Fake vaccine cards are everywhere. It's a public health nightmare (2022). https://www.grid.news/story/science/2022/01/25/fake-vaccine-cards-are-everywhere-its-a-public-health-nightmare/
22. Bruggeman, L., Pezenik, S.: Emergent biosolutions discarded ingredients for 400 million covid-19 vaccines, probe finds (2022). https://abcnews.go.com/US/emergent-biosolutions-discarded-ingredients-400-million-covid-19/story?id=84604285
23. Aborode, A.T., Awuah, W.A., Talukder, S., Oyeyemi, A.A., Nansubuga, E.P., Machai, P., Tillewein, H., Oko, C.I.: Fake covid-19 vaccinations in Africa. Postgrad. Med. J. **98**(1159), 317–318 (2022)
24. Choudhary, O.P., Priyanka, Singh, I., Mohammed, T.A., Rodriguez-Morales, A.J.: Fake covid-19 vaccines: scams hampering the vaccination drive in India and possibly other countries. Hum. Vaccines Immunother., 1–2 (2021)
25. World Health Organization: Medical product alert n°5/2021: Falsified covishield vaccine (2021). https://www.who.int/news/item/31-08-2021-medical-product-alert-n-5-2021-falsified-covishield-vaccine
26. Schiffling, S., Valantasis Kanellos, N.: Shanghai: world's biggest port is returning to normal, but supply chains will get worse before they get better (2022). https://theconversation.com/shanghai-worlds-biggest-port-is-returning-to-normal-but-supply-chains-will-get-worse/before-they-get-better-182720
27. Benigno, G., di Giovanni, J., Groen, J.J., Noble, A.: Global supply chain pressure index: May 2022 update (2022). https://libertystreeteconomics.newyorkfed.org/2022/05/global-supply-chain-pressure-index-may-2022-update/
28. BBC News: Coronavirus: pfizer confirms fake versions of vaccine in Poland and Mexico (2021). https://www.bbc.com/news/world-56844149
29. Amankwah-Amoah, J.: Covid-19 and counterfeit vaccines: global implications, new challenges and opportunities. Health Policy Technol., 100630 (2022)

30. Owen, P.: Vaccine supply under threat from theft and counterfeits (2021). https://www.ttclub.com/news-and-resources/news/press-releases/2021/vaccine-supply-under-threat-from-theft-and-counterfeits/
31. World Health Organization et al.: A study on the public health and socioeconomic impact of substandard and falsified medical products (2017)
32. Vaccines Europe (VE): Vaccines manufacturing: how are vaccines produced? (2016) https://www.vaccineseurope.eu/about-vaccines/how-are-vaccines-produced
33. Dwork, C., Lynch, N., Stockmeyer, L.: Consensus in the presence of partial synchrony. J. ACM (JACM) **35**(2), 288–323 (1988)
34. Dolev, D., Dwork, C., Stockmeyer, L.: On the minimal synchronism needed for distributed consensus. J. ACM (JACM) **34**(1), 77–97 (1987)
35. Evans, D., Kolesnikov, V., Rosulek, M.: A pragmatic introduction to secure multi-party computation. Found. Trends® Priv. Secur.**2**(2–3) (2017)
36. Archer, D.W., Bogdanov, D., Lindell, Y., Kamm, L., Nielsen, K., Pagter, J.I., Smart, N.P., Wright, R.N.: From keys to databases-real-world applications of secure multi-party computation. Comput. J. **61**(12), 1749–1771 (2018)
37. Kosba, A., Papamanthou, C., Shi, E.: xjsnark: a framework for efficient verifiable computation. In: IEEE Symposium on Security and Privacy (SP), pp. 944–961. IEEE (2018)
38. Maller, M., Bowe, S., Kohlweiss, M., Meiklejohn, S.: Sonic: zero-knowledge snarks from linear-size universal and updatable structured reference strings. In: Conference on Computer and Communications Security (CCS), pp. 2111–2128. ACM (2019)
39. Gabizon, A., Williamson, Z.J.: Plonk: permutations over lagrange-bases for oecumenical non-interactive arguments of knowledge (2019)
40. Zakhary, V., Agrawal, D., El Abbadi, A.: Atomic commitment across blockchains. Proc. VLDB Endowment **13**, 1319–1331 (2020)
41. Herlihy, M., Liskov, B., Shrira, L.: Cross-chain deals and adversarial commerce (2019). arXiv preprint arXiv:1905.09743
42. Bracha, G., Toueg, S.: Asynchronous consensus and broadcast protocols. J. ACM (JACM) **32**(4), 824–840 (1985)
43. Khan, M., Babay, A.: Toward intrusion tolerance as a service: confidentiality in partially cloud-based bft systems. In: International Conference on Dependable Systems and Networks (DSN), pp. 14–25. IEEE (2021)
44. Vassantlal, R., Alchieri, E., Ferreira, B., Bessani, A.: Cobra: dynamic proactive secret sharing for confidential bft services. In: Symposium on Security and Privacy (SP), pp. 1528–1528. IEEE (2022)
45. Padilha, R., Pedone, F.: Belisarius: BFT storage with confidentiality. In: 2011 IEEE 10th International Symposium on Network Computing and Applications, pp. 9–16. IEEE (2011)
46. Bessani, A.N., Alchieri, E.P., Correia, M., Fraga, J.S.: Depspace: a byzantine fault-tolerant coordination service. In: European Conference on Computer Systems (EuroSys), pp. 163–176 (2008)
47. Marsh, M.A., Schneider, F.B.: Codex: a robust and secure secret distribution system. Trans. Dependable Secure Comput. **1**(1), 34–47 (2004)
48. Bessani, A., Correia, M., Quaresma, B., André, F., Sousa, P.: Depsky: dependable and secure storage in a cloud-of-clouds. Trans. Storage (TOS) **9**(4), 12 (2013)
49. Fischer, M.J., Lynch, N.A., Paterson, M.S.: Impossibility of distributed consensus with one faulty process. J. ACM (JACM) **32**(2), 374–382 (1985)
50. Castro, M., Liskov, B.: Practical byzantine fault tolerance. In: Symposium on Operating Systems Design and Implementation (OSDI), pp. 173–186. USENIX Association (1999)
51. Amiri, M.J., Lai, Z., Patel, L., Loo, B.T., Lo, E., Zhou, W.: Saguaro: an edge computing-enabled hierarchical permissioned blockchain. In: International Conference on Data Engineering (ICDE), pp. 259–272. IEEE (2023)

52. Nawab, F., Sadoghi, M.: Blockplane: a global-scale byzantizing middleware. In: International Conference on Data Engineering (ICDE), pp. 124–135. IEEE (2019)
53. Lamport, L.: Paxos made simple. ACM SIGACT News **32**(4), 18–25 (2001)

Verifiability 7

7.1 Introduction

The rise of the "gig" or *platform economy* [1, 2] is reshaping work all around the world. Crowdsourcing platforms dedicated to work (also called *crowdworking platforms* [3]) are online intermediaries between *requesters* and *workers*, where requesters propose *tasks* while *workers* propose skills and time. By providing requesters (resp. workers) 24/7 access to a worldwide workforce (resp. worldwide task market), crowdworking platforms have grown in numbers, diversity, and adoption.[1] Today, crowdworkers come from countries spread all over the world, and work on several, possibly competing, platforms [3]. The use of crowdworking platforms is expected to continue growing [4], and in fact, they are envisioned as key technological components of the future of work [5–7].

Crowdworking platforms, however, challenge national boundaries and weaken the formal relationships between the platforms, workers and task requesters. Guaranteeing the compliance of crowdworking platforms with national or regional labor laws is hard[2] [4] despite the stringent need for regulating work. For example, the preamble of the 1919 constitution of the International Labor Organization [8], written in the ruins of World War I, states that: *"Whereas universal and lasting peace can be established only if it is based upon social justice; (...) an improvement of those conditions is urgently required; as, for example, by the regulation of the hours of work, including the establishment of a maximum working day and week, the regulation of the labor supply (...)".* The total work hours of a worker per week

[1] See for example: Amazon Mechanical Turk (https://www.mturk.com/), Wirk (https://www.wirk.io/), or Appen (https://appen.com/) for micro-tasks, Uber (https://www.uber.com/) or Lyft (https://www.lyft.com/) for rides, TaskRabbit (https://www.taskrabbit.com/) for home maintenance, Kicklox (https://www.kicklox.com/) for collaborative engineering.

[2] See, e.g., the `Otey V Crowdflower` class action against a famous microtask platform for "*sub-standard wages and oppressive working hours*" (http://casetext.com/case/otey-v-crowdflower-1).

M. J. Amiri et al., *Blockchain-Enabled Large-Scale Transaction Management*,
Synthesis Lectures on Data Management,
https://doi.org/10.1007/978-3-031-91058-6_7

may not exceed 40 hours to follow *Fair Labor Standards Act*[3] (FLSA). The global regulation of the work hours represents the *minimal* and *maximal* number of hours that participants, i.e., worker, requester, and platform, can spend on crowdworking platforms. While legal tools are currently being investigated [4, 9], there is a stringent need for technical tools allowing official institutions to enforce regulations.

Some platforms have already started implementing self-defined *local regulations*. For example, Uber[4] and Lyft[5] force drivers to rest at least 6 h for every 12 h in driver mode, or Wirk.io[6] prevent micro-workers from earning more than 3000 euros per year. However, since workers and requesters can simply switch platforms when a local limit is reached, no global cross-platform regulation can be enforced. Moreover, participants in a crowdworking task may also behave maliciously or act as adversaries, e.g., violate the privacy of participants or the regulations for their benefits. The privacy of participants and the global consistency of regulations are considered as critical needs for future of work crowdworking environments [6].

Most current crowdworking platforms are independent of each other. However, the emergence of complex tasks that may need multiple contributions from possibly different platforms, on one hand, and more importantly, the enforcement of legal regulations, on the other hand, highlights the need for collaboration between crowdworking platforms, thus resulting in *multi-platform crowdworking systems*. For example, many drivers work for both Uber and Lyft concurrently,[7] while a requester may also request multiple rides from both Uber and Lyft concurrently. The observation holds also for on-demand services,[8] as well as microtask platforms [3] where a requester who has registered on *Amazon Mechanical Turk* and *Prolific* might need hundreds of contributions for a single microtask at the same time and accept these contributions from workers regardless of the platforms the microtasks are performed on. Since workers from different platforms might want to perform these contributions, the system needs to establish consensus among the various microtask platforms to assign workers and provide the specified number of contributions while ensuring minimal and maximum hourly regulations on workers without revealing any private information about the workers to competing platforms.

Our overall vision for multi-platform crowdworking environments needs to address three main dimensions: *regulations*, *privacy*, and *architecture*. First, a multi-platform crowdworking system must clearly define the *types of regulations* supported in terms of the *complexity* of the regulation (e.g., a simple or a chain of interactions) as well as the *aggregate* requirements of the regulation (e.g., no aggregation or `SUM` aggregations). For example, California

---

[3] https://www.dol.gov/agencies/whd/flsa.

[4] https://www.uber.com/en-ZA/blog/driving-hours-limit/.

[5] https://help.lyft.com/hc/articles/115012926787-Taking-breaks-and-time-limits.

[6] https://www.wirk.io/50k-freelances-en-france/.

[7] For example, `rideshareapps.com` provides tutorials to help drivers manage apps to optimize their earnings https://rideshareapps.com/drive-for-uber-and-lyft-at-the-same-time/.

[8] See, e.g., https://tinyurl.com/nytgigmult.

Proposition 22, which states "if a driver works at least 25 hours per week, companies (i.e., platforms) require to provide healthcare subsidies ...", is a simple, SUM-aggregate regulation. Second, the threat model (e.g., *honest-but-curious*, *covert*, *fully malicious*) as well as the privacy guarantees provided to each entity must be clearly specified. Finally, from an architecture design point of view, any multi-platform crowdworking environment consists of two critical components: *regulation management* that models and enforces regulations and *global state management* that manages the global states of all participants as well as tasks. Each of these components can be implemented in a centralized or decentralized approach.

This chapter presents a vision for the future of work multi-platform crowdworking environments together with Separ [10] a possible instance of a precise point in the design space of multi-platform crowdworking systems. Separ results from choices, guided by cutting-edge real-life regulation proposals, on all three regulations, privacy and architecture dimensions of the design space. First, Separ focuses on managing lower and upper bounds on aggregate-based regulations. Second, Separ considers that any participant in a crowdworking environment may act as a *covert adversary* [11] and ensures that no participant obtains or infers any information about a crowdworking task beyond what is strictly needed for accomplishing its local crowdworking task and for the distributed enforcement of regulations. Finally, in Separ, we opted for simplicity and rapid prototyping by using a centralized (but fault-tolerant) component to manage regulations. However, we use a decentralized component to manage the global state of the system. In particular, Separ uses a *permissioned blockchain* as an underlying infrastructure that is shared among all involved platforms.

The complexity of the conjunction of the required properties makes the problem non-trivial. First, the regulations need to be expressed in a *simple* and *non-ambiguous* manner. Second, while enforcing regulations over multiple crowdworking platforms requires the global state of the system to be *transparent*, the *privacy* of participants needs to be preserved, hence Separ needs to reconcile *transparency* with *privacy*. Finally, the decentralized management of the global state among a distributed set of crowdworking platforms requires distributed consensus protocols.

Separ is a two-level solution consisting of a *privacy-preserving token-based system* (i.e., the application level) on top of a *blockchain ledger* shared across platforms (i.e., the infrastructure level). First, at the application level, global regulations are modeled using *lightweight and anonymous tokens* distributed to workers, platforms, and requesters. The information shared among platforms and participants is limited to the minimum necessary for performing the tasks against *adversarial participants acting as covert adversaries*. Second, at the infrastructure level, the blockchain ledger allows Separ to provide transparency across platforms. Nonetheless, for the sake of privacy and to improve performance, the ledger is *not maintained* by any platform and each platform maintains only a view of the ledger. We then design a suite of consensus protocols for coping with the concurrency issues inherent to a multi-platform context. Salient features of Separ include the simplicity of its building blocks (e.g., usual signature schemes) and its compatibility with today's platforms (e.g., it does not jeopardize their privacy requirements of requesters and workers for enforcing the regulation).

In a nutshell, the contributions of this chapter are two-folds:

1. A vision for the design space of regulation systems for the future of work multi-platform crowdworking environments. In particular, we (1) express regulations as SQL constraints and categorize them according to their SQL expression, (2) propose a formal privacy model for multi-platform regulated crowdworking systems based on the well-known simulatability paradigm, and (3) discuss critical components of their architecture.
2. Separ, a two-level *privacy-preserving transparent* multi-platform proof-of-concept crowdworking system that enforces a precise point in the design space guided by cutting-edge practical regulations currently discussed by societal organizations, legal entities and enterprises. Separ uses a simple language for expressing *global regulations* and mapping them to SQL constraints to ensure semantic clarity. It ensures privacy using *lightweight and anonymous tokens*, while transparency is achieved using a *blockchain* shared across platforms for both crash-only and Byzantine nodes.

The chapter is organized as follows. The overall vision of the design space for regulation systems is presented in Sect. 7.2. Section 7.3 presents the Separ model within the design space. The implementation of regulations in Separ is discussed in Sect. 7.4. The blockchain ledger and consensus protocols are presented in Sects. 7.5, and 7.6 concludes the chapter.

7.2 Design Space of Regulation Systems

Designing a system for regulating crowdworking platforms mandates three main choices. First, given the large variety of regulations that apply to working environments, any given regulation system must clearly define the *types of regulations* it supports. Second, a crowdworking environment involves a set of distributed entities (platforms, workers, requesters) that cannot fully trusted each other. The *privacy guarantees* provided to each entity must be rigorously stated (e.g., computational guarantees). Third, the distributed nature of a crowdworking environment requires various *architectural choices* that range from fully decentralized approaches (e.g., peer-to-peer architectures) to the traditional centralized architecture. In this section, we first define the crowdworking environment that we consider and then characterize the design space for crowdworking regulation systems.

7.2.1 Crowdworking Environment

A *crowdworking environment* consists of a set of workers $\mathcal{W}$ interacting with a set of requesters $\mathcal{R}$ through a set of competing platforms $\mathcal{P}$. We refer to the workers, platforms, and requesters of a crowdworking environment as *participants*. Each worker $w \in \mathcal{W}$ (1) registers to one or more platforms $\mathcal{P}_w \subset \mathcal{P}$ according to her preferences and, through the latter, (2) accesses the set of tasks available on $\mathcal{P}_w$, (3) submits each *contribution* to the platform $p \in \mathcal{P}_w$ she elects, and (4) obtains a *reward* for her work. On the other hand, each requester $r \in \mathcal{R}$ similarly (1) registers to one or more platforms $\mathcal{P}_r \subset \mathcal{P}$, (2) issues a *submission* which contains her tasks $\mathcal{T}_r$ to one or more platforms $p \in \mathcal{P}_r$, (3) receives the contributions of each worker w registered to $\mathcal{P}_r \cap \mathcal{P}_w$ having elected a task $t \in \mathcal{T}_r$, and (4) launches the distribution of rewards. Platforms are thus in charge of facilitating the interactions between workers and requesters. A *crowdworking process* π connects three participants—a workers w, a platform p, and a requester r—and aims to facilitate the execution of a task $t \in \mathcal{T}_r$ through platform p via a worker w. For simplicity and without loss of generality, we assume that each process corresponds to a time unit of work (e.g., 1 hour). Figure 7.1 shows a crowdworking infrastructure with four platforms, four workers and four requesters.

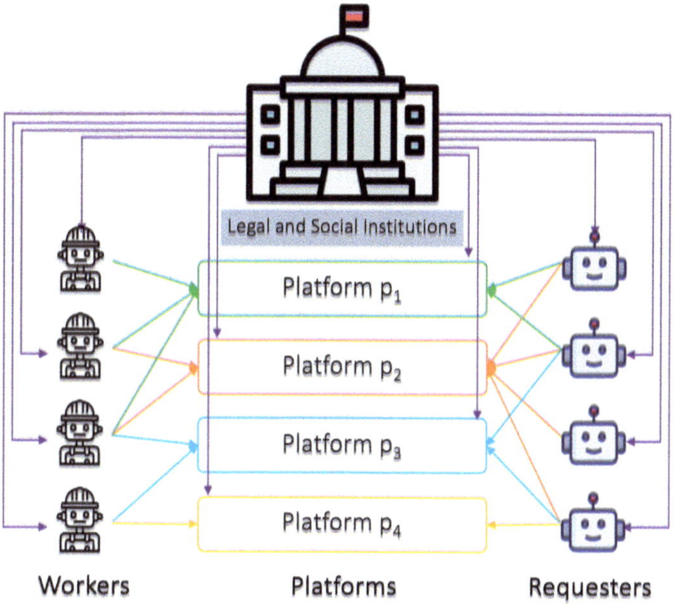

Fig. 7.1 A crowdworking infrastructure with four platforms, four workers, and four requesters. Each requester can send its requests to multiple platforms and each worker can work for multiple platforms

7.2.2 Types of Regulation

The space of possible regulations can be structured based on two orthogonal dimensions: the *complexity* of the regulation, e.g., constraints on a single process versus constraints that apply to multiple processes that are transitively related, and the *aggregate* nature of the regulation, e.g., no aggregation versus restrictions involving `SUM` aggregate.

In order to give a clear semantics to each dimension and to rigorously map regulations to points in this space, we express regulations by `SQL` constraints over a *universal virtual table* storing information about all crowdworking processes having been performed. We denote this table by `U-TABLE` and emphasize that it is *virtual* (we use it only for clarifying the various types of regulations, it is never instantiated). The attributes of `U-TABLE` refer to meta-data about the interactions (i.e., at least the worker, requester, and platform involved in a process, and also possibly additional metadata such as begin and end timestamps) and information about the contents (e.g., the time estimate for the task[9]—the `TIMECOST` attribute below, the proposed wage, the worker's contribution). For simplicity, we focus below on the attributes of the `U-TABLE` relevant to our illustrative examples: (1) `TS_BEGIN`, `TS_END`, `WORKER`, `PLATFORM`, and `REQUESTER`, and (2) `TIMECOST`, `WAGE`, and `CONTRIBUTION`. Finally, a regulation is simply a Boolean `SQL` expression nested within the usual `CHECK` clause: `ALTER TABLE U ADD CONSTRAINT r CHECK ( ... )`.

The complexity and aggregate dimensions of a regulation can both be deduced from its `SQL` expression. The complexity is given by the presence of *join* operations while the aggregate dimension is given by the presence of *aggregate* function(s), possibly with `GROUP BY` and `HAVING` clause(s). For simplicity, we consider a coarse grain characterization of these two dimensions. A regulation is `simple` if there is no join and `complex` otherwise. A regulation is `row-only` if it does not involve any aggregate function, `aggregate-only` if it involves only comparison(s) over aggregate(s), and `mixed` if it involves comparisons over rows and aggregates.

We illustrate the possible types of regulations based on simple examples extracted from real-life crowdworking regulations or from real-life proposals of regulation. First, we consider a regulation r_1 requiring the wage proposed by each task to be at least a given amount θ. It illustrates the (`simple`, `row-only`) type of regulation.

```
ALTER TABLE U-TABLE ADD CONSTRAINT r1 CHECK (
  NOT EXISTS (
    SELECT * FROM U
    WHERE TIMECOST ≤ θ
  ) );
```

[9] Future regulation systems will need to design technical means to guarantee the reliability of the time estimates for tasks (e.g., privacy-preserving feedback systems from workers, automatic time estimation by analyzing task descriptions).

Second, we consider a regulation r_2 requiring each worker to work at most a given amount of time units θ per time period ρ. It illustrates the (simple, mixed with SUM-aggregate) type of regulation. It is similar to the regulation followed by the wirk.io platform that limits the crowdworking gains of any worker on the platform to 3000 euros per year. The following SQL constraint expresses r_2, assuming that current_time() gives the current time in the same unit as the period ρ.

```
ALTER TABLE U-TABLE ADD CONSTRAINT r2 CHECK (
  NOT EXISTS (
    SELECT * FROM U
    WHERE WORKER=w AND current_time()-TS_BEGIN ≤ ρ
    GROUP BY WORKER
    HAVING SUM(TIMECOST) ≥ θ
  ) );
```

Finally, we complete our illustrations by considering a regulation r_3 that prevents any worker to submit two similar contributions to the same requester (even through two distinct platforms). We assume that the sim function computes the similarity between two contributions and that θ is the threshold above which we consider that two contributions are too similar. This illustrates the (complex, row-only) type of regulation.

```
ALTER TABLE U-TABLE ADD CONSTRAINT r3 CHECK (
  NOT EXISTS (
    SELECT *
    FROM U U1 JOIN U U2 ON
        U1.WORKER=U2.WORKER
        AND U1.REQUESTER=U2.REQUESTER
        AND sim(U1.CONTRIBUTION, U2.CONTRIBUTION) ≥ θ
  ) );
```

Although most regulations must always hold (e.g., a lower than constraint on a (simple, SUM-aggregate) regulation, a (complex, row-only) regulation), some regulations, inherently, *cannot* always hold. Similar to deferred SQL constraints, they must only hold after a given time period. For example, a periodic greater than constraint on a (simple, SUM-aggregate) regulation cannot hold initially, but must hold at the end of a given period (e.g., a constraint that requires a worker to work at least 25 h per week to qualify for healthcare subsidies). We call *enforceable* the regulations that must always hold and *verifiable* the regulations that eventually hold. The verifiable/enforceable property of a regulation is only due to its nature not to its implementation (but it impacts it directly). Future crowdworking regulation systems need to determine the enforceable/verifiable properties of the regulations they support.

7.2.3 Threat Model and Privacy Model

Crowdworking environments are open environments that connect possibly adversarial participants. Any regulation system must clearly specify both the threat model (e.g., *honest-but-curious*, *covert*, *fully malicious*) and the privacy model. While the threat model only depends on the underlying system, the privacy model can be based on a common formal requirement parameterized for each system by the leaks it tolerates. The possible leakage ranges from no information leaked to any participant (similar to usual *secure multi-party computation* algorithms) to full disclosure (of all the information discussed above) to all participants (e.g., in current crowdworking platforms, the underlying system often requires full disclosure to the platform). The disclosures tolerated by future regulation systems will fall within this range.

We formalize below a common privacy model based on the well-known simulatability paradigm often used by secure multi-party computation algorithms. The proposed model guarantees that nothing leaks, with computational guarantees[10], except the *pluggable* system-dependent tolerated *disclosures*.

Consider a crowdworking process π between worker w, platform p, and requester r for solving a task t. The task may have been sent to several platforms and, depending on the underlying crowdworking platforms, might have been accessed by several workers before being picked and solved. The information generated by the execution of π consists, similarly to the information captured by the `U-TABLE`, of information about interactions (e.g., at least w, r, and p, the participants directly involved in π) and information about content (e.g., description of t, contribution, proposed wage). We propose to define the sets of disclosure according to the involvement of a participant in π. Indeed, the platforms not involved in π (i.e., different from p) but that received t may need to learn that t has been completed (e.g., to manage their local copy of the task). Similarly, workers who are not involved in a task t might still need to know that it has been executed, while potentially preserving the privacy of worker w who executed the task. The three sets of disclosures defined below cover all these cases.[11] Future regulation systems have to specify clearly the content of each disclosure set.

- Disclosures to the participants that are **not involved** in π and that have **not received** task t from requester r: $\delta^{\pi}_{\neg R \neg I}$

[10] The majority of data protection techniques used in real-life are based on encryption schemes that provide guarantees against computationally-bounded adversaries but the model can be easily adapted to information theoretic attackers.

[11] This can be extended by tuning the disclosure sets (e.g., by distinguishing the requesters from the platforms in the set of involved participants).

- Disclosures to the platforms and workers that have **received** the task t from r but that are **not involved** in π: $\delta^{\pi}_{R\neg I}$
- Disclosures to the participants that are directly **involved** in π (and have thus **received** task t): δ^{π}_{RI}

Definition 7.1 Let Π be a set of crowdworking processes executed by ς a regulation system over a set of participants. We say that ς is δ^{Π}-*Private* if, for all $\pi \in \Pi$, for all computationally-bounded adversaries $\mathtt{A}$, the sets of disclosures $(\delta^{\pi}_{\neg R\neg I}, \delta^{\pi}_{R\neg I}, \delta^{\pi}_{RI})$, assuming arbitrary background knowledge $\chi \in \{0, 1\}^*$, the distribution representing the adversarial knowledge over the input dataset in the real setting is *computationally indistinguishable* from the distribution representing the adversarial knowledge in an ideal setting in which a trusted third party $\mathtt{cp}$ executes the crowdworking process π of ς:

$$\mathtt{REAL}_{\varsigma,\mathtt{A}(\chi,\delta^{\pi}_{i})}(\mathcal{W}, \mathcal{P}, \mathcal{R}, \mathcal{T}) \overset{c}{\equiv} \mathtt{IDEAL}_{\mathtt{cp},\mathtt{A}(\chi,\delta^{\pi}_{i})}(\mathcal{W}, \mathcal{P}, \mathcal{R}, \mathcal{T})$$

where $i \in \{\neg R\neg I, R\neg I, RI\}$, and $\mathtt{REAL}$ denotes the adversarial knowledge in the real setting and $\mathtt{IDEAL}$ its counterpart in the ideal setting.

7.2.4 Architecture

The architecture of a multi-platform crowdworking system consists of two main building blocks: *Regulation Management* and *Global State Management*. Regulation management *models* the regulations among the participants and *ensures* that the modeled regulations are adhered to by all participants. Global state management, on the other hand, stores the global states of the system including all information related to the participants and tasks. To implement these two components, similar to all distributed systems, either a centralized or a decentralized approach can be employed. Centralization is typically easier to rapid prototype, while requiring additional technologies to ensure fault-tolerance, privacy, and trustworthiness. A decentralized approach, on the other hand, is more compatible with the setting consisting of diverse organizational entities, while resulting in more overhead and complex communication protocols among entities.

The verifiable/enforceable property of a regulation is another architectural challenge. While enforceable regulations could be enforced within the multi-platform system, verifiable regulations might be of interest to an outside entity, e.g., legal courts or insurance companies. In the latter case, the system needs to provide evidence to an outside entity demonstrating that the regulation was adhered to and hence resolve any disputes that may arise.

7.3 Separ: Design Choices

We present Separ as a possible instance of a precise point in the design space of regulation systems. Separ results from choices, guided by cutting-edge real-life regulation proposals, on the three dimensions of the design space: supported regulations, disclosures tolerated, and architecture.

7.3.1 Supported Regulations

Separ focuses on enforcing lower and upper bounds on the aggregated working time spent on crowdworking platforms,[12] a consensual societal need. The necessary information are the participants to crowdworking processes and the (discrete) time estimation of tasks[13]: for Separ, the `U-TABLE` thus consists of the `WORKER`, `PLATFORM`, `REQUESTER`, and `TIMECOST` attributes. Separ does not consider joins. As a result, the kind of regulations supported by Separ is (`simple`, `mixed` with `SUM`-aggregate). The enforceable/verifiable nature of the regulations supported by Separ is easy to determine: lower-than regulations are enforceable because the upper-bound guarantee must always hold, and greater-than regulations are verifiable because the lower-bound guarantee cannot always hold (but will have to hold eventually, e.g., at the end of each time period).

For simplicity, we propose to express such regulations by (1) a triple (w, p, r) that associates a worker w, a platform p, and a requester r, (2) a comparison operator $<$ or $>$, and (3) a threshold value θ (an integer) that defines the lower/upper bound that needs to hold. Intuitively, a regulation $((w, p, r), <, \theta)$ states that there must not be more than θ time spent by worker w on platform p for requester r. We also allow two wildcards to be written in any position of a triple: $*$ and $\forall$. First, the $*$ wildcard allows ignoring one or more elements of a triple.[14] For example, $(*, p, r)$ means the regulation applies to the pair (p, r). A triple may contain up to three $*$ wildcards. An element of a triple that is not a $*$ wildcard is called a *target* of the regulation. Second, the $\forall$ wildcard allows a regulation to express a constraint that must hold for all participants in the same group of participants.[15] For example, $(\forall, p, r)$ represents the following set of triples: $\{(w, p, r)\}, \forall w \in \mathcal{W}$. As a result, enforceable regulations are expressed by $((w, p, r), <, \theta)$ tuples (possibly with wildcards), and verifiable regulations by $((w, p, r), >, \theta)$ tuples (possibly with wildcards).

Examples. The semantics of an enforceable regulation without any wildcard, e.g., $e \leftarrow ((w, p, r), <, 26)$ expressing a higher bound on the number of time units spent (i.e., 25-time units) by worker w for requester r on platform p, is the same as the following `SQL` query:

---

[12] Regulating the wages earned through crowdworking platforms can be dealt with similarly.

[13] Extending regulations with validity periods (e.g., "one week"), is straightforward.

[14] Intuitively, the $*$ wildcard means "whatever".

[15] Intuitively, the $\forall$ wildcard means "for each".

```
ALTER TABLE U-TABLE ADD CONSTRAINT e CHECK (
  NOT EXISTS (
    SELECT * FROM U-TABLE
    WHERE WORKER=w AND PLATFORM=p AND REQUESTER=r
    GROUP BY WORKER, PLATFORM, REQUESTER
    HAVING SUM(TIMECOST) ≥ 26
  ) );
```

The weekly FLSA limit on the total work hours per worker can easily be expressed as $((\forall, *, *), <, 40)$. A social security institution can request each worker w applying for insurance coverage to prove that she worked more than 5 hours: $((w, *, *), >, 5)$ is both necessary and sufficient. Similarly, the regulation $((*, p, *), >, 1000)$ allows a tax institution to require from each platform p applying for a tax refund that the total work hours of all its workers is at least 1000 hours.

7.3.2 Threat Model and Disclosure Sets

Separ considers that any participant in a crowdworking environment (worker, requester, platform) may act as a *covert adversary* [11] that aims at inferring anything that can be inferred from the execution sequence and that is able to deviate from the protocol if no other participant detects it. For simplicity, we assume in Separ that adversarial participants do not collude (although extending Separ to cope with colluding covert adversaries is easy (see Sect. 7.4)).

Consider a crowdworking process π between worker w, platform p, and requester r for solving task t. The information generated by the execution of π consists of the relationship between the three participants (w, p, and r) with the task t. Additionally, we also consider the information that π starts or ends through a starting event BEGIN and an ending event END. They may be determined, for example, by exchanging messages among the participants of π, and may include additional concrete information, e.g., timestamps, IP address. (BEGIN, END, w, p, r, t) denotes the information generated by π. Separ does not leak any information about the worker and the requester involved in π when it is not needed by π. It tolerates the disclosure of the {BEGIN, END} events and of the platform p to all participants, whatever their involvement in π. This allows platforms to share information for enforcing regulations (e.g., check that all participants satisfy the regulations before executing π), and to collaborate for correctly managing cross-platforms tasks. Note that for simplicity we use the same notation δ for disclosures concerning *sets* of crowdworking processes as well.

The resulting disclosure sets of Separ are instantiated as follows:

- The participants that are **not involved** in π and that have **not received** task t from requester r must not learn anything about the worker, the task, and the requester involved in π: $\delta^{\pi}_{\neg R \neg I} = (\texttt{BEGIN}, \texttt{END}, p)$
- The platforms and workers that have **received** task t from r but that are **not involved** in π must be aware that t has been performed (e.g., for not contributing to t) but must not know that it has been performed by worker w: $\delta^{\pi}_{R \neg I} = (\texttt{BEGIN}, \texttt{END}, p, r, t)$
- The participants that are directly **involved** in π (and have thus **received** task t) learn the complete 6-tuple: $\delta^{\pi}_{RI} = (\texttt{BEGIN}, \texttt{END}, w, p, r, t)$

7.3.3 Architecture

Separ has two main components. The centralized *Registration Authority (RA)* and the decentralized *Multi-Platform Infrastructure (MPI)*. Although centralized, the RA can be made fault-tolerant using standard replication [12] techniques. RA registers the participants to the crowdworking environment, models the regulations, and distributes to participants the cryptographic material necessary for enforcing or verifying regulations in a secure manner.

MPI, on the other hand, is a decentralized component that maintains the global state of the system including all operations performed by the participants. This state is maintained within a distributed persistent transparent *ledger*. MPI consists of a set of collaborating crowdworking platforms connected by an asynchronous distributed network. Due to the unique features of blockchains such as transparency, provenance, and fault tolerance, the MPI is implemented as a *permissioned blockchain*.

MPI processes two types of tasks: *internal* and *cross-platform*. Internal tasks are submitted to the ledger of a single platform, whereas cross-platform tasks are submitted to the ledgers of multiple platforms (i.e., involved platforms). Separ does not make any assumptions on the implementation of crowdworking processes by platforms, e.g., task assignment algorithm and workers contribution delivery. However, processing a task (either internal or cross-platform) requires agreement from the involved platform(s). To establish agreement among the nodes within or across platforms, Separ uses *local* and *cross-platform* consensus protocols. Furthermore, in both internal and cross-platform tasks, Separ enables all platforms to check the fulfillment of regulations using a *global* consensus protocol among *all* platforms (irrespective of whether they are involved in the execution of task).

7.4 Separ: Application Level

Separ can be viewed as a *two-level* system consisting of an application level, i.e., *privacy-preserving token-based system*, on top of an infrastructure level, i.e., *blockchain ledger* shared across platforms. This section presents the application level of Separ and Sect. 7.5

presents the infrastructure level. Inspired by e-cash systems, Separ implements both enforceable and verifiable regulations by managing two *budgets* per participant while guaranteeing both privacy and correctness. The overall system is conceptually simple and only relies on the correct use of individual and group signatures. The registration authority (RA, see Sect. 7.3.3) bootstraps Separ, its participants, and refreshes their budgets periodically, but is not involved in the continuous execution of crowdworking processes and their regulations.

7.4.1 Individual and Group Signatures

Workers, requesters, and platforms are all equipped by the registration authority with the following cryptographic material: a pair of *individual* public/private asymmetric keys (e.g., RSA) and a pair of public/private asymmetric *group* keys (e.g., [13]) where the union of all workers forms a group (in the sense of group signatures), the union of all requesters forms another group, and the union of all platforms forms the last group. A group signature scheme respects three main properties [14]: (1) only members of the group can sign messages, (2) the receiver of the signature can verify that it is a valid signature for the group but cannot discover which member of the group computed it, and (3) in case of dispute later on, the signature can be "opened" (with or without the help of the group members) to reveal the identity of the signer. A common way to enforce the third property is to rely on a *group manager* that can add new members to the group or revoke the anonymity of a signature. Instances of such schemes are proposed in [14], but also in [13, 15]. In Separ, we use the protocol proposed in [13] and denote $\sigma_w^g(m)$ the group signature of the worker w (with her group private key) for message m. We use equivalent notations for requester r and platform p (i.e., respectively $\sigma_r^g(m)$ and $\sigma_p^g(m)$). The notation $\sigma_w^i(m)$ is used to refer to an individual asymmetric signature (e.g., RSA) of worker w (with her individual (non-group) private key) for message m. We use equivalent notations for requester r and platform p (i.e., respectively $\sigma_r^i(m)$ and $\sigma_p^i(m)$). The registration authority is the group manager for the three groups (workers $\mathcal{W}$, requesters $\mathcal{R}$, platforms $\mathcal{P}$) and is also equipped with her own individual cryptographic keys for signing her messages : $\sigma_{RA}^i(m)$.

7.4.2 A Simple Token-Based System

To regulate crowdworking processes, our token-based system is defined by five functions: `GENERATE` for initializing the budgets with the correct number of tokens and refilling them, `SPEND` for spending portions of the budgets, `PROVE` for providing proofs for verifying verifiable regulations (e.g., to a third party), `CHECK` for checking whether a given spending is allowed or not, and `ALERT` for reporting dubious spending. Since the execution of these functions changes the global state of the system, the data involved in the execution (e.g., tasks, tokens, signatures) must be appended to the distributed ledger of the platforms.

The GENERATE Function

The registration authority uses the GENERATE function to create tokens for all participants (i.e., workers, platforms, requesters) according to the set of regulations. We call *e-tokens* the tokens implementing enforceable regulations and *v-tokens* the tokens implementing verifiable regulations.[16]

e-tokens. For each enforceable regulation $((w, p, r), <, \theta + 1)$, the registration authority generates θ e-tokens and sends a copy of each token to each target of the regulation. An e-token consists of a *public component*—i.e., a pair made of a *number used only once* (referred to as a *nonce* below) generated by the registration authority and a signature of the nonce by the registration authority[17]—and a *private component*—an index for selecting the correct set of tokens given the other targets, i.e., their public keys.[18] Let e-τ be an e-token, e-τ_{pub} be its public component, e-τ_{priv} be its private component, N be a nonce and λ the list of public keys of the targets of the corresponding regulation. The e-token is thus the pair (e-τ_{pub},e-τ_{priv}) where e-$\tau_{pub} = (N, \sigma^i_{RA}(N))$ and e-$\tau_{priv} = \lambda$.

v-Tokens. Similar to an e-token, a v-token consists of a public and a private component. The public component is a nonce together with its signature from the registration authority. The private component is simply a triplet of signatures, from the registration authority, binding the recipient of the v-token (called *owner* below) to each of the other targets of the verifiable regulation.[19] More formally, let v-τ be a v-token, v-τ_{pub} be its public component, v-τ_{priv} be its private component, N be a nonce, o be the identity of the participant owner of the token, and (w, p, r) be the related triplet. The v-token is thus the pair (v-τ_{pub},v-τ_{priv}) where v-$\tau_{pub} = (N, \sigma^i_{RA}(N))$ and v-$\tau_{priv} = (\sigma^i_{RA}(N, o, w), \sigma^i_{RA}(N, o, p), \sigma^i_{RA}(N, o, r))$. The number of v-tokens to produce initially can be easily deduced from the lowest higher bound in enforceable regulations[20]

16 Although it is technically possible to use a unified token structure for both enforceable and verifiable regulations, using two different tokens reduces computation and communication costs.

17 Extending tokens with labels and timestamps to support validity periods is straightforward.

18 The use of a public key generated by the registration authority is important here because (1) it can be shared among participants without disclosing their identities, i.e., it is a pseudonym, (2) the corresponding private key can be used by participants for mutual authentication in order to guarantee the correctness of the index and consequently of the choice of tokens.

19 Binding recipients to their v-tokens allows to trace possible malicious leakages of v-tokens (they strongly bind a participant to a crowdworking process, contrary to e-tokens) and consequently to prevent them (our participants act as covert adversaries).

20 For simplicity, we assume that there is at least one enforceable regulation in the system, and that the smallest threshold for all enforceable regulations is θ_{min}. Then, θ_{min} is a sufficient upper bound of the time that can be spent by any given triplet of participants. It is therefore enough to produce $\theta_{min} \times |\mathcal{W}| \times |\mathcal{P}| \times |\mathcal{R}|$ v-tokens. In practice, the number of v-tokens produced can be drastically reduced in a straightforward manner by letting participants declare to the registration authority the subset of participants they may work with (e.g., selecting a subset of platforms or a few domains of interest).

The SPEND Function

Requesters create and send their tasks to a platform and the platform appends the tasks to either its own ledger (for local tasks) or the ledgers of all involved platforms (for cross-platform tasks). Once the task is published, the workers can indicate their intent to perform the task by sending a *contribution intent* to their platforms. If a contribution is still needed for the task, the crowdworking process π starts with the `SPEND` function, performed as follows. Without loss of generality, we assume below that the given task has a time cost equal to 1. First, for each enforceable regulation, the platform requests the public component of one e-token from a participant to the crowdworking process, whatever its group, i.e., worker, platform, or requester, that is also a target of the regulation. We call this participant *the initiator*. For a verifiable regulation, the platform is the initiator and consequently does not request any v-token to the corresponding worker and requester. For each regulation (each enforceable regulation and each verifiable regulation), the initiator then chooses one token, not spent yet, and sends it to the platform. Once the platform receives it, it forwards the full token to all the targets and requests two signatures (see below). The platform includes in its request message the task (or a hash of it), an identifier for the contribution (e.g., a nonce, or when possible a hash of the contribution), and a signature of the two, concatenated, so that the worker and the requester involved will be able to prove that they were asked for signatures, even if the platform fails. The platform requires the worker and the requester to send back two signatures: (1) a group signature of the public component of the token and (2) a group signature of the public component of the token concatenated to the task (or to its hash). The two signatures per participant will be used later for guaranteeing the correctness of the spending (see the CHECK function below). Finally, the platform appends to the common datastore the public parts of the tokens (τ_{pub} for both e-tokens and v-tokens) and the signatures of the targets ($(\sigma_w^g(\tau_{pub}||t), \sigma_r^g(\tau_{pub}||t), \sigma_p^g(\tau_{pub}||t))$ for both e-tokens and v-tokens). Note that since only the public component of tokens is maintained in the ledgers, the number of tokens that a participant has spent cannot be learned from the ledgers.

The PROVE Function

Participants use the `PROVE` function to provide proofs for guaranteeing verifiable regulations (e.g., to a third party). The use of v-tokens is relatively straightforward. During the crowdworking processes, participants simply store the private components of v-tokens and deliver them at the end of the validity periods of verifiable regulations. As an example, for a $((w, p, r), >, 4)$ verifiable regulation, the worker w sends the private components of 5 v-tokens.[21] The entity in charge of guaranteeing the verifiable regulation checks the signature of the registration authority—to verify that the participant was involved in the task—and the

[21] For minimal disclosure purposes, participants are allowed to send only the parts of the private components of v-tokens that are relevant to the verifiable regulations being verified: verifiable regulations that do not specify all the targets, e.g., $((w, *, *), >, \theta)$ only require the private components involving the worker w, i.e., $\theta + 1$ distinct $\sigma_{RA}^i(N, o, w)$ signatures where $o == w$ here.

nonce stored in the ledger—to ensure that the token has been indeed spent and committed to the ledgers of all platforms.

The CHECK and ALERT Functions

These functions are used to detect and report either the malicious behavior of participants resulting in an invalid consumption of tokens or the failure of a platform. The complete set of verifications protects against (1) the forgery of tokens (verification of the signatures), (2) the replay of tokens (verification of the absence of double-spending), (3) the relay of tokens (verification of the absence of usurpation), and (4) the illegitimate invalidation of tokens (timeout against malicious platform failures). The first two verifications are straightforward and are performed during global consensus. Verifications (3) and (4) are similar, and we explain here case (3). When a token is appended to the ledgers of all platforms, any participant (whether involved in the corresponding crowdworking process or not) can `CHECK` its nonce. If a participant detects a nonce that was received from the registration authority but not spent (or spent on a wrong task), it `ALERT`s the registration authority. The registration authority will de-anonymize the group signature of the corresponding participant, i.e., the worker's group signature if the alert comes from a worker, and check whether it has been signed by the same participant that sent the token. Depending on the result, the registration authority will take adequate sanctions against the fraudulent participant (true positive) or the alert-riser (false positive).

Platform failure. If a platform fails after it requested *e*-tokens or signatures and does not recover (e.g., tokens are not appended to the ledger), the *e*-tokens revealed to the platform are lost: they cannot be used in any other crowdworking process because they are not anonymous anymore (i.e., the platform knows the association between them and the corresponding participants), and they are not spent either. In that case, workers or requesters send an `ALERT` to the registration authority including (1) the public key of the platform, (2) the task (or a hash of it), and (3) all the requests received from the platform. The registration authority then checks whether the number of requests sent by the platform for the given task matches the corresponding number of matching messages committed in the ledger of all participants. If there are more requests, the registration authority sets a timeout (e.g., to let unfinished transactions end or the platform to recover from a failure).

7.4.3 Task Processing Sequence

The processing of a crowdworking task involves the following five main phases, as depicted in Fig. 7.2.

Initialization. The registration authority provides all parties with their keys and tokens.

Publication. Requesters create and send their tasks to platforms. If a requester wants to publish its task on more than one platform (i.e., a cross-platform task), the involved platforms

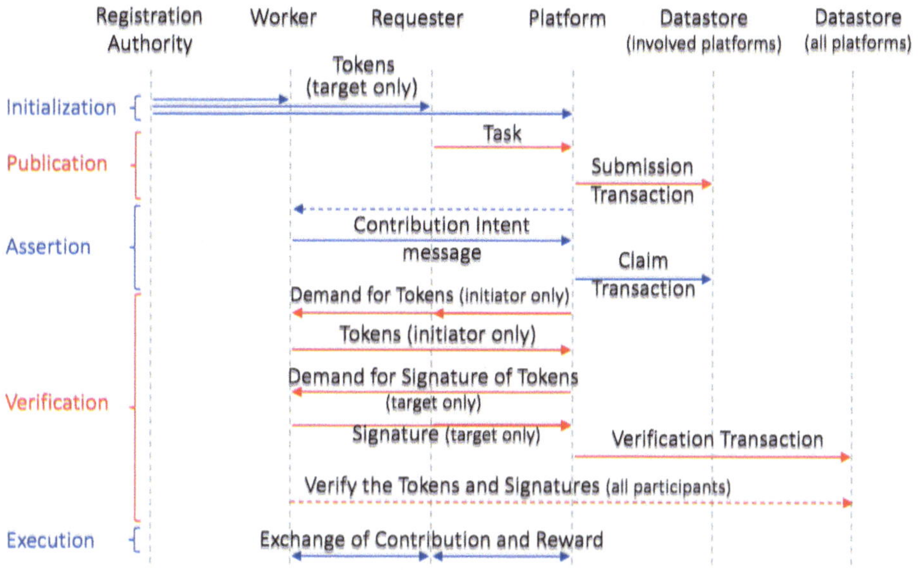

Fig. 7.2 Sequence chart (references to targets include all participants for v-tokens)

collaborate with each other to create a common instance of the task (e.g., a common task identifier). The involved platforms then append the task to their ledgers through submission transactions and inform their workers in their preferred manner for accessing tasks.

Assertion. After a worker has retrieved a task, the worker sends a *contribution intent* message to the platform without revealing the actual contribution. The platform then updates the number of required contributions for the task and appends the contribution intent to its ledger through a claim transaction. For cross-platform tasks, the platform informs other involved platforms about the received contribution intent, so that all involved platforms agree with the number (and order) of the received contribution intents (i.e., claim transactions) and append the claim transaction to their ledgers. If the desired number of contributions for the task has not been achieved, the contribution intent is refused.

Note that while the requester does not choose the workers, it is possible to enforce a selection with *a priori* criteria, passed through the platform. Another straightforward enhancement would be to add a communication step, by forwarding the contribution intent, together with the worker's identity to the requester, and allowing it to approve or deny. This communication, however, requires the disclosure of the worker's identity to requesters even before a contribution is accepted.

Verification. Once the contribution intent has been accepted by the platform(s), the platform asks the corresponding requester and worker to send the required tokens and signatures, through the SPEND function (see above). Upon receiving all tokens and signatures, the platform shares them with all platforms and the e-tokens and their signatures are appended to the ledgers of all platforms through verification transactions. From this point, anyone can check the validity of requirements with the CHECK function (and ALERT if required), as developed above.

Execution. Once all parties have checked the validity of the task, the tokens, and the group signatures, the contribution can be delivered to the requester and the reward to the worker.

7.4.4 Privacy Analysis

We show below in the suite of Theorems 7.1, 7.2, Lemmas 7.1 and 7.2 that the global execution of Separ satisfies the δ^{Π}*-privacy* model against covert adversaries (where the disclosure sets are defined in Sect. 7.3).

First, Theorem 7.1 restricts the adversarial behavior to inferences (i.e., similar to a *honest-but-curious* adversary) and shows that the execution of Separ satisfies δ^{Π}-privacy (where the disclosure sets are defined in Sect. 7.3).

Theorem 7.1 (Privacy (inferences)) For all sets of crowdworking processes Π executed over participants $\mathcal{W}$, $\mathcal{P}$, and $\mathcal{R}$ by an instance of Separ ς, then it holds that ς is δ^{Π}-Private against covert adversaries restricted to inferences (where the disclosure sets are defined in Sect. 7.3).

Proof (Sketch) First, we focus on the content of tokens and show that it is harmless. For each crowdworking process π, the information contained within the tokens exchanged and stored in the common datastore is made of (1) the public components $e\text{-}\tau_{pub}$ and $v\text{-}\tau_{pub}$ of the tokens involved (i.e., a nonce and a signature) and (2) of the group signatures of the participants to π. The nonce is generated by the registration authority independently from π, thus do not leak any information about π[22]. Since the group signatures are generated by a semantically-secure group signature scheme, they do not leak anything to the real adversary (computationally bounded) beyond the groups of the signers, which is also available to the ideal adversary.

Second, we concentrate on the information disclosed along the execution sequence of crowdworking processes. We consider below each disclosure set δ_i^{π} in turn and show that the computational indistinguishability requirement between the ideal setting and the real setting (where the instance of Separ ς executes Π) is satisfied in all cases. *Disclosure set* $\delta^{\pi}_{\neg R \neg I}$. The $\delta^{\pi}_{\neg R \neg I}$ disclosure set contains the information allowed to be disclosed to the participants that are not involved in a crowdworking process $\pi \in \Pi$ and that have not received the related task (i.e., (BEGIN, END, p)). First, we focus on the subset of such participants

[22] Including a generation timestamp into the public component of tokens, for supporting validity periods, would not leak information about π beyond its probable execution timeframe, which is already captured by the $BEGIN$ and END events allowed to leak in the δ^{Π}-privacy model. Indeed, the timestamps would be generated by the registration authority independently from π.

that are requesters or workers. In the ideal settings, these participants learn nothing beyond the information contained in $\delta^{\pi}_{\neg R \neg I}$. In the real setting, when π is executed by ς, these participants are not involved in any consensus. They are only able to observe the state of the datastore. The latter is updated exactly once for π, when π ends, for storing the tokens spent: only the ending event (END) is disclosed, which is already contained within $\delta^{\pi}_{\neg R \neg I}$. Second, we focus on the platforms. In the ideal setting, they are given $\delta^{\pi}_{\neg R \neg I}$. In the real setting, they participate to the global consensus and are able to observe the state of the datastore. Consequently, they learn p from the global consensus (i.e., the platform that initiates the global consensus) and the ending event END.[23] Both are already contained within $\delta^{\pi}_{\neg R \neg I}$.

Disclosure set $\delta^{\pi}_{R \neg I}$. The $\delta^{\pi}_{R \neg I}$ disclosure set contains the information allowed to be disclosed to the workers and platforms that have received the task t from r but that are not involved in the crowdworking process $\pi \in \Pi$ (*i.e.,* (BEGIN, END, p, r, t)). First, we focus on the subset of such participants that are workers. In the ideal settings, they learn nothing beyond the information contained in $\delta^{\pi}_{R \neg I}$. In the real setting, we see from the global execution sequence of Separ that (1) they are not involved in any consensus, (2) but are able to observe the state of the common datastore, (3) have received the task t, and (4) may receive an abort from their platform if they contribute to t while t has already been solved. From (2) and (4), they are able to learn the ending events of crowdworking processes, from (3) they learn t, and from (1) they do not learn any other information. As a result, they learn (END, t), which is contained in $\delta^{\pi}_{R \neg I}$. Second, we focus on the subset of participants that are platforms. In the ideal settings, they learn nothing beyond the information contained in $\delta^{\pi}_{R \neg I}$. In the real setting, (1) they receive the tasks from the requesters, (2) they participate to the cross-platform consensuses and to the global consensuses in addition to (3) observing the same information as the workers. From (1) they learn t and r for each process $\pi \in \Pi$. From (2), they learn p, BEGIN, and END because: the cross-platform consensus discloses the initiating platform and the starting event, and the global consensus discloses the initiating platform together with the ending event. From (3), they learn the ending event and the task. As a result, such platforms learn about all $\pi \in \Pi$ the following information (BEGIN, END, r, p, t), which is exactly $\delta^{\pi}_{R \neg I}$.

Disclosure set δ^{π}_{RI}. The computational indistinguishability requirement between the real setting and the ideal setting is trivially satisfied for the δ^{π}_{RI} set of disclosures because δ^{π}_{RI} contains all the information about the execution of the crowdworking process π so ς does not (and cannot) disclose more information. □

Second, we extend possible behavior to malicious behaviors aiming at jeopardizing regulations and show that they are systematically detected by Separ (Lemma 7.1 focuses on

[23] The verifications performed by the worker and the requester involved in π are performed on the instance of the datastore stored on p. Indeed, the block resulting from the global consensus contains all the necessary information both for performing the verification and for checking that it results from the global consensus.

enforceable regulations and Lemma 7.2 on verifiable regulations). This prevents covert adversaries from performing malicious actions, limiting them to inferences.

Lemma 7.1 (Detection of malicious behavior (enforceable regulations)) *A crowdworking process π executed over participants $\mathcal{W}$, $\mathcal{P}$, and $\mathcal{R}$ by an instance of Separ ς, completes successfully without raising a legitimate alert if and only if π does not jeopardize any enforceable regulation.*

Proof (Sketch) We have to show first that the *e*-tokens allocated to participants can be spent, and second that participants cannot spend more.

Participants can spend their *e*-tokens. In order to prevent participants from spending their *e*-tokens, an attacker has three main possibilities. First, she can try to acquire tokens belonging to another participant and to spend them (i.e., relay attack). However, this rises an `ALERT` with certainty. Indeed, if a token is spent by an illegitimate participant, it is stored on the datastore and is thus accessible to the legitimate participant who is able to detect it through the nonce and to rise an `ALERT` to the registration authority (including the group signatures stored along the token). Second, the attacker (platform only) could try to misuse tokens by spending them in a way that was not intended by the legitimate owner (i.e., relay attack). However, this would be detected by participants as well because the signature of the task would not be valid. Third, the attacker (platform only) may abort the process after having received tokens but before performing the global consensus (i.e., illegitimate invalidation). However, after a timeout, the other involved participants simply send an `ALERT` to the registration authority and prove that their tokens were requested by the platform (signatures of the requests for tokens and signatures), and therefore that the platform behaves illegitimately.

Participants cannot spend more. First, an attacker may produce additional *e*-tokens (i.e., forge attack). However, the public parts of *e*-tokens must contain valid signatures produced by the registration authority. Second, an attacker may try to spend an *e*-token more than once (i.e., replay attack). However, the nonce of an *e*-token that must be spent must not already be in the datastore. Finally, an attacker may simply omit sending any *e*-token. However, the public parts of *e*-tokens are required for the successful completion of the global consensus. □

Lemma 7.2 (Detection of malicious behavior (verifiable regulations)) *Participant P can produce a proof about process π executed over participants $\mathcal{W}$, $\mathcal{P}$, and $\mathcal{R}$ by an instance of Separ ς if and only if P was involved in π* **and** *π completed successfully.*

Proof (Sketch) First, a proof about a crowdworking process π that completed successfully can always be produced by the participants involved in π. Indeed, the *v*-tokens are produced by the registration authority and sent to all participants (i.e., the number of *v*-tokens is correct), and only the successful crowdworking processes store the *v*-tokens in the datastore.

Second, participants cannot spend a υ-token more than once because the nonce of a token that must be spent must not already be in the common datastore. Third, participants cannot produce any υ-token by themselves because their public parts must contain valid signatures produced by the RA. □

Since Theorem 7.1 shows that Separ is δ^{Π}-private against adversaries restricted to inferences, and Lemma 7.1 and Lemma 7.2 show that malicious behaviors are prevented, it follows that Separ is δ^{Π}-private against covert adversaries (Theorem 7.2).

Theorem 7.2 (Privacy (inferences and malicious behavior)) *For all sets of crowdworking processes* Π *executed over participants* $\mathcal{W}$, $\mathcal{P}$, *and* $\mathcal{R}$ *by an instance of Separ* ς, *then* ς *is* δ^{Π}*-private against covert adversaries (where the disclosure sets are defined in Sect. 7.3).*

Proof Theorem 7.1 shows that the execution of Separ satisfies δ^{Π}-privacy against covert adversaries restricted to inferences, while Lemmas 7.1 and 7.2 show that malicious behaviors aiming at jeopardizing the regulations guaranteed are detected and consequently prevented within Separ. As a result it follows directly that the execution of Separ satisfies δ^{Π}-privacy against covert adversaries (where the disclosure sets are defined in Sect. 7.3). □

7.5 Separ: Infrastructure Level

Section 7.4 provides an abstract design for implementing regulations. In this section, we show how Separ supports the execution of transactions on multiple globally distributed platforms that do not necessarily trust each other. In Separ and in order to provide fault tolerance, each platform consists of a set of nodes (i.e., replicas) that store copies of the platform's ledger. Separ uses a *permissioned blockchain* as its underlying infrastructure (i.e., MPI). The unique features of blockchain such as transparency, provenance, fault tolerance, and authenticity are used by many systems to deploy a wide range of distributed applications in permissioned settings. In particular and for a crowdworking system, the *transparency* of blockchains is useful for checking integrity constraints, *provenance* enables Separ to trace how data is transformed, *fault tolerance* helps to enhance reliability and availability, and finally, *authenticity* guarantees that signatures and transactions are valid.

7.5.1 Blockchain Ledger

The blockchain ledger in Separ maintains the global state of the system, encompassing all submission, claim, and verification transactions related to both internal and cross-platform tasks. Separ establishes an ordering for transactions involving any platform to ensure data consistency. Given that multiple platforms participate in each cross-platform transaction, the

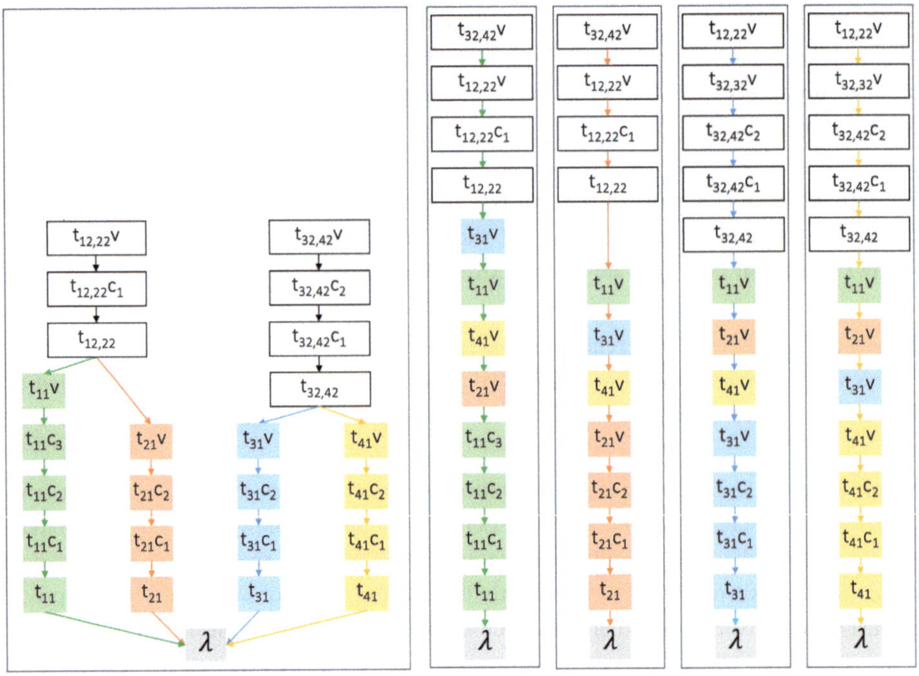

(a) The Global View (b) platform p_1 (c) platform p_2 (d) platform p_3 (e) platform p_4

Fig. 7.3 **a** The ledger of Separ with 4 platforms, **b–e** The views of the ledger from different platforms

ledger is structured as a directed acyclic graph (DAG), similar to the designs in Caper [16] and SharPer [17]. In this DAG structure, each node represents a transaction block containing a single transaction, while edges dictate the order of these transaction blocks.

Figure 7.3a shows a blockchain ledger created in the Separ model for a blockchain infrastructure consisting of four platforms p_1, p_2, p_3, and p_4. In this figure, λ is the genesis block, t_i's are submission transactions, $t_i c_j$ is the j-th claim transaction of task t_i, and $t_i v$ is the verification transaction of task t_i. In Fig. 7.3a, t_{11}, t_{21}, t_{31}, and t_{41} are internal submission transactions of different platforms that can be appended to the ledger in parallel. As shown, t_{11} requires 3 contributions (thus 3 claim transactions $t_{11}c_1$, $t_{11}c_2$, and $t_{11}c_3$) whereas each of t_{21}, t_{31}, and t_{41} needs two contributions. blocks $t_{11}v$, $t_{21}v$, $t_{31}v$, and $t_{41}v$ are the corresponding verification transactions. $t_{12,22}$ is a cross-platform submission among platforms p_1 and p_2. Similarly, $t_{32,42}$ is a cross-platform submission among platforms p_3 and p_4. Here, $t_{12,22}$ and $t_{32,42}$ require one and two contributions respectively. Note that the claim transactions of a cross-platform task might be initiated by different platforms and, as mentioned earlier, the order of these claim transactions is important (to recognize the first n claim transactions).

This global directed acyclic graph blockchain ledger includes all transactions required for internal as well as cross-platform tasks initiated by all platforms. However, to ensure data privacy, each platform should only access the transactions in which the platform is involved. As a result, in Separ, similar to Caper, the entire blockchain ledger is not maintained by any specific platform and each platform p_i, as shown in Fig. 7.3b–e, only maintains its own view of the blockchain ledger including (1) all submission and claim transactions of its internal tasks, (2) all submission and claim transactions of the cross-platform tasks involving the platform, and (3) verification transactions of all tasks. Note that verification transactions are replicated on every platform to enable all platforms to check the satisfaction of global regulations. The global DAG ledger (e.g., Fig. 7.3a) is the union of all these physical views (e.g., Fig. 7.3b–e). Note that, since there is no data dependency between the tasks that platform p is involved in and the verification transactions of the tasks that platform p is *not* involved in, the verification transactions might be appended to the ledgers in different orders, e.g., $t_{21}v$ (of p_2) and $t_{41}v$ (of p_4) are appended to the ledger of platforms p_1 and p_3 in different orders.

7.5.2 Consensus in Separ

In Separ, each platform consists of a (disjoint) set of nodes (i.e., replicas) where the platform replicates its own view of the blockchain ledger on those nodes to achieve fault tolerance. Nodes follow either the crash or Byzantine failure model. Figure 7.4 shows the crowdworking infrastructure of Fig. 7.1 where each platform consists of 4 replicas (assuming Byzantine failure model and $f = 1$) and replicas use blockchain to store data.

Completion of a crowdworking task, as discussed earlier, requires a single submission transaction, one or more claim transactions (depending on the requested number of contributions), and a verification transaction. For an internal task of a platform, submission and claim transactions are replicated only on the nodes of the platform, hence, *local consensus* among nodes of the platform on the order of the transaction is needed. For a cross-platform task, on the other hand, submission and claim transactions are replicated on every node of all involved platforms. As a result, *cross-platform consensus* among the nodes of only the *involved* platforms is needed. Finally, verification transactions are appended to the ledger of all platforms, therefore, all nodes of *every* platform participate in a *global consensus* protocol. In this section, we show how local, cross-platform, and global consensus are established with crash-only or Byzantine nodes.

Local Consensus

Processing a submission or a claim transaction of an internal task requires local consensus where nodes of a single platform, *independent* of other platforms, establish agreement on the order of the transaction. The local consensus protocol in Separ is pluggable and depending on the failure model of nodes, i.e., crash-only or Byzantine, a platform uses a crash fault-tolerant protocol, e.g., Paxos [18], or a Byzantine fault-tolerant protocol, e.g., PBFT [19].

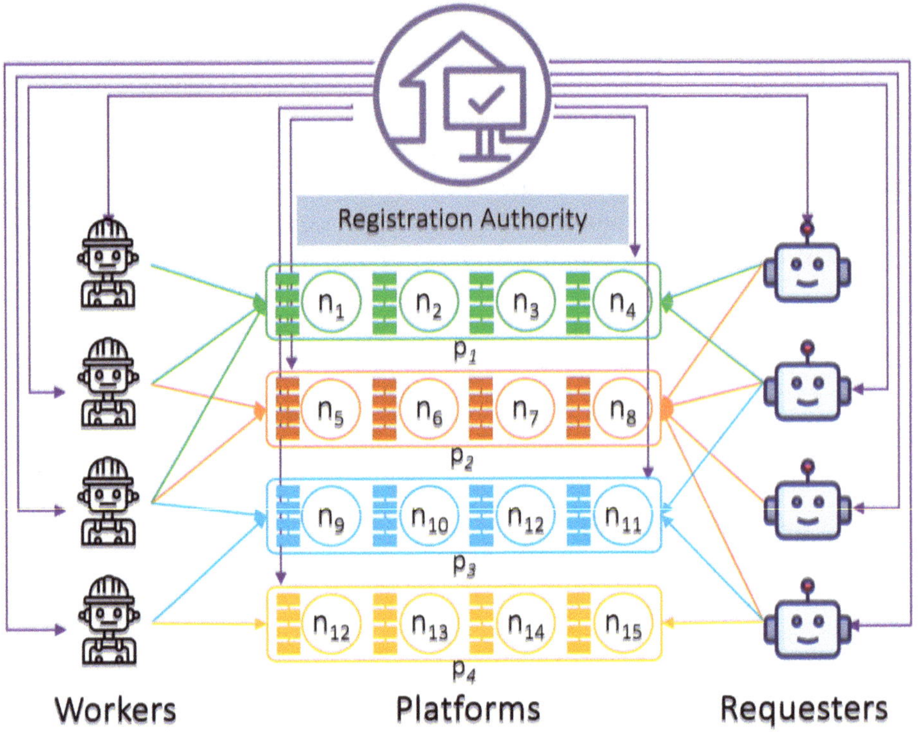

Fig. 7.4 Separ infrastructure

The local consensus protocol is initiated by the primary node. When the primary *p* receives a valid internal transaction (either submission or claim), it initiates a local consensus algorithm by multicasting a message, e.g., accept message in Paxos or pre-prepare message in PBFT, including the requested transaction to other nodes of the platform. To provide a total order among transaction blocks, the primary also assigns a sequence number to the request. If the transaction is a claim transaction, the primary includes the cryptographic hash of the corresponding submission transaction. The nodes of the platform then establish agreement on a total order of transactions using the utilized consensus protocol and append the transaction to the blockchain ledger.

Cross-Platform and Global Consensus

Both cross-platform consensus and global consensus require collaboration between multiple platforms. Since platforms do not trust each other and the primary node that initiates the transaction might behave maliciously, Separ uses Byzantine fault-tolerant protocols in both cross-platform and global consensus. cross-platform and global consensus, however, are different in two aspects. First, in cross-platform consensus, only the involved platforms participate, whereas global consensus is established among all platforms, and second, at the platform level, while cross-platform consensus requires agreement from *every* involved platform, in global consensus, agreement from *two-thirds* of all platforms is sufficient. Cross-platform consensus requires agreement from every involved platform to ensure data consistency due to the possible data dependency between the cross-platform transaction and other transactions of an involved platform. Note that if an involved platform (as a set of nodes) behaves maliciously by not sending an agreement for a cross-platform transaction initiated by another platform, e.g., a claim transaction, its malicious behavior can be detected and penalties imposed. In global consensus, however, the goal is to check the correctness of the transaction. To provide safety for global consensus at the platform level, we assume that at most $\lfloor \frac{|P|-1}{3} \rfloor$ platforms might behave maliciously. As a result, to commit a transaction, by a similar argument as in PBFT [20], at least two-thirds ($\lfloor \frac{2|P|}{3} \rfloor + 1$) of the platforms must agree on the order of the transaction.

Cross-Platform Consensus. Processing submission and claim transactions of a cross-platform task requires cross-platform consensus among *all* involved platforms where due to the untrustworthiness of platforms, a Byzantine fault-tolerant protocol is used. Since the number of nodes within each platform depends on the failure model of nodes of a platform (i.e. $2f + 1$ crash-only or $3f + 1$ Byzantine nodes), the required number of matching replies from each platform, i.e., the quorum size, to ensure the safety of protocol is different for different platforms. We define *local-majority* as the required number of matching replies from the nodes of a platform. For a platform with crash-only nodes, local-majority is $f + 1$ (from the total $2f + 1$ nodes), whereas for a platform with Byzantine nodes, local-majority is $2f + 1$ (from the total $3f + 1$ nodes).

Inspired by SharPer [17], Separ processes cross-platform transactions in four phases: prepare, propose, accept, and commit, using a flattened approach.

Algorithm 10 presents the normal case of *cross-platform consensus* in Separ. Although not explicitly mentioned, every sent and received message is logged by nodes. As shown in lines 1–6 of the algorithm, p_i is the platform that initiates the transaction, $\pi(p)$ represents the primary node of platform p, and P is the set of involved platforms in the transaction.

Once the primary $\pi(p_i)$ of the initiator platform p_i (called the *initiator primary*) receives a valid submission or claim transaction, as presented in lines 6–9, the initiator primary node assigns sequence number h_i to the request and multicasts a *signed* prepare message $\langle\langle \text{PREPARE}, h_i, d\rangle_{\sigma_{\pi(p_i)}}, m\rangle$ to all nodes of every involved platform where m is the received message (either submission or claim) and $d = D(m)$ is the digest of m. The sequence number h_i represents the correct order of the transaction block in the initiator platform p_i. If the transaction is a claim transaction, the primary includes the cryptographic hash of the corresponding submission transaction as well. The prepare message is sent to all nodes enabling them to detect possible malicious behaviors of their cluster's primary node. The initiator primary node also multicasts a *signed* propose message $\langle \text{PROPOSE}, h_i, d\rangle_{\sigma_{\pi(p_i)}}$ to the nodes of its platform where $d = D(m)$ is the digest of m. Since the actual message m has been sent in the prepare message, the primary does not send it again.

Algorithm 10 Cross-Platform Consensus

1: **init()**:
2: r := *node_id*
3: p_i := the platform that initiates the consensus instance
4: $\pi(p)$:= the primary node of cluster p
5: P := set of all nodes in the involved platforms
6: **if** $r == \pi(p_i)$ and receiving valid cross-platform transaction m **then**
7: multicast $\langle\langle \text{PREPARE}, h_i, d\rangle_{\sigma_{\pi(p_i)}}, m\rangle$ to P
8: multicast $\langle \text{PROPOSE}, h_i, d\rangle_{\sigma_{\pi(p_i)}}$ to all nodes of p_i
9: **end if**
10: **if** $r == \pi(p_j)$ and receiving valid $\langle\langle \text{PREPARE}, h_i, d\rangle_{\sigma_{\pi(p_i)}}, m\rangle$ and r is not involved in any uncommitted request m' where m and m' intersect in some other platform p_k **then**
11: multicast $\langle \text{PROPOSE}, h_i, h_j, d\rangle_{\sigma_{\pi(p_j)}}$ to all nodes of p_j
12: multicast $\langle \text{ACCEPT}, h_i, h_j, d, r\rangle_{\sigma_{\pi(p_j)}}$ to P
13: **end if**
14: **if** $r \in p_i$ and receiving valid $\langle \text{PROPOSE}, h_i, d\rangle_{\sigma_{\pi(p_i)}}$ **then**
15: multicast $\langle \text{ACCEPT}, h_i, d, r\rangle_{\sigma_r}$ to P
16: **end if**
17: **if** $r \in p_j$ and receiving valid $\langle \text{PROPOSE}, h_i, h_j, d\rangle_{\sigma_{\pi(p_i)}}$ **then**
18: multicast $\langle \text{ACCEPT}, h_i, h_j, d, r\rangle_{\sigma_r}$ to P
19: **end if**
20: **if** $r \in P$ and receiving matching accept from *local-majority* of every platform in P **then**
21: multicast $\langle \text{COMMIT}, h_i, h_j, ..., h_k, d, r\rangle_{\sigma_r}$ to P
22: **end if**
23: **if** $r \in P$ and receiving matching commit from *local-majority* of every platform in P **then**
24: append the transaction block to the ledger
25: **end if**

Upon receiving a valid prepare message from the initiator primary, as indicated in lines 10–13, the primary node of platform p_j checks whether it is currently waiting for a commit message of some cross-platform transaction m' where the involved platforms of the two requests m and m' intersect in p_j as well as some other platform p_k. If yes, the node does not process the new transaction m before the earlier transaction m' gets committed. This ensures that requests are committed in the same order on overlapping platforms (consistency), e.g., m and m' are committed in the same order on both p_j and p_k (Separ addresses deadlock situations where different platforms receive prepare messages in a different order in the same way as SharPer [17]). If the primary is not waiting for an uncommitted transaction, it assigns sequence number h_j to the message and multicasts a *signed* propose message to the nodes of its platform. The primary node $\pi(p_j)$ also multicasts a signed accept message to *every* node of *all* involved platforms.

When node r of an involved platform receives a valid propose message, as indicated in lines 14–19, the node multicasts a signed accept message including the corresponding sequence number, e.g., h_j (that represents the order of m in platform p_j), and the digest $d =$

$D(m)$ to *every* node of *all* involved platforms. Note that if a platform behaves maliciously by not sending accept messages to other involved platforms, the initiator platform can report the malicious behavior of the platform by sending an ALERT message (similar to Sect. 7.4.2) to the registration authority.

As presented in lines 20–22, each node waits for valid matching accept messages from a local-majority (i.e., either $f + 1$ or $2f + 1$ depending on the failure model) of *every* involved platform with h_i and d that matches the propose message which was sent by primary $\pi(p_i)$. We define the predicate accepted-local$_{p_j}(m, h_i, h_j, r)$ to be true if and only if node r has received the request m, a propose for m with sequence number h_i from the initiator platform p_i and accept messages from a local-majority of an involved platform p_j that match the propose message. The predicate accepted(m, h, r) where $h = [h_i, h_j, ..., h_k]$ is then defined to be true on node r if and only if accepted-local$_{p_j}$ is true for *every* involved platform p_j in cross-platform request m. The order of sequence numbers in the predicate is an ascending order determined by their platform ids. The propose and accept phases of the algorithm basically guarantee that non-faulty nodes agree on a total order for the transactions. When accepted(m, h, r) becomes true, node r multicasts a signed commit message to all nodes of every involved platform.

Finally, as shown in lines 23–25, node r waits for valid matching commit messages from a local-majority of *every* involved platform that matches its commit message. The predicate committed-local$_{p_j}(m, h, r)$ is defined to be true on node r if and only if accepted(m, h, r) is true and node r has received valid matching commit messages from a local-majority of platform p_j that match the propose message for cross-platform transaction m. The predicate committed(m, h, r) is then defined to be true on node r if and only if committed-local$_{p_j}$ is true for *every* involved platform p_j in cross-platform transaction m. The committed predicate certifies that at least $f + 1$ nodes of each involved platform have multicast valid commit messages. When the committed predicate becomes true, the node considers the transaction as committed.

If all transactions with lower sequence numbers than h_j have already been appended to the leader, the node appends a transaction block including the transaction as well as the corresponding commit messages to its copy of the ledger. Note that since commit messages include the digest (cryptographic hash) of the corresponding transactions, appending valid signed commit messages to the blockchain ledger in addition to the transactions, provides the same level of *immutability* guarantee as including the cryptographic hash of the previous transaction in the transaction block, i.e., any attempt to alter the block data can easily be detected.

Figure 7.5 shows the normal case operation for Separ to execute two concurrent cross-platform transactions in the presence of Byzantine nodes where each transaction accesses two disjoint platforms. The network consists of four platforms and each platform includes four nodes ($f = 1$).

Global Consensus The verification transactions include group signatures and all tokens that are consumed by different participants to perform a particular task. In Separ and in order

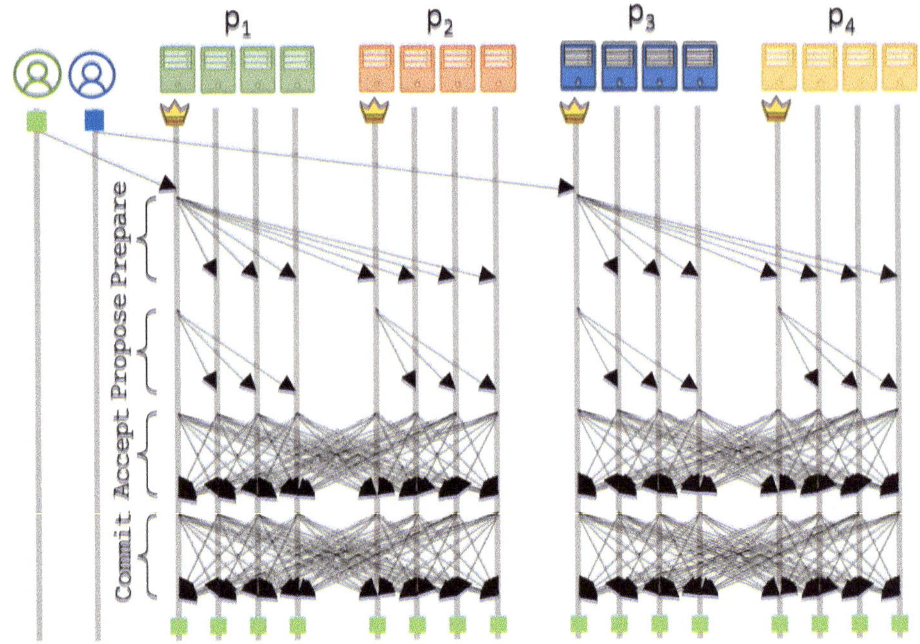

Fig. 7.5 Two concurrent cross-platform transaction flows in Separ where two disjoint sets of platforms are involved in each task

to enable all platforms to check constraints, verification transactions are appended to the blockchains of all platforms. To do so, a Byzantine fault-tolerant protocol is run among all nodes of every platform where the protocol needs agreement from the *local-majority* of the nodes of *two-thirds* of the platforms ($2f + 1$ out of $3f + 1$). The local-majority, similar to cross-platform consensus, is defined based on the utilized consensus protocol within each platform. However, there are two main differences between cross-platform consensus and global consensus. First, in cross-platform consensus only the involved platforms participate, whereas, in global consensus, every platform verifies transactions by checking the group signatures and consumed tokens. Second, cross-platform consensus requires agreement from *every* platform, whereas, in global consensus, agreement from only *two-thirds* of platforms is needed. In cross-platform consensus, there might be some dependency between cross-platform transactions and internal ones, thus, to ensure data consistency, every involved platform must agree on the order of the cross-platform transaction. However, in global consensus, the goal is to verify the correctness of the transaction and as soon as two-thirds of platforms verify that (assuming at most one-third of platforms might behave maliciously), the transaction can be appended to the blockchain ledger.

Algorithm 11 shows the normal case of *global consensus* in Separ where a Byzantine protocol is run among all nodes of every platform (in contrast to the cross-platform consensus protocol where only the involved platforms participate). The protocol, similar to cross-

Algorithm 11 Global Consensus

1: **init()**:
2: $r := node\_id$
3: $p_i :=$ the platform that initiates the consensus
4: $\pi(p) :=$ the primary node of cluster p
5: **if** $r == \pi(p_i)$ and receiving valid verification transaction m **then**
6: multicast $\langle\langle \text{PREPARE}, h_i, d\rangle_{\sigma_{\pi(p_i)}}, m\rangle$ to all nodes
7: multicast $\langle \text{PROPOSE}, h_i, d\rangle_{\sigma_{\pi(p_i)}}$ to all nodes of p_i
8: **end if**
9: **if** $r == \pi(p_j)$ and receiving valid $\langle\langle \text{PREPARE}, h_i, d\rangle_{\sigma_{\pi(p_i)}}, m\rangle$ and r is not involved in any uncommitted request m' where m and m' intersect in some other platform p_k **then**
10: multicast $\langle \text{PROPOSE}, h_i, h_j, d\rangle_{\sigma_{\pi(p_j)}}$ to all nodes of p_j
11: multicast $\langle \text{ACCEPT}, h_i, h_j, d, r\rangle_{\sigma_{\pi(p_j)}}$ to all nodes
12: **end if**
13: **if** $r \in p_i$ and receiving valid $\langle \text{PROPOSE}, h_i, d\rangle_{\sigma_{\pi(p_i)}}$ **then**
14: multicast $\langle \text{ACCEPT}, h_i, d, r\rangle_{\sigma_r}$ to all nodes
15: **end if**
16: **if** $r \in p_j$ and receiving valid $\langle \text{PROPOSE}, h_i, h_j, d\rangle_{\sigma_{\pi(p_i)}}$ **then**
17: multicast $\langle \text{ACCEPT}, h_i, h_j, d, r\rangle_{\sigma_r}$ to all nodes
18: **end if**
19: **if** $r \in P$ and receiving matching accept from *local-majority* of **two-thirds** of platforms **then**
20: multicast $\langle \text{COMMIT}, h_i, h_j, ..., h_k, d, r\rangle_{\sigma_r}$ to all nodes
21: **end if**
22: **if** $r \in P$ and receiving matching commit from *local-majority* of **two-thirds** of platforms **then**
23: append the transaction block to the ledger
24: **end if**

platform consensus, processes a transaction in four phases of prepare (lines 5–8), propose (lines 9–12), accept (lines 13–18), and commit (lines 19–24). However, each node waits for matching accept and commit messages from the local-majority of only *two-thirds* of the platforms (as shown in lines 19 and 22).

Figure 7.6 presents the normal case operation of global consensus in Separ. Here the nodes of all platforms follow the Byzantine failure model where $f = 1$ and the network consists of four platforms.

Primary Failure Handling

In both cross-platform and global consensus protocols, in addition to the normal case operation, Separ has to deal with node failures. We use the technique, discussed in Chap. 4, to address such situations. Note that for local consensus, since the consensus protocol is pluggable, Separ follows the primary failure handling of the plugged protocol.

The primary failure handling routine provides liveness by allowing the system to make progress when a primary fails. The routine is triggered by timeout. When node r of some

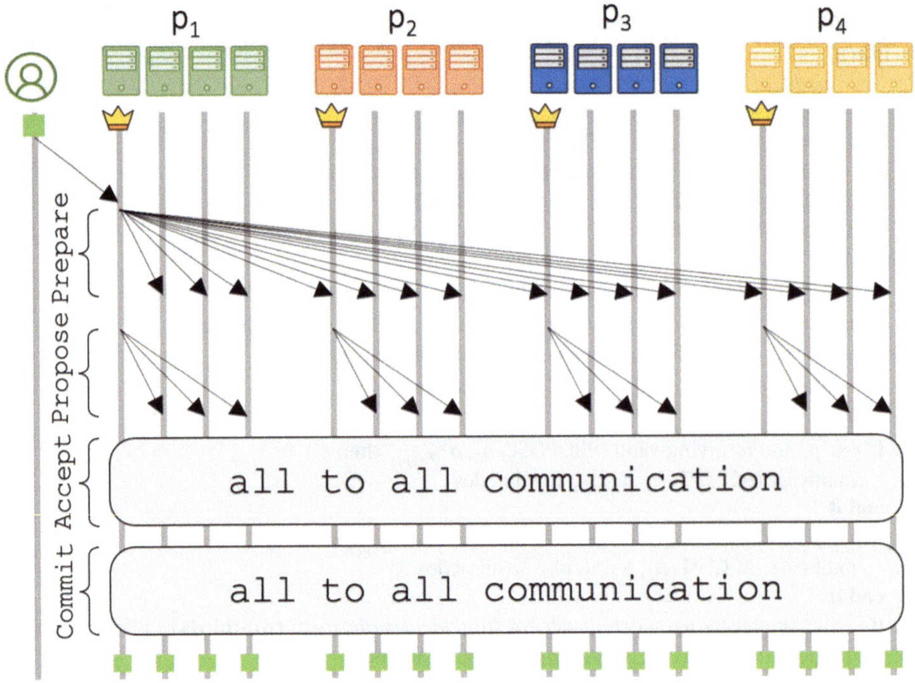

Fig. 7.6 Global consensus in Separ

platform p_j receives a valid propose message from its primary for either an internal or a cross-platform transaction, it starts a timer that expires after some predefined time τ (time τ is longer for cross-platform and verification transactions). If the timer has expired and the node has not committed the message, the node suspects that the primary is faulty. Similarly, if nodes of the initiator platform receive accept messages from other platforms with sequence numbers that are different from their sequence number h_i (that they have received from the initiator primary in the propose message), they suspect that the initiator primary is faulty (i.e., a malicious initiator primary might assign different sequence numbers to the same transaction and send non-matching prepare messages to different platforms). Note that nodes within other platforms are also able to detect conflicting messages and send an accept-query message $\langle \text{ACCEPT}-\text{QUERY}, h_i, h_j, d, r\rangle$ message to every node of the initiator platform p_i (the platform of the faulty primary). When node r (of the initiator platform) suspects that the initiator primary is faulty, it initiates the routine by multicasting a view-change message (with the same structure as PBFT [20] view-change messages) including all processed internal as well as cross-platform transactions to every node within the platform. Upon receiving $2f$ view-change message, the next primary (determined in the round-robin manner based on the id of nodes) handles transactions by multicasting a new-view message including $2f + 1$ view-change messages and a propose message for each request to every node within the platform. For cross-platform and verification transactions also, the new primary multicasts a new-view message including $2f + 1$ view-change messages and related prepare messages to the primary nodes of all involved platforms.

Separ may encounter deadlock situations when nodes fail to receive accept messages from a local-majority of either all participating platforms (for cross-platform consensus) or two-thirds of the platforms (for global consensus). A deadlock can occur if the primary nodes of different platforms multicast their prepare messages simultaneously, leading to overlapping platforms receiving these messages in differing orders. This situation will prevent them from sending accept messages for the second transaction, as they need to ensure consistency. By implementing timeouts, such deadlock scenarios can be detected, hence, aborting the deadlocked transactions.

Correctness. Given that Separ utilizes a blockchain infrastructure comparable to that of SharPer, the safety properties (agreement, validity, and consistency) as well as the liveness property of Separ's consensus protocols can be demonstrated using analogous reasoning, as outlined in Sect. 4.4.5.

7.6 Summary

This chapter outlines a comprehensive vision for the future of work multi-platform crowdworking environments, focusing on three primary dimensions: regulations, security, and architecture. We introduced Separ, which is to our knowledge the first solution designed to enforce global regulations in these environments while preserving privacy. Separ enables official institutions to express global regulations in simple and unambiguous terms, ensures compliance with these regulations by design, and enables participants to demonstrate their engagement in crowdworking tasks to external parties, all in a privacy-preserving manner. Additionally, Separ employs transparent blockchain ledgers that are shared across multiple platforms and facilitates collaboration among these platforms through a set of distributed consensus protocols.

References

1. Cohen, J.E.: Law for the platform economy. UCDL Rev. **51**, 133 (2017)
2. Kenney, M., Zysman, J.: The rise of the platform economy. Issues Sci. Technol. **32**(3), 61 (2016)
3. Berg, J., Furrer, M., Harmon, E., Rani, U., Silberman, M.S.: Digital labour platforms and the future of work: towards decent work in the online world. International Labour Office Geneva (2018)
4. On the Future of Work, G.C.: Work for a brighter future. Technical Report. ISBN 978-92-2-132796-7, International Labour Organization (2019)
5. Fow Participants: Imagine all the people and AI in the future of work. ACM SIGMOD blog post (2019)

6. Bourhis, P., Demartini, G., Elbassuoni, S., Hoareau, E., Rao, H.R.: Ethical challenges in the future of work. Bull. Techn. Committee Data Eng. (2019)
7. Gross-Amblard, D., Morishima, A., Thirumuruganathan, S., Tommasi, M., Yoshida, K.: Platform design for crowdsourcing and future of work. Bull. Techn. Committee Data Eng. **42**(4) (2019)
8. International Labour on Legislation Constitution: Constitution of the International Labour Organization (1919)
9. National du numérique, C.: Travail à l'ère des plateformes. mise à jour requise (2020). https://cnnumerique.fr/publication-du-rapport-travail-lere-des-plateformes-mise-jour-requise-en-presence-de-cedric-o (in French)
10. Amiri, M.J., Duguépéroux, J., Allard, T., Agrawal, D., El Abbadi, A.: Separ: towards regulating future of work multi-platform crowd working environments with privacy guarantees. In: The Web Conference (WWW), pp. 1891–1903 (2021)
11. Aumann, Y., Lindell, Y.: Security against covert adversaries: efficient protocols for realistic adversaries. In: Theory of Cryptography Conference (TCC), pp. 137–156. Springer (2007)
12. Lamport, L.: The implementation of reliable distributed multiprocess systems. Comput. Netw. (1976) **2**(2), 95–114 (1978)
13. Camenisch, J., Groth, J.: Group signatures: better efficiency and new theoretical aspects. In: International Conference on Security in Communication Networks (SecureComm), pp. 120–133. Springer (2004)
14. Chaum, D., Van Heyst, E.: Group signatures. In: Workshop on the Theory and Application of Cryptographic Techniques, pp. 257–265. Springer (1991)
15. Ateniese, G., Camenisch, J., Joye, M., Tsudik, G.: A practical and provably secure coalition-resistant group signature scheme. In: Annual International Cryptology Conference (CRYPTO), pp. 255–270. Springer (2000)
16. Amiri, M.J., Agrawal, D., El Abbadi, A.: CAPER: a cross-application permissioned blockchain. Proc. VLDB Endowment **12**(11), 1385–1398 (2019)
17. Amiri, M.J., Agrawal, D., El Abbadi, A.: SharPer: sharding permissioned blockchains over network clusters. In: SIGMOD International Conference on Management of Data, pp. 76–88. ACM (2021)
18. Lamport, L.: Paxos made simple. ACM SIGACT News **32**(4), 18–25 (2001)
19. Castro, M., Liskov, B.: Practical byzantine fault tolerance and proactive recovery. Trans. Comput. Syst. (TOCS) **20**(4), 398–461 (2002)
20. Castro, M., Liskov, B.: Practical byzantine fault tolerance. In: Symposium on Operating Systems Design and Implementation (OSDI), pp. 173–186. USENIX Association (1999)

Conclusion 8

8.1 Summary and Concluding Remarks

Today's large-scale distributed data management systems need to deal with untrustworthy environments where multiple mutually distrustful entities communicate with each other, and maintain data on untrusted infrastructure. By relying on Byzantine fault-tolerant (BFT) protocols, permissioned blockchain systems, have enabled a large class of distributed applications ranging from contact tracing [1], crowdworking [2], supply chain assurance [3, 4], and federated learning [5]. In fact, the popularity of these services has motivated cloud providers (e.g., Amazon [6, 7], IBM [8], Oracle [9], Alibaba [10]) to offer Blockchains-as-a-Service (BaaS) [11]. The unique features of blockchain such as transparency, provenance, and authenticity, are appealing to a wide range of large-scale data management applications in permissioned settings. However, these applications deal with four main challenges, *performance*, *scalability*, *confidentiality*, and *verifiability*, that need to be supported by blockchain systems [12, 13]. While confidentiality and verifiability are needed in multi-application systems (to preserve the confidentiality of application data and to enable verifiability of the transactions of an application for other applications without revealing any information), performance and scalability are required in systems with either a single application or multiple applications. In this monograph, we proposed different techniques to address these challenges. A permissioned blockchain system can utilize any of these techniques to address its challenges.

M. J. Amiri et al., *Blockchain-Enabled Large-Scale Transaction Management*,
Synthesis Lectures on Data Management,
https://doi.org/10.1007/978-3-031-91058-6_8

8.1.1 Large-Scale Transaction Management Challenges

Performance. Distributed applications require high performance in terms of throughput and latency, e.g., financial applications need to process tens of thousands of requests every second with very low latency. Existing blockchain systems, however, suffer from architectural limitations resulting in performance issues. While recent permissioned blockchain systems, e.g., Hyperledger Fabric, have tried to overcome these limitations, their focus has mainly been on workloads with no contention, i.e., no conflicting transactions. In this monograph, we introduced OXII, a new paradigm for permissioned blockchains to support distributed applications that execute concurrently. OXII is designed for workloads with (different degrees of) contention. We then presented ParBlockchain, a permissioned blockchain designed specifically in the OXII paradigm.

Scalability. Scalability is one of the main obstacles to business adoption of blockchain systems. Scalability is the ability of a blockchain system to process a growing number of transactions by adding resources to the system. Partitioning the data into multiple shards that are maintained by different subsets of nodes is a proven approach to enhance the scalability of databases [14]. Despite recent intensive research on using sharding techniques to enhance the scalability of blockchain systems, existing solutions do not efficiently address the efficient processing of cross-shard transactions. In this monograph, we introduced SharPer, a permissioned blockchain system that improves scalability by clustering (partitioning) the nodes and assigning different data shards to different clusters where each data shard is replicated on the nodes of a cluster. SharPer supports both intra-shard and cross-shard transactions and processes intra-shard transactions of different clusters as well as cross-shard transactions with non-overlapping clusters simultaneously. SharPer also incorporates a flattened protocol to establish consensus among clusters on the order of cross-shard transactions.

Confidentiality. Confidentiality of data is required in distributed applications consisting of a set of collaborating enterprises. In such applications, enterprises collaborate with each other following Service Level Agreements (SLAs) to provide different services. While collaboration between enterprises, e.g., cross-enterprise transactions, should be visible to all enterprises, the internal data of each enterprise, e.g., internal transactions, might be confidential. In this monograph, we presented Caper, a permissioned blockchain system that supports both internal and cross-enterprise transactions of collaborating enterprises. In Caper, the blockchain ledger is not maintained by any node and each enterprise maintains its own local view of the ledger including its internal and all cross-enterprise transactions. Caper also distinguishes between trust at the node level and trust at the enterprise level and allows an enterprise to behave maliciously for its benefit while its nodes are non-malicious. Furthermore, Caper introduces three consensus protocols to globally order cross-enterprise transactions: using a separate set of orderers, hierarchical consensus, and one-level consensus.

While Caper's solution is simple and suitable for collaboration workflows with internal and public transactions, Caper does not support confidential collaboration among subsets of enterprises (i.e., it only supports internal or public transactions) To support confidential collaboration (i.e., data sharing), in addition to public transactions among all enterprises and internal transactions within each enterprise, any subset of enterprises might process transactions *confidentially* from other enterprises. To address this problem, we presented Qanaat [4], a more generalized confidentiality solution for scalable multi-enterprise applications. Qanaat presents *data collections* that enable any subset of enterprises involved in a collaboration workflow to keep their collaboration private from other enterprises.

Verifiability. Verifiability deals with checking the satisfaction of predefined global constraints on the entire system in a privacy-preserving manner. In many multi-application systems, participants need to verify all or some of the transactions that are initiated by other applications (platforms/enterprises) to ensure the satisfaction of some predefined constraints. In particular, crowdworking platforms need to interface with legal and social institutions. Global regulations must be enforced, such as minimal and maximal work hours that participants can spend on crowdworking platforms. Moreover, while collaborating to enforce global regulations or while processing complex tasks that require the *transparent* sharing of information about the tasks, the system needs to preserve the *privacy* of all participants. In this monograph, we presented Separ, a blockchain-based multi-platform crowdworking system that enforces global constraints on distributed independent entities. In Separ, privacy is ensured using lightweight and anonymous tokens, while transparency is achieved using a permissioned blockchain shared across multiple platforms. To support fault tolerance and support collaboration among platforms, Separ provided a suite of distributed consensus protocols.

8.1.2 Large-Scale Transaction Management Applications

We now discuss several large-scale transaction management applications and show how the presented techniques can be used to satisfy the requirements of these applications.

Supply Chain Management. Lack of trust between different parties is one of the most important problems in supply chain management. To address such issues, a permissioned blockchain can be used to *monitor* the execution of the collaborative process and *check compliance* between the execution and SLAs. The utilized blockchain system needs to support both internal and cross-enterprise transactions where in contrast to the cross-enterprise transactions which are visible to all participants, the internal transactions of each enterprise are confidential, e.g., the internal transactions of the Manufacturer show its internal process for producing a product that the Manufacturer might intend to keep as a secret. To address the confidentiality challenge of Supply Chain Management applications, Caper or Qanaat can be used.

Large-Scale Databases. Sharding techniques are extensively used in distributed databases such as Google's Spanner [14] and Facebook's Tao [15] to address the scalability issue.

Such systems mainly assume a crash failure model and rely on a trusted coordinator to process cross-shard transactions. In a blockchain-based data management system that needs to tolerate malicious failures, however, the scalability issue can be addressed using SharPer. Note that if the confidentiality of shards is required, Qanaat would be an appropriate choice.

Multi-Platform Crowdsourcing. Crowdsourcing empowers open collaboration over the Internet. A crowdsourcing system includes platforms, requesters, and workers where requesters submit their tasks and workers send their contributions for a particular task to the platform. A crowdsourcing system might need to perform thousands of transactions per second, thus, has to be high *performance*. In addition, a multi-platform crowdsourcing system should scale appropriately with the increasing number of platforms, workers, and requesters, thus requires *scalability*. Moreover, the system has to provide *verifiability* of transactions against the predefined global constraints, e.g., a worker can work *no more* than 40 hours per week or a framework should process *no less than* 100 tasks per week, while preserving the *confidentiality* of transactions. To implement such a complex system, we have presented Separ. While the main focus of Separ was on the verifiability requirement, it uses the blockchain ledger view that is presented in Caper to ensure confidentiality. In addition, the sharding technique of SharPer as well as the parallel execution of ParBlockchain can be integrated with Separ to provide higher performance and scalability.

8.2 Future Directions

This section summarizes some of the future directions that we think will be areas of active research pursuit in the coming years.

8.2.1 Full Stack Adaptivity in Permissioned Blockchains

As novel smart contracts, modern hardware, and new cloud platforms arise, future permissioned blockchain systems need to be designed with *full-stack adaptivity* in mind. Recently, a wide range of decentralized applications has flourished on top of blockchains, encompassing real-world asset tokenization, gaming, supply chain assurance, crowdworking, central bank digital currencies, and decentralized AI inference. At the same time, a proliferation of blockchain systems has been proposed. This rapid growth presents challenges at every layer of the system stack:

Challenge 1: No One-Size-Fits-All transaction management paradigm. Permissioned blockchain systems, e.g., Tendermint [16], Fabric [17], Fabric++ [18], Fabric# [19], Streamchain [20], ParBlockchain [21], and BIDL [22], as discussed in Chapter 3, present different transaction management paradigms, including the sequence in which ordering, execution, and validation are performed, the number of transactions in a block, stream processing, and the use of reordering and early aborts, etc. Our experimental studies [23] have shown that different transaction management paradigms are optimal for different workloads. Unfortunately, current users have to choose a fixed paradigm prior to application development. Choosing the right configuration is not easy even for experienced users, due to the vast search space of paradigms and their internal parameters. Furthermore, client requests fluctuate with different patterns throughout the day, and workloads may permanently shift as business evolves. These dynamic factors are especially pronounced in decentralized applications, resulting in poor performance of the chosen system, since no single configuration provides dominant performance.

Challenge 2: No One-Size-Fits-All consensus protocol. Each transaction management paradigm can be further customized with a broad spectrum of Byzantine fault-tolerant (BFT) consensus protocols. Over the past two decades, the BFT protocol landscape has surged from a handful to over a hundred protocols, each embodying different design choices, including commitment strategies, number of communication phases, and leader replacement mechanism, etc. [24–27]. Selecting the right protocol and properly configuring its parameters from this vast search space is critical for end-to-end system performance. However, users are continually challenged by dynamic client workloads, failures, and network conditions, as no single protocol consistently performs well in all scenarios. To make matters worse, migrating between these siloed protocols dynamically—each with its own code base and distinct interfaces—is difficult, if not impossible [28–30].

Challenge 3: No One-Size-Fits-All resource provisioning. With machine learning increasingly integrated on-chain, decentralized applications might perform memory-intensive operations, compute-intensive operations, or a mix of both at different times and execution stages. Although Blockchains-as-a-Service (BaaS) offers a convenient way for users to manage their resources, the current rigid BaaS infrastructure poorly supports such heterogeneous resource demands. First, to ensure high-throughput services over various workloads, servers are usually over-provisioned, leading to low utilization of certain or all types of resources. Second, as workloads evolve, it is hard to scale up/down resources independently and seamlessly, e.g., expanding/shrinking memory resources independent of CPUs without pausing transactions. Such limitations require a radical rethinking of how resources are arranged for BaaS infrastructure [31].

Addressing all three challenges together requires an adaptive framework that leverages machine learning techniques and is designed with *full-stack adaptivity* in mind. First, the framework must not only dynamically select the most effective transaction management paradigm to optimize performance for varying workloads but also rapidly adjust to new hardware and unforeseen changes in workload in real time. Second, the BFT protocol chosen for consensus should also automatically adapt to dynamic workloads, ever-changing faulty conditions, and network configurations while maintaining safety and liveness. Third, at the infrastructure level, the framework needs to leverage resource disaggregation [32–35] in order to adapt to diverse resource demands. Interestingly, some paradigms and workloads benefit immensely from a resource-disaggregated setting, while others may backfire – motivating the need for a cross-layer adaptation strategy.

8.2.2 Privacy-Preserving Management of Regulated Dynamic Data

Data privacy has garnered significant attention recently due to various applications that store sensitive data in untrusted infrastructures. Data privacy and enabling secure query processing on data using cryptographic techniques have been addressed in several systems [36–48]. As an example, Prism [46] presents a secret-sharing-based technique to answer queries in the form of private set operations as well as aggregation functions over outsourced databases belonging to multiple owners. The focus of such private database systems, however, is mainly on static databases and they do not support updates on dynamically evolving databases in a satisfactory manner [49].

Privacy-preserving dynamic data management has been addressed in a few systems where the focus is on answering queries in a privacy-preserving manner (e.g., [48, 50–54]), in supporting high insertion rates (e.g., [55]), or in strengthening the privacy model [49]. For instance, DP-Sync [49] addresses the problem of hiding timing database update patterns and guarantees that the entire update history over the outsourced data (in which only a single table schema is supported) is protected using differential privacy techniques. None of these dynamic data management systems, however, support regulated data where data are being updated frequently and updates must satisfy predefined constraints before being incorporated into the data while the privacy of updates, regulations, and/or data needs to be preserved.

Regulated dynamic data have a wide range of applications from single-enterprise settings, where the enterprise data is typically maintained in an outsourced database within an untrusted infrastructure, to multi-enterprise settings, where data is maintained in multiple independent databases owned by a set of mutually distrustful parties. Constraints might be internal constraints defined by the data owners or global regulations defined by external authorities, e.g., some national or governmental institutions. For example, in supply chain management, as discussed in Chapters 5 and 6, terms of collaborations are internal constraints defined in service level agreements (SLAs) which all involved participants agree upon while in a crowdworking environment, as discussed in Chapter 7, the Fair Labor Standards Act (FLSA) is a global regulation that limits the total work hours of a worker per week to not exceed 40 hours.

Verifying incoming updates with respect to such constraints and incorporating the verified updates into data maintained by either untrusted or mutually distrustful infrastructures, on the one hand, and guaranteeing the integrity of the stored data, on the other hand, while preserving the privacy of updates, constraints, and data makes the problem challenging. The challenge with respect to privacy is that data managers may not be allowed to (1) view the update, (2) view the data itself and (3) be necessarily aware of the constraints that allow or disallow updates to be incorporated into the databases.

Another future direction in the context of this monograph could be the development of a universal framework for managing regulated dynamic data in a privacy-preserving manner. Once data is stored, managing data requires the support of privacy-preserving queries as well as privacy-preserving updates. The underlying infrastructure might consist of a single database owned by a data owner, e.g., an enterprise, or multiple independent databases owned by different distrustful data owners, e.g., different enterprises in a supply chain management. Furthermore, data might be stored remotely on untrusted providers, e.g., cloud servers. While outsourcing data to third parties like the cloud results in higher availability, ease of maintenance, and lower costs, the privacy concerns of data owners need to be addressed. In fact, depending on the application and the underlying infrastructure, the content of the stored data, the content of the updates, and the constraints may be private or public. In addition to privacy, the framework must address *integrity* to manage regulated dynamic data. Integrity ensures the checking of updates against constraints and incorporating them into data and enforces the consistency and accuracy of the stored data.

Such a framework enables database researchers to explore how to support the scalable efficient execution of private updates on private datasets with constraints. Addressing this challenge requires providing support for the private verifiability of updates on data that is regulated by private or public constraints in a scalable manner as well as a better understanding of information leakage when updates are verified with respect to constraints, where the updates or the constraints may be private or public. This framework can be instantiated using data that is both private or public and where the data is either centralized or sharded across multiple entities in a federated setting. Finally, solutions can be both centralized or distributed, thus providing designers with a range of challenges to explore, especially given the need for practical scalable performance [56].

8.2.3 Designing Efficient BFT Consensus Protocols

Byzantine fault-tolerant (BFT) protocols play a crucial role in distributed systems operating within untrustworthy environments, such as permissioned blockchains. Despite extensive research on BFT protocols over the last forty years, challenges remain in designing efficient BFT protocols that must be tackled. In this section, we explore two key dimensions for designing new BFT consensus protocols.

Achieving order-fairness in BFT Consensus Protocols. Consensus protocols use the State Machine Replication (SMR) paradigm [57, 58] to ensure that all honest replicas execute transactions in the same order (safety), and all correct transactions are eventually executed (liveness). Existing consensus protocols typically include a designated leader replica that receives transactions from clients, assigns an order (e.g., a sequence number) to each transaction, which represents the position of the transaction in the final log, and initiates agreement on the order of transactions among all replicas. However, a malicious leader can control the inclusion and final ordering of transactions without violating safety or liveness. Most existing BFT protocols do not prevent such adversarial order manipulations. Adversarial manipulation of transaction order is studied in the decentralized finance (DeFi) domain

[59–65] where transaction proposers make profit by including, excluding, or reordering transactions within blocks, known as maximal extractable value (MEV) [60].

Different techniques, such as censorship resistance, random leader election, and threshold encryption, have been proposed to prevent transaction ordering manipulation. Censorship resistance [66] only ensures that correct transactions are eventually ordered, i.e., not censored. However, the reordering of transactions, e.g., sandwich attacks, is still possible. Similarly, reputation-based systems [67–70] only detect unfair censorship. Random leader (committee) election or, in general, participation equity, on the other hand, provides opportunities for every replica to propose and commit its transactions, e.g., by becoming the proposer [67, 69, 71–79]. However, a malicious proposer can still unfairly order transactions. Finally, using threshold encryption [66, 67, 80, 81], transactions are encrypted, and their content is revealed once their order is fixed. This technique suffers from (1) metadata leakage and (2) collusion attacks between clients and the leader, where the leader becomes aware of a client transaction before ordering it and manipulates its order [82–84].

Recently, the notion of *order-fairness* was proposed to address the manipulation of transaction ordering [82–88]. Intuitively, order-fairness ensures that if a sufficiently large number of replicas (known as γ-fraction) receive a transaction t before another transaction t', then t must be ordered before t' [82]. To support order-fairness, clients broadcast their transactions to all replicas. In each round, every replica locally orders each transaction according to the time it was received and sends its ordering to the designated leader of that particular round. The leader then constructs a fair-ordered proposal from the received orderings and initiates consensus on the transaction block.

Existing fair ordering protocols, e.g., Wendy [84, 86], Pompe [85], Aequitas [82], Themis [83], Rashnu [88] and Quick-order-fairness [87], however, suffer from serious limitations. First, both Wendy [84, 86] and Pompe [85] rely on synchronized clocks between replicas, making these protocols impractical in asynchronous networks. Pompe [85] also determines a fair order using the median of timestamps assigned by replicas. The median value, however, can be easily manipulated by faulty replicas. Similarly, in Wendy, if the local clocks of the honest nodes are far apart, no fairness guarantees can be provided [83]. Second, Aequitas [82], and Quick-order-fairness [87] only guarantee weak liveness and transactions might need to wait an arbitrarily long time before being committed [83]. Finally, while Themis [83], which bootstraps from HotStuff [89], does not assume synchronized clocks, it suffers from significant performance overhead. Rashnu [88] tries to mitigate the performance overhead associated with Themis by focusing on data dependencies among transactions and introducing the concept of *data-dependent order-fairness* to maintain the order of data-dependent transactions. However, in environments with a high level of contention, Rashnu needs to preserve the order for a large volume of transactions, which leads to considerable performance overhead. Additionally, system performance is often constrained by the underlying consensus protocol, e.g., HotStuff. Employing a more efficient Byzantine Fault Tolerance (BFT) consensus protocol, like a DAG-based protocol, could potentially reduce this overhead.

Enhancing performance by parallel transaction orderings. Transaction processing involves two primary phases: ordering and execution. While executing transactions in parallel can enhance the performance of blockchain systems, the requirement for sequential ordering often leads to inefficiencies. In a blockchain environment, nodes reach consensus on the total order of transaction blocks to ensure data consistency, particularly when there are dependencies among transactions. However, many applications do not require all transactions to be ordered sequentially. A key research objective is to improve the performance of permissioned blockchain systems by facilitating parallel transaction orderings.

Recent research indicates that allowing multiple nodes to propose blocks concurrently—rather than one at a time—can significantly boost overall system performance. This approach results in a Directed Acyclic Graph (DAG) structure for blocks, where edges represent multiple references to previous blocks. Since traditional state machine replication (SMR) solutions operate solely on linear blockchains, new BFT consensus protocols based on DAG structures are gaining traction. Notable examples include Aleph [90], DAG-Rider [78], Narwhal and Tusk [79], and Bullshark [77].

In these DAG-based BFT consensus protocols, leader election occurs in rounds from previous rounds without prior knowledge of who will lead any given round. This unpredictability enhances resilience against attacks and deters malicious actors from launching assaults. Although attackers are less likely to manipulate the order of transactions within individual blocks due to this structure's rules, it remains susceptible to interblock reordering attacks where an attacker attempts to position their own blocks ahead of those belonging to legitimate users' transactions.

References

1. Peng, Z., Xu, C., Wang, H., Huang, J., Xu, J., Chu, X.: P2b-trace: privacy-preserving blockchain-based contact tracing to combat pandemics. In: SIGMOD International Conference on Management of Data, pp. 2389–2393. ACM (2021)
2. Amiri, M.J., Duguépéroux, J., Allard, T., Agrawal, D., El Abbadi, A.: Separ: towards regulating future of work multi-platform crowd working environments with privacy guarantees. In: The Web Conference (WWW), pp. 1891–1903 (2021)
3. Tian, F.: A supply chain traceability system for food safety based on HACCP, blockchain & internet of things. In: International Conference on Service Systems and Service Management (ICSSSM), pp. 1–6. IEEE (2017)
4. Amiri, M.J., Loo, B.T., Agrawal, D., El Abbadi, A.: Qanaat: a scalable multi-enterprise permissioned blockchain system with confidentiality guarantees. Proc. VLDB Endowment **15**(11), 2839–2852 (2022)
5. Peng, Z., Xu, J., Chu, X., Gao, S., Yao, Y., Gu, R., Tang, Y.: Vfchain: enabling verifiable and auditable federated learning via blockchain systems. IEEE Trans. Netw. Sci. Eng. (2021)
6. Blockchain on AWS enterprise blockchain made real. https://aws.amazon.com/blockchain/
7. AWS. amazon quantum ledger database (qldb). https://aws.amazon.com/qldb/
8. IBM blockchain platform. https://www.ibm.com/cloud/blockchain-platform
9. Oracle blockchain. https://www.oracle.com/blockchain/

10. Yang, X., Zhang, Y., Wang, S., Yu, B., Li, F., Li, Y., Yan, W.: Ledgerdb: a centralized ledger database for universal audit and verification. Proc. VLDB Endowment **13**(12), 3138–3151 (2020)
11. Daley, S.: 18 blockchain-as-a-service companies making the DLT more accessible (2021). https://builtin.com/blockchain/blockchain-as-a-service-companies
12. Amiri, M.J., Agrawal, D., El Abbadi, A.: Permissioned blockchains: properties, techniques and applications. In: SIGMOD International Conference on Management of Data, pp. 2813–2820. ACM (2021)
13. Amiri, M.J.: Large-Scale Data Management using Permissioned Blockchains. University of California, Santa Barbara (2020)
14. Corbett, J.C., Dean, J., Epstein, M., Fikes, A., Frost, C., Furman, J.J., Ghemawat, S., Gubarev, A., Heiser, C., Hochschild, P.: Spanner: google's globally distributed database. Trans. Comput. Syst. (TOCS) **31**(3), 8 (2013)
15. Bronson, N., Amsden, Z., Cabrera, G., Chakka, P., Dimov, P., Ding, H., Ferris, J., Giardullo, A., Kulkarni, S., Li, H.: Tao: Facebook's distributed data store for the social graph. In: Annual Technical Conference (ATC), pp. 49–60. USENIX Association (2013)
16. Kwon, J.: Tendermint: consensus without mining (2014)
17. Androulaki, E., Barger, A., Bortnikov, V., Cachin, C., Christidis, K., De Caro, A., Enyeart, D., Ferris, C., Laventman, G., Manevich, Y.: Hyperledger fabric: a distributed operating system for permissioned blockchains. In: European Conference on Computer Systems (EuroSys), pp. 30:1–30:15. ACM (2018)
18. Sharma, A., Schuhknecht, F.M., Agrawal, D., Dittrich, J.: Blurring the lines between blockchains and database systems: the case of hyperledger fabric. In: SIGMOD International Conference on Management of Data, pp. 105–122. ACM (2019)
19. Ruan, P., Loghin, D., Ta, Q.T., Zhang, M., Chen, G., Ooi, B.C.: A transactional perspective on execute-order-validate blockchains. In: SIGMOD International Conference on Management of Data, pp. 543–557. ACM (2020)
20. István, Z., Sorniotti, A., Vukolić, M.: Streamchain: do blockchains need blocks? In: Workshop on Scalable and Resilient Infrastructures for Distributed Ledgers (SERIAL), pp. 1–6. ACM (2018)
21. Amiri, M.J., Agrawal, D., El Abbadi, A.: ParBlockchain: leveraging transaction parallelism in permissioned blockchain systems. In: International Conference on Distributed Computing Systems (ICDCS), pp. 1337–1347. IEEE (2019)
22. Qi, J., Chen, X., Jiang, Y., Jiang, J., Shen, T., Zhao, S., Wang, S., Zhang, G., Chen, L., Au, M.H., et al.: Bidl: A high-throughput, low-latency permissioned blockchain framework for datacenter networks. In: Symposium on Operating Systems Principles (SOSP), pp. 18–34. ACM (2021)
23. Wu, C., Mehta, B., Amiri, M.J., Marcus, R., Loo, B.T.: AdaChain: a learned adaptive blockchain. Proc. VLDB Endowment **16**(8), 2033–2046 (2023)
24. Amiri, M.J., Wu, C., Agrawal, D., El Abbadi, A., Loo, B.T., Sadoghi, M.: The bedrock of byzantine fault tolerance: a unified platform for {BFT} protocols analysis, implementation, and experimentation. In: Symposium on Networked Systems Design and Implementation (NSDI), pp. 371–400. USENIX Association (2024)
25. Gupta, S., Amiri, M.J., Sadoghi, M.: Chemistry behind agreement. In: Conference on Innovative Data Systems Research (CIDR) (2023)
26. Amiri, M.J., Agrawal, D., El Abbadi, A.: Modern large-scale data management systems after 40 years of consensus. In: International Conference on Data Engineering (ICDE), pp. 1794–1797. IEEE (2020)
27. Amiri, M.J., Agrawal, D., El Abbadi, A., Loo, B.T.: Distributed transaction processing in untrusted environments. In: SIGMOD Conference Companion, pp. 570–579 (2024)
28. Wu, C., Qin, H., Amiri, M.J., Loo, B.T., Malkhi, D., Marcus, R.: Bftbrain: Adaptive bft consensus with reinforcement learning. In: Symposium on Networked Systems Design and Implementation (NSDI). USENIX Association (2025)

29. Wu, C., Qin, H., Amiri, M.J., Loo, B.T., Malkhi, D., Marcus, R.: Towards truly adaptive byzantine fault-tolerant consensus. ACM SIGOPS Oper. Syst. Rev. **58**(1), 15–22 (2024)
30. Qin, H., Wu, C., Amiri, M.J., Marcus, R., Loo, B.T.: BFTGym: an interactive playground for BFT protocols. Proc. VLDB Endowment **17**(12), 4261–4264 (2024)
31. Wu, C., Amiri, M.J., Asch, J., Nagda, H., Zhang, Q., Loo, B.T.: FlexChain: an elastic disaggregated blockchain. Proc. VLDB Endowment **16**(01), 23–36 (2022)
32. Shan, Y., Huang, Y., Chen, Y., Zhang, Y.: {LegoOS}: A disseminated, distributed {OS} for hardware resource disaggregation. In: Symposium on Operating Systems Design and Implementation (OSDI), pp. 69–87. USENIX Association (2018)
33. Zhang, Q., Cai, Y., Chen, X., Angel, S., Chen, A., Liu, V., Loo, B.T.: Understanding the effect of data center resource disaggregation on production dbmss. Proc. VLDB Endowment 13(9) (2020)
34. Zhang, Q., Cai, Y., Angel, S., Chen, A., Liu, V., Loo, B.T.: Rethinking data management systems for disaggregated data centers. In: Conference on Innovative Data Systems Research (CIDR) (2020)
35. Gao, P.X., Narayan, A., Karandikar, S., Carreira, J., Han, S., Agarwal, R., Ratnasamy, S., Shenker, S.: Network requirements for resource disaggregation. In: Symposium on Operating Systems Design and Implementation (OSDI), pp. 249–264. USENIX Association (2016)
36. Roy Chowdhury, A., Wang, C., He, X., Machanavajjhala, A., Jha, S.: Cryptϵ: Crypto-assisted differential privacy on untrusted servers. In: SIGMOD International Conference on Management of Data, pp. 603–619. ACM (2020)
37. Hacigümüş, H., Iyer, B., Li, C., Mehrotra, S.: Executing SQL over encrypted data in the database-service-provider model. In: SIGMOD International Conference on Management of Data, pp. 216–227. ACM (2002)
38. Dwork, C., Naor, M., Pitassi, T., Rothblum, G.N.: Differential privacy under continual observation. In: Symposium on Theory of computing (STOC), pp. 715–724. ACM (2010)
39. Kellaris, G., Kollios, G., Nissim, K., O'Neill, A.: Accessing data while preserving privacy (2017). arXiv preprint arXiv:1706.01552
40. Bater, J., He, X., Ehrich, W., Machanavajjhala, A., Rogers, J.: Shrinkwrap: efficient sql query processing in differentially private data federations. Proc. VLDB Endowment **12**(3), 307–320 (2018)
41. Poddar, R., Boelter, T., Popa, R.A.: Arx: a strongly encrypted database system. IACR Cryptol. ePrint Arch. **2016**, 591 (2016)
42. Hore, B., Mehrotra, S., Canim, M., Kantarcioglu, M.: Secure multidimensional range queries over outsourced data. VLDB J. **21**(3), 333–358 (2012)
43. Chen, Y., Machanavajjhala, A., Hay, M., Miklau, G.: Pegasus: data-adaptive differentially private stream processing. In: Conference on Computer and Communications Security (CCS), pp. 1375–1388. ACM (2017)
44. Bellare, M., Boldyreva, A., O'Neill, A.: Deterministic and efficiently searchable encryption. In: Annual International Cryptology Conference (CRYPTO), pp. 535–552. Springer (2007)
45. Arasu, A., Kaushik, R.: Oblivious query processing, pp. 26–37 (2014)
46. Li, Y., Ghosh, D., Gupta, P., Mehrotra, S., Panwar, N., Sharma, S.: Prism: Private verifiable set computation over multi-owner outsourced databases. In: SIGMOD International Conference on Management of Data, pp. 1116–1128. ACM (2021)
47. Agarwal, A., Herlihy, M., Kamara, S., Moataz, T.: Encrypted databases for differential privacy. Priv. Enhanc. Technol. **2019**(3), 170–190 (2019)
48. Sahin, C., Allard, T., Akbarinia, R., Abbadi, A.E., Pacitti, E.: A differentially private index for range query processing in clouds. In: International Conference on Data Engineering (ICDE), pp. 857–868 (2018)

49. Wang, C., Bater, J., Nayak, K., Machanavajjhala, A.: Dp-sync: hiding update patterns in secure outsourced databases with differential privacy. In: SIGMOD International Conference on Management of Data, pp. 1892–1905. ACM (2021)
50. Curtmola, R., Garay, J., Kamara, S., Ostrovsky, R.: Searchable symmetric encryption: improved definitions and efficient constructions. J. Comput. Secur. **19**(5), 895–934 (2011)
51. Popa, R.A., Redfield, C.M., Zeldovich, N., Balakrishnan, H.: Cryptdb: processing queries on an encrypted database. Commun. ACM **55**(9), 103–111 (2012)
52. Hahn, F., Kerschbaum, F.: Searchable encryption with secure and efficient updates. In: Conference on Computer and Communications Security (CCS), pp. 310–320. ACM (2014)
53. Kamara, S., Moataz, T.: Sql on structurally-encrypted databases. In: International Conference on the Theory and Application of Cryptology and Information Security, pp. 149–180. Springer (2018)
54. Stefanov, E., Papamanthou, C., Shi, E.: Practical dynamic searchable encryption with small leakage. In: Network and Distributed System Security Symposium (NDSS), vol. 71, pp. 72–75 (2014)
55. Tran, H., Allard, T., d'Orazio, L., Abbadi, A.E.: Fresque: a scalable ingestion framework for secure range query processing on clouds. In: International Conference on Extending Database Technology (EDBT) (2021)
56. Amiri, M.J., Allard, T., Agrawal, D., El Abbadi, A.: PReVer: Towards private regulated verified data. In: International Conference on Extending Database Technology (EDBT), pp. 2:454–2:461 (2022)
57. Lamport, L.: Time, clocks, and the ordering of events in a distributed system. Commun. ACM **21**(7), 558–565 (1978)
58. Schneider, F.B.: Implementing fault-tolerant services using the state machine approach: a tutorial. Comput. Surv. (CSUR) **22**(4), 299–319 (1990)
59. Eskandari, S., Moosavi, S., Clark, J.: Sok: transparent dishonesty: front-running attacks on blockchain. In: International Conference on Financial Cryptography and Data Security (FC), pp. 170–189. Springer (2019)
60. Daian, P., Goldfeder, S., Kell, T., Li, Y., Zhao, X., Bentov, I., Breidenbach, L., Juels, A.: Flash boys 2.0: frontrunning in decentralized exchanges, miner extractable value, and consensus instability. In: Symposium on Security and Privacy (SP), pp. 910–927. IEEE (2020)
61. Klages-Mundt, A., Minca, A.: (In)stability for the blockchain: deleveraging spirals and stablecoin attacks (2019). arXiv preprint arXiv:1906.02152
62. Qin, K., Zhou, L., Gervais, A.: Quantifying blockchain extractable value: how dark is the forest? In: Symposium on Security and Privacy (SP), pp. 198–214. IEEE (2022)
63. Zhou, L., Qin, K., Torres, C.F., Le, D.V., Gervais, A.: High-frequency trading on decentralized on-chain exchanges. In: Symposium on Security and Privacy (SP), pp. 428–445. IEEE (2021)
64. Baum, C., Chiang, J.H.Y., David, B., Frederiksen, T.K., Gentile, L.: Sok: mitigation of front-running in decentralized finance. Cryptology ePrint Archive (2021)
65. Heimbach, L., Wattenhofer, R.: Sok: preventing transaction reordering manipulations in decentralized finance. In: Conference on Advances in Financial Technologies (AFT), pp. 1–14. ACM (2022)
66. Miller, A., Xia, Y., Croman, K., Shi, E., Song, D.: The honey badger of bft protocols. In: Conference on Computer and Communications Security (CCS), pp. 31–42. ACM (2016)
67. Asayag, A., Cohen, G., Grayevsky, I., Leshkowitz, M., Rottenstreich, O., Tamari, R., Yakira, D.: A fair consensus protocol for transaction ordering. In: International Conference on Network Protocols (ICNP), pp. 55–65. IEEE (2018)
68. Kokoris-Kogias, E., Jovanovic, P., Gasser, L., Gailly, N., Syta, E., Ford, B.: Omniledger: a secure, scale-out, decentralized ledger via sharding. In: Symposium on Security and Privacy (SP), pp. 583–598. IEEE (2018)

69. Lev-Ari, K., Spiegelman, A., Keidar, I., Malkhi, D.: Fairledger: a fair blockchain protocol for financial institutions. In: International Conference on Principles of Distributed Systems (OPODIS). Schloss Dagstuhl-Leibniz-Zentrum fuer Informatik (2019)
70. Crain, T., Natoli, C., Gramoli, V.: Red belly: a secure, fair and scalable open blockchain. In: Symposium on Security and Privacy (SP). IEEE (2021)
71. Kiayias, A., Russell, A., David, B., Oliynykov, R.: Ouroboros: a provably secure proof-of-stake blockchain protocol. In: Annual International Cryptology Conference, pp. 357–388. Springer (2017)
72. Abraham, I., Malkhi, D., Nayak, K., Ren, L., Spiegelman, A.: Solida: a blockchain protocol based on reconfigurable byzantine consensus. In: International Conference on Principles of Distributed Systems (OPODIS). Schloss Dagstuhl-Leibniz-Zentrum fuer Informatik (2017)
73. Gilad, Y., Hemo, R., Micali, S., Vlachos, G., Zeldovich, N.: Algorand: scaling byzantine agreements for cryptocurrencies. In: Symposium on Operating Systems Principles (SOSP), pp. 51–68. ACM (2017)
74. Pass, R., Shi, E.: Hybrid consensus: efficient consensus in the permission less model. In: International Symposium on Distributed Computing (DISC), p. 6 (2017)
75. Yakira, D., Asayag, A., Cohen, G., Grayevsky, I., Leshkowitz, M., Rottenstreich, O., Tamari, R.: Helix: a fair blockchain consensus protocol resistant to ordering manipulation. IEEE Trans. Netw. Serv. Manage. **18**(2), 1584–1597 (2021)
76. Malkhi, D., Szalachowski, P.: Maximal extractable value (mev) protection on a dag (2022). arXiv preprint arXiv:2208.00940
77. Spiegelman, A., Giridharan, N., Sonnino, A., Kokoris-Kogias, L.: Bullshark: Dag bft protocols made practical. In: ACM SIGSAC Conference on Computer and Communications Security (CCS), pp. 2705–2718 (2022)
78. Keidar, I., Kokoris-Kogias, E., Naor, O., Spiegelman, A.: All you need is dag. In: Symposium on Principles of Distributed Computing (PODC), pp. 165–175. ACM (2021)
79. Danezis, G., Kokoris-Kogias, L., Sonnino, A., Spiegelman, A.: Narwhal and tusk: a dag-based mempool and efficient bft consensus. In: European Conference on Computer Systems (EuroSys), pp. 34–50 (2022)
80. Cachin, C., Kursawe, K., Petzold, F., Shoup, V.: Secure and efficient asynchronous broadcast protocols. In: Annual International Cryptology Conference, pp. 524–541. Springer (2001)
81. Stathakopoulou, C., Rüsch, S., Brandenburger, M., Vukolić, M.: Adding fairness to order: preventing front-running attacks in BFT protocols using tees. In: International Symposium on Reliable Distributed Systems (SRDS), pp. 34–45. IEEE (2021)
82. Kelkar, M., Zhang, F., Goldfeder, S., Juels, A.: Order-fairness for byzantine consensus. In: Annual International Cryptology Conference, pp. 451–480. Springer (2020)
83. Kelkar, M., Deb, S., Long, S., Juels, A., Kannan, S.: Themis: fast, strong order-fairness in byzantine consensus. In: SIGSAC Conference on Computer and Communications Security (CCS), pp. 475–489. ACM (2023)
84. Kursawe, K.: Wendy, the good little fairness widget: achieving order fairness for blockchains. In: Conference on Advances in Financial Technologies (AFT), pp. 25–36. ACM (2020)
85. Zhang, Y., Setty, S., Chen, Q., Zhou, L., Alvisi, L.: Byzantine ordered consensus without byzantine oligarchy. In: Symposium on Operating Systems Design and Implementation (OSDI), pp. 633–649. USENIX Association (2020)
86. Kursawe, K.: Wendy grows up: more order fairness. In: International Conference on Financial Cryptography and Data Security (FC), pp. 191–196. Springer (2021)
87. Cachin, C., Mićić, J., Steinhauer, N.: Quick order fairness. In: International Conference on Financial Cryptography and Data Security (FC), pp. 1–18. Springer (2022)
88. Nagda, H., Singhal, S.P., Amiri, M.J., Loo, B.T.: Rashnu: data-dependent order-fairness. Proc. VLDB Endowment **17**(9), 2335–2348 (2024)

89. Yin, M., Malkhi, D., Reiter, M.K., Gueta, G.G., Abraham, I.: Hotstuff: BFT consensus with linearity and responsiveness. In: Symposium on Principles of Distributed Computing (PODC), pp. 347–356. ACM (2019)
90. Gągol, A., Leśniak, D., Straszak, D., Świętek, M.: Aleph: efficient atomic broadcast in asynchronous networks with byzantine nodes. In: Conference on Advances in Financial Technologies, pp. 214–228. ACM (2019)

MIX
Papier aus verantwortungsvollen Quellen
Paper from responsible sources
FSC® C105338

If you have any concerns about our products, you can contact us on
ProductSafety@springernature.com

In case Publisher is established outside the EU, the EU authorized representative is:
Springer Nature Customer Service Center GmbH
Europaplatz 3, 69115 Heidelberg, Germany

Printed by Libri Plureos GmbH
in Hamburg, Germany